PROPERTY OF
John L. Fox

D1257266

The Autobiography of Theodore Roosevelt

CENTENNIAL EDITION

The Autobiography
of Theodore Roosevelt

Condensed from the original edition, supplemented by letters,

speeches, and other writings, and edited with an introduction by

WAYNE ANDREWS

Charles Scribner's Sons   New York

ACKNOWLEDGMENTS

For permission to quote briefly from the following sources, the editor and publisher make grateful acknowledgment.

To Harvard University Press (Cambridge, Massachusetts) for excerpts from THE LETTERS OF THEODORE ROOSEVELT (8 volumes), edited by Elting Elmore Morison, copyright 1951, 1952, 1954 by the President and Fellows of Harvard College.

To Houghton Mifflin Company to quote an excerpt from the biography, CHARLES W. ELIOT, Volume II by Henry James.

To William M. Cruikshank, literary executor of the estate of Theodore Roosevelt to quote from FEAR GOD AND TAKE YOUR OWN PART by Theodore Roosevelt (George H. Doran & Company, 1916).

CONTENTS

1 Boyhood and Youth, 3
2 The Vigor of Life, 26
3 Practical Politics, 36
4 In Cowboy Land, 58
5 Applied Idealism, 86
6 The New York Police, 100
7 The War of America the Unready, 117
8 The New York Governorship, 146
9 Outdoors and Indoors, 170
10 The Presidency: Making an Old Party Progressive, 192
11 The Natural Resources of the Nation, 209
12 The Big Stick and the Square Deal, 222
13 Social and Industrial Justice, 249
14 The Monroe Doctrine and the Panama Canal, 268
15 The Peace of Righteousness, 286
16 Hunter and Historian, 298
17 Armageddon and Afterward, 326
   Sources, 359
   Index, 363

Theodore Roosevelt was an important President of the United States, the first since Andrew Jackson to remind the people that our government was a flexible instrument. This was a revolutionary notion in 1901, when he succeeded McKinley. For the men who occupied the White House since Lincoln's time had rarely listened to the murmur of discontent.

TR always listened, much as he might disapprove of the rhetoric of William Jennings Bryan or of the lonely moral fervor of Governor Altgeld of Illinois. Unimpressed by the very rich and easily provoked by reformers who preached a gospel to the left of his own, he made it possible for the nation to steer a middle course that answered many of the questions raised by discontented citizens. In other words, he was an enlightened conservative, a man who made Americans realize that their government was the most exciting business on earth.

In his time the White House was not a mausoleum. It was a place where prizefighters and cowpunchers sat down to dinner with elder statesmen, and where children at any moment might start a pillow-fight. There were those who were appalled by the energy TR displayed even at the dinner table. "You must always remem-

ber," *remarked British Ambassador Cecil Spring-Rice, "that Theodore is about six." Spring-Rice's comment is worth recalling. But
so are Henry Adams' last words when TR left Washington. "I
shall miss you very much," admitted the intellectual of intellectuals.*

*The charm of Theodore Roosevelt was not a legend. It was a
fact. Though he made plain to Edith Wharton that one of her
novels was immoral, she was not offended. How could she be, in
the light of his unqualified admiration for Lewis Carroll? "Well,"
he told her, "I am glad to welcome to the White House some one
to whom I can quote* The Hunting of the Snark *without being
asked what I mean. . . . Would you believe it, no one in the
Administration has ever heard of Alice, much less of the Snark!"*

*An author himself, TR presumed that any intelligent caller
would have heard of his writings and digested at least one volume.
"What book of mine do you like the best?" he asked one visitor
to Sagamore Hill. The visitor, fortunately, was pleased to be asked.*

*Though TR diligently re-read Euripides in between stalking lions
in Africa, it would be doing his memory—and his charm—a dis-
service to emphasize his contribution to American history at the
expense of his contribution to American humor. He had a sense
of humor, even if, like many of us, he occasionally misplaced it.*

In this new edition of the Autobiography *supplemented by selections from his letters, his speeches, and his historical and nature
writings, TR holds forth on every important reform of his administration, on every move of our diplomacy that came into his ken,
and on his hopes for the future of America. But he also talks of
the fads he endorsed and the notions that raised his wrath. He was
a man of violent likes and dislikes. If he had not been, he would
not have captured the sympathy of the American people.*

*Since the President's autobiography is by all means the most
important source, it has been abridged as little as possible; pertinent*

letters and other material have been placed at the end of chapters. Footnotes have been largely eliminated, and scholarly references have been trimmed. This would not have displeased Theodore Roosevelt. He believed that the greatest historians traveled with the lightest baggage.

The Autobiography of Theodore Roosevelt

CHAPTER 1

Boyhood and Youth

My grandfather on my father's side was of almost purely Dutch blood. When he was young he still spoke some Dutch, and Dutch was last used in the services of the Dutch Reformed Church in New York while he was a small boy.

About 1644 his ancestor Klaes Martensen van Roosevelt came to New Amsterdam as a "settler"—the euphemistic name for an immigrant who came over in the steerage of a sailing ship in the seventeenth century instead of the steerage of a steamer in the nineteenth century. From that time for the next seven generations from father to son every one of us was born on Manhattan Island.

My father's paternal ancestors were of Holland stock; except that there was one named Waldron, a wheelwright, who was one of the Pilgrims who remained in Holland when the others came over to found Massachusetts, and who then accompanied the Dutch adventurers to New Amsterdam. My father's mother was a Pennsylvanian. Her forebears had come to Pennsylvania with William

Penn, some in the same ship with him; they were of the usual type of the immigration of that particular place and time. They included Welsh and English Quakers, an Irishman—with a Celtic name, and apparently not a Quaker—and peace-loving Germans, who were among the founders of Germantown, having been driven from their Rhineland homes when the armies of Louis the Fourteenth ravaged the Palatinate; and, in addition, representatives of a by-no-means altogether peaceful people, the Scotch-Irish, who came to Pennsylvania a little later, early in the eighteenth century. My grandmother was a woman of singular sweetness and strength, the keystone of the arch in her relations with her husband and sons. Although she was not herself Dutch, it was she who taught me the only Dutch I ever knew, a baby song of which the first line ran, "Trippe troppa tronjes." I always remembered this, and when I was in East Africa it proved a bond of union between me and the Boer settlers, not a few of whom knew it, although at first they always had difficulty in understanding my pronunciation—at which I do not wonder. It was interesting to meet these men whose ancestors had gone to the Cape about the time that mine went to America two centuries and a half previously, and to find that the descendants of the two streams of emigrants still crooned to their children some at least of the same nursery songs. . . .

My mother's people were predominantly of Scotch, but also of Huguenot and English, descent. She was a Georgian, her people having come to Georgia from South Carolina before the Revolution. The original Bulloch was a lad from near Glasgow, who came hither a couple of centuries ago, just as hundreds of thousands of needy, enterprising Scotchmen have gone to the four quarters of the globe in the intervening two hundred years. My mother's great-grandfather, Archibald Bulloch, was the first Revolutionary "President" of Georgia. My grandfather, her father, spent the winters in Savannah and the summers at Roswell, in the Georgia uplands near Atlanta, finally making Roswell his permanent home. He used to travel thither with his family and their belongings in his own carriage, followed by a baggage wagon. I never saw Roswell until I was President, but my mother told me so much about the place that when I did see it I felt as if I already knew every nook and corner of it, and as if it were haunted by the ghosts of all the men and women who had lived there. . . .

On October 27, 1858, I was born at No. 28 East Twentieth Street, New York City,* in the house in which we lived during the time that my two sisters and my brother and I were small children. It was furnished in the canonical taste of the New York which George William Curtis described in the *Potiphar Papers*. The black haircloth furniture in the dining-room scratched the bare legs of the children when they sat on it. The middle room was a library, with tables, chairs, and bookcases of gloomy respectability. It was without windows, and so was available only at night. The front room, the parlor, seemed to us children to be a room of much splendor, but was open for general use only on Sunday evening or on rare occasions when there were parties. The Sunday-evening family gathering was the redeeming feature in a day which otherwise we children did not enjoy—chiefly because we were all of us made to wear clean clothes and keep neat. The ornaments of that parlor I remember now,

* The headquarters today of The Theodore Roosevelt Association. Open to the public. [*Editor's note*]

including the gas chandelier decorated with a great quantity of cut-glass prisms. These prisms struck me as possessing peculiar magnificence. One of them fell off one day, and I hastily grabbed it and stowed it away, passing several days of furtive delight in the treasure, a delight always alloyed with fear that I would be found out and convicted of larceny. There was a Swiss wood-carving representing a very big hunter on one side of an exceedingly small mountain, and a herd of chamois, disproportionately small for the hunter and large for the mountain, just across the ridge. This always fascinated us; but there was a small chamois kid for which we felt agonies lest the hunter might come on it and kill it. There was also a Russian moujik drawing a gilt sledge on a piece of malachite. Some one mentioned in my hearing that malachite was a valuable marble. This fixed in my mind that it was valuable exactly as diamonds are valuable. I accepted that moujik as a priceless work of art, and it was not until I was well in middle age that it occurred to me that I was mistaken.

Now and then we children were taken round to our grandfather's house; a big house for the New York of those days, on the corner of Fourteenth Street and Broadway, fronting Union Square. Inside there was a large hall running up to the roof; there was a tessellated black-and-white marble floor, and a circular staircase round the sides of the hall, from the top floor down. We children much admired both the tessellated floor and the circular staircase. I think we were right about the latter, but I am not so sure as to the tessellated floor.

The summers we spent in the country, now at one place, now at another. We children, of course, loved the country beyond anything. We disliked the city. We were always wildly eager to get to the country when spring came, and very sad when in the late fall the family moved back to town. In the country we of course had all kinds of pets—cats, dogs, rabbits, a coon, and a sorrel Shetland pony named General Grant. . . .

My father, Theodore Roosevelt, was the best man I ever knew. He combined strength and courage with gentleness, tenderness, and great unselfishness. He would not tolerate in us children selfishness or cruelty, idleness, cowardice, or untruthfulness. As we grew older he made us understand that the same standard of clean living was demanded for the boys as for the girls; that what was wrong in a woman could not be right in a man. With great love and patience, and the most understanding sympathy and consideration, he combined insistence on discipline. He never physically punished me but once, but he was the only man of whom I was ever really afraid. I do not mean that it was a wrong fear, for he was entirely just, and we children adored him. We used to wait in the library in the evening until we could hear his key rattling in the latch of the front hall, and then rush out to greet him; and we would troop into his room while he was dressing, to stay there as long as we were permitted, eagerly examining anything which came out of his pockets which could be regarded as an attractive novelty. Every child has fixed in his memory various details which strike it as of grave importance. The trinkets he used to keep in a little box on his dressing-table we children always used to speak of as "treasures." The word, and some of the trinkets themselves, passed on to the next generation. My own children, when small, used to troop into my room while I was dressing, and the gradually accumulating trinkets in the "ditty-box"—the gift of an enlisted man in the navy—always excited rapturous joy. On occasions of solemn festivity each child would receive a trinket for his or her "very own." . . .

The punishing incident I have referred to happened when I was four years old. I bit my elder sister's arm. I do not remember biting her arm, but I do remember running down to the yard, perfectly conscious that I had committed a crime. From the yard I went into the kitchen, got some dough from the cook, and crawled under the kitchen table. In a minute or two my father entered from the yard and asked where I was. The warm-hearted Irish cook had a characteristic contempt for "informers," but although she said nothing she compromised between informing and her conscience by casting a look under the table. My father immediately dropped on all fours and darted for me. I feebly heaved the dough at him, and, having the advantage of him because I could stand up under the table, got a fair start for the stairs, but was caught half-way up them. The punishment that ensued fitted the crime, and I hope—and believe—that it did me good.

I never knew any one who got greater joy out of living than did my father, or any one who more whole-heartedly performed every duty; and no one whom I have ever met approached his combination of enjoyment of life and performance of duty. He and my mother were given to a hospitality that at that time was associated more commonly with Southern than Northern households; and, especially in their later years when they had moved uptown, in the neighborhood of Central Park, they kept a charming, open house.

My father worked hard at his business, for he died when he was forty-six, too early to have retired. He was interested in every social reform movement, and he did an immense amount of practical charitable work himself. He was a big, powerful man, with a leonine face, and his heart filled with gentleness for those who needed help or protection, and with the possibility of much wrath against a bully or an oppressor. . . .

When in the city on Thanksgiving or Christmas, my father was very apt to drive my mother and a couple of friends up to the racing park to take lunch. But he was always back in time to go to the dinner at the Newsboys' Lodging-House, and not infrequently also to Miss Sattery's Night School for little Italians. At a very early age we children were taken with him and were required to help. He was a stanch friend of Charles Loring Brace, and was particularly interested in the Newsboys' Lodging-Houses and in the night schools and in getting the children off the streets and out on farms in the West. When I was President, the Governor of Alaska under me, Governor Brady, was one of these ex-newsboys who had been sent from New York out West by Mr. Brace and my father. My father was greatly interested in the societies to prevent cruelty to children and cruelty to animals. On Sundays he had a mission class. On his way to it he used to drop us children at our Sunday-school in Doctor Adams' Presbyterian Church on Madison Square; I remember hearing my aunt, my mother's sister, saying that when he walked along with us children he always reminded her of Greatheart in Bunyan. Under the spur of his example I taught a mission class myself for three years before going to college, and for all four years that I was in college. I do not think I made much of a success of it. But the other day on getting out of a taxi in New York the chauffeur spoke to me and told me that he was one of my old Sunday-school pupils. I remembered him well, and was much pleased to find that he was an ardent Bull Mooser!

My mother, Martha Bulloch, was a sweet, gracious, beautiful Southern woman, a delightful companion and beloved by everybody. She was entirely "unreconstructed" to the day of her death. Her mother, my grandmother, one of the dearest of old ladies, lived with us, and was distinctly overindulgent to us children, being quite unable to harden her heart toward us even when the occasion demanded it. Toward the close of the Civil War, although a very small boy, I grew to have a partial but alert understanding of the fact that the family were not one in their views about that conflict, my father being a strong Lincoln Republican; and once, when I felt that I had been wronged by maternal discipline during the day, I attempted a partial vengeance by praying with loud fervor for the success of the Union arms, when we all came to say our prayers before my mother in the evening. She was not only a most devoted mother, but was also blessed with a strong sense of humor, and she was too much amused to punish me; but I was warned not to repeat the offense, under penalty of my father's being informed—he being the dispenser of serious punishment. Morning prayers were with my father. We used to stand at the foot of the stairs, and when father came down we called out, "I speak for you and the cubby-hole too!" There were three of us young children, and we used to sit with father on the sofa while he conducted morning prayers. The place between father and the arm of the sofa we called the "cubby-hole." The child who got that place we regarded as especially favored both in comfort and somehow or other in rank and title. The two who were left to sit on the much wider expanse of sofa on the other side of father were outsiders for the time being.

My aunt Anna, my mother's sister, lived with us. She was as devoted to us children as was my mother herself, and we were equally devoted to her in return. She taught us our lessons while we were little. She and my mother used to entertain us by the hour with tales of life on the Georgia plantations; of hunting fox, deer, and wildcat; of the long-tailed driving-horses, Boone and Crockett, and of the riding-horses, one of which was named Buena Vista in a fit of patriotic exaltation during the Mexican War; and of the queer goings-on in the negro quarters. She knew all the "Br'er Rabbit" stories, and I was brought up on them. One of my uncles, Robert Roosevelt, was much struck with them, and took them down from her dictation, publishing them in *Harper's*, where they fell flat. This was a good many years before a genius arose who in "Uncle Remus" made the stories immortal.

My mother's two brothers, James Dunwoodie Bulloch and Irvine Bulloch, came to visit us shortly after the close of the war. Both came under assumed names, as they were among the Confederates who were at that time exempted from the amnesty. "Uncle Jimmy" Bulloch was a dear old retired sea-captain, utterly unable to "get on" in the worldly sense of that phrase, as valiant and simple and upright a soul as ever lived, a veritable Colonel Newcome. He was an admiral in the Confederate navy, and was the builder of the famous Confederate war-vessel *Alabama*. My uncle Irvine Bulloch was a midshipman on the *Alabama*, and fired the last gun discharged from her batteries in the fight with the *Kearsarge*. Both of these uncles lived in Liverpool after the war. . . .

I was a sickly, delicate boy, suffered much from asthma,

and frequently had to be taken away on trips to find a place where I could breathe. One of my memories is of my father walking up and down the room with me in his arms at night when I was a very small person, and of sitting up in bed gasping, with my father and mother trying to help me. I went very little to school. I never went to the public schools, as my own children later did . . . For a few months I attended Professor McMullen's school in Twentieth Street near the house where I was born, but most of the time I had tutors. As I have already said, my aunt taught me when I was small. At one time we had a French governess, a loved and valued "mam'selle," in the household.

When I was ten years old I made my first journey to Europe. My birthday was spent in Cologne, and in order to give me a thoroughly "party" feeling I remember that my mother put on full dress for my birthday dinner. I do not think I gained anything from this particular trip abroad. I cordially hated it, as did my younger brother and sister. Practically all the enjoyment we had was in exploring any ruins or mountains when we could get away from our elders, and in playing in the different hotels. Our one desire was to get back to America, and we regarded Europe with the most ignorant chauvinism and contempt. Four years later, however, I made another journey to Europe, and was old enough to enjoy it thoroughly and profit by it.

While still a small boy I began to take an interest in natural history. I remember distinctly the first day that I started on my career as zoologist. I was walking up Broadway, and as I passed the market to which I used sometimes to be sent before breakfast to get strawberries I suddenly saw a dead seal laid out on a slab of wood. That seal filled me with every possible feeling of romance and adventure. I asked where it was killed, and was informed in the harbor. I had already begun to read some of Mayne Reid's books and other boys' books of adventure, and I felt that this seal brought all these adventures in realistic fashion before me. As long as that seal remained there I haunted the neighborhood of the market day after day. I measured it, and I recall that, not having a tape measure, I had to do my best to get its girth with a folding pocket footrule, a difficult undertaking. I carefully made a record of the utterly useless measurements, and at once began to write a natural history of my own, on the strength of that seal. This, and subsequent natural histories, were written down in blank books in simplified spelling, wholly unpremeditated and unscientific. I had vague aspirations of in some way or another owning and preserving that seal, but they never got beyond the purely formless stage. I think, however, I did get the seal's skull, and with two of my cousins promptly started what we ambitiously called the "Roosevelt Museum of Natural History." The collections were at first kept in my room, until a rebellion on the part of the chamber-maid received the approval of the higher authorities of the household and the collection was moved up to a kind of bookcase in the back hall up-stairs. It was the ordinary small boy's collection of curios, quite incongruous and entirely valueless except from the standpoint of the boy himself. My father and mother encouraged me warmly in this, as they always did in anything that could give me wholesome pleasure or help to develop me. . . .

Quite unknown to myself, I was, while a boy, under a hopeless disadvantage in studying nature. I was very near-sighted, so that the only things I could study were those I ran against or stumbled over. When I was about thirteen I was allowed to take lessons in taxidermy from a Mr. Bell, a tall, clean-shaven, white-haired old gentleman, as straight as an Indian, who had been a companion of Audubon's. He had a musty little shop, somewhat on the order of Mr. Venus's shop in "Our Mutual Friend," a little shop in which he had done very valuable work for science. This "vocational study," as I suppose it would be called by modern educators, spurred and directed my interest in collecting specimens for mounting and preservation. It was this summer that I got my first gun, and it puzzled me to find that my companions seemed to see things to shoot at which I could not see at all. One day they read aloud an advertisement in huge letters on a distant billboard, and I then realized that something was the matter, for not only was I unable to read the sign, but I could not even see the letters. I spoke of this to my father, and soon afterwards got my first pair of spectacles, which literally opened an entirely new world to me. I had no idea how beautiful the world was until I got those spectacles. I had been a clumsy and awkward little boy, and while much of my clumsiness and awkwardness was doubtless due to general characteristics, a good deal of it was due to the fact that I could not see and yet was wholly ignorant that I was not seeing. The recollection of this experience gives me a keen sympathy with those who are trying in our public schools and elsewhere to remove the physical causes of deficiency in children, who are often unjustly blamed for being obstinate, or unambitious, or mentally stupid.

This same summer, too, I obtained various new books on mammals and birds. . . . I did not accomplish much in outdoor study because I did not get spectacles until late in the fall, a short time before I started with the rest of the family for a second trip to Europe. We were living at Dobbs Ferry, on the Hudson. My gun was a breech-loading, pin-fire double-barrel, of French manufacture. It was an excellent gun for a clumsy and often absent-minded boy. There was no spring to open it, and if the mechanism became rusty it could be opened with a brick without serious damage. When the cartridges stuck they could be removed in the same fashion. If they were loaded, however, the result was not always happy, and I tattooed myself with partially unburned grains of powder more than once.

When I was fourteen years old, in the winter of '72 and '73, I visited Europe for the second time, and this trip formed a really useful part of my education. We went to Egypt, journeyed up the Nile, travelled through the Holy Land and part of Syria, visited Greece and Constantinople; and then we children spent the summer in a German family in Dresden. My first real collecting as a student of natural history was done in Egypt during this journey. By this time I had a good working knowledge of American bird-life from the superficially scientific standpoint. I had no knowledge of the ornithology of Egypt, but I picked up in Cairo a book by an English clergyman, whose name I have now forgotten, who described a trip up the Nile, and in an appendix to his volume gave an account of his bird collection. I wish I could remember the name of the author now, for I owe that book very much. Without it I should have been collecting entirely in the dark, whereas with its aid I could generally find out what the birds were. My first knowledge of Latin was obtained by learning the scientific names of the birds and mammals which I collected and classified by the aid of such books as this one.

The birds I obtained up the Nile and in Palestine represented merely the usual boy's collection. Some years afterward I gave them, together with the other ornithological specimens I had gathered, to the Smithsonian Institution in Washington, and I think some of them also to the American Museum of Natural History in New York. I am told that the skins are to be found yet in both places and in other public collections. I doubt whether they have my original labels on them. With great pride the directors of the "Roosevelt Museum," consisting of myself and the two cousins aforesaid, had printed a set of Roosevelt Museum labels in pink ink preliminary to what was regarded as my adventurous trip to Egypt. This bird-collecting gave what was really the chief zest to my Nile journey. I was old enough and had read enough to enjoy the temples and the desert scenery and the general feeling of romance; but this in time would have palled if I had not also had the serious work of collecting and preparing my specimens. Doubtless the family had their moments of suffering—especially on one occasion when a well-meaning maid extracted from my taxidermist's outfit the old tooth-brush with which I put on the skins the arsenical soap necessary for their preservation, partially washed it, and left it with the rest of my wash-kit for my own personal use. I suppose that all growing boys tend to be grubby; but the ornithological small boy, or indeed the boy with the taste for natural history of any kind, is generally the very grubbiest of all. . . .

When we reached Dresden we younger children were left to spend the summer in the house of Herr Minckwitz, a member of either the Municipal or the Saxon Government—I have forgotten which. It was hoped that in this way we would acquire some knowledge of the German language and literature. They were the very kindest family imaginable. I shall never forget the unwearied patience of the two daughters. The father and mother, and a shy, thin, student cousin who was living in the flat, were no less kind. Whenever I could get out into the country I collected specimens industriously and enlivened the household with hedge-hogs and other small beasts and reptiles which persisted in escaping from partially closed bureau drawers. The two sons were fascinating students from the University of Leipsic, both of them belonging to duelling corps, and much scarred in consequence. One, a famous swordsman, was called *Der Rothe Herzog* (the Red Duke), and the other was nicknamed *Herr Nasehorn* (Sir Rhinoceros) because the tip of his nose had been cut off in a duel and sewn on again. I learned a good deal of German here, in spite of myself, and above all I became fascinated with the Nibelungenlied. German prose never became really easy to me in the sense that French prose did, but for German poetry I cared as much as for English poetry. Above all, I gained an impression of the German people which I never got over. From that time to this it would have been quite impossible to make me feel that the Germans were really foreigners. The affection, the *Gemüthlichkeit* (a quality which cannot be exactly expressed by any single English word), the capacity for hard work, the sense of duty, the delight in studying literature and science, the pride in the new Germany, the more than kind and friendly interest in three strange children—all these manifestations of the German character and of German family life made a subconscious impression upon me which I did not in the least define at the time, but which is very vivid still forty years later.

When I got back to America, at the age of fifteen, I began serious study to enter Harvard under Mr. Arthur Cutler, who later founded the Cutler School in New York. I could not go to school because I knew so much less than most boys of my age in some subjects and so much more in others. In science and history and geography and in unexpected parts of German and French I was strong, but lamentably weak in Latin and Greek and mathematics. My grandfather had made his summer home in Oyster Bay a number of years before, and my father now made Oyster Bay the summer home of his family also. Along with my college preparatory studies I carried on the work of a practical student of natural history. I worked with greater industry than either intelligence or success, and made very few additions to the sum of human knowledge; but to this day certain obscure ornithological publications may be found in which are recorded such items as, for instance, that on one occasion a fish-crow, and on another an Ipswich sparrow, were obtained by one Theodore Roosevelt, Jr., at Oyster Bay, on the shore of Long Island Sound.

In the fall of 1876 I entered Harvard, graduating in 1880. I thoroughly enjoyed Harvard, and I am sure it did me good, but only in the general effect, for there was very little in my actual studies which helped me in afterlife. More than one of my own sons have already profited by their friendship with certain of their masters in school or college. I certainly profited by my friendship with one of my tutors, Mr. Cutler; and in Harvard I owed much to the professor of English, Mr. A. S. Hill. Doubtless through my own fault, I saw almost nothing of President Eliot and very little of the professors. I ought to have gained much more than I did gain from writing the themes and forensics. My failure to do so may have been partly due to my taking no interest in the subjects. Before I left Harvard I was already writing one or two chapters of a book I afterward published on the naval war of 1812. Those chapters were so dry that they would have made a dictionary seem light reading by comparison. Still, they represented purpose and serious interest on my part, not the perfunctory effort to do well enough to get a certain mark; and corrections of them by a skilled older man would have impressed me and have commanded my respectful attention. But I was not sufficiently developed to make myself take an intelligent interest in some of the subjects assigned me—the character of the Gracchi, for instance. A very clever and studious lad would no doubt have done so, but I personally did not grow up to this particular subject until a good many years later. The frigate and sloop actions between the American and British sea-tigers of 1812 were much more within my grasp. I worked drearily at the Gracchi because I had to; my conscientious and much-to-be-pitied professor dragging me through the theme by main strength, with my feet firmly planted in dull and totally idea-proof resistance. . . .

I was a reasonably good student in college, standing just within the first tenth of my class, if I remember rightly; although I am not sure whether this means the tenth of the whole number that entered or of those that graduated. I was given a Phi Beta Kappa "key." My chief interests were scientific. When I entered college, I was devoted to out-of-doors natural history, and my ambition was to be a scientific man of the Audubon, or Wilson, or Baird, or Coues type—a man like Hart Merriam, or Frank Chapman, or Hornaday, to-day. My father had from the earliest days instilled into me the knowledge that I was to work and to make my own way in the world, and I had always supposed that this meant that I must enter business. But in my freshman year (he died when I was a sophomore) he told me that if I wished to become a scientific man I could do so. He explained that I must be sure that I really intensely desired to do scientific work, because if I went into it I must make it a serious career; that he had made enough money to enable me to take up such a career and do non-remunerative work of value *if I intended to do the very best work there was in me*; but that I must not dream of taking it up as a dilettante. He also gave me a piece of advice that I have always remembered, namely, that, if I was not going to earn money, I must even things up by not spending it. As he expressed it, I had to keep the fraction constant, and if I was not able to increase the numerator, then I must reduce the denominator. In other words, if I went into a scientific career, I must definitely abandon all thought of the enjoyment that could accompany a money-making career, and must find my pleasures elsewhere.

After this conversation I fully intended to make science my life-work. I did not, for the simple reason that at that time Harvard, and I suppose our other colleges, utterly ignored the possibilities of the faunal naturalist, the outdoor naturalist and observer of nature. They treated biology as purely a science of the laboratory and the microscope, a science whose adherents were to spend their time in the study of minute forms of marine life, or else in section-cutting and the study of the tissues of the higher organisms under the microscope. This attitude was, no doubt, in part due to the fact that in most colleges then there was a not always intelligent copying of what was done in the great

German universities. The sound revolt against superficiality of study had been carried to an extreme; thoroughness in minutiæ as the only end of study had been erected into a fetich. There was a total failure to understand the great variety of kinds of work that could be done by naturalists, including what could be done by outdoor naturalists —the kind of work which Hart Merriam and his assistants in the Biological Survey have carried to such a high degree of perfection as regards North American mammals. In the entirely proper desire to be thorough and to avoid slipshod methods, the tendency was to treat as not serious, as unscientific, any kind of work that was not carried on with laborious minuteness in the laboratory. My taste was specialized in a totally different direction, and I had no more desire or ability to be a microscopist and section-cutter than to be a mathematician. Accordingly I abandoned all thought of becoming a scientist. Doubtless this meant that I really did not have the intense devotion to science which I thought I had; for, if I had possessed such devotion, I would have carved out a career for myself somehow without regard to discouragements. . . .

The teaching which I received was genuinely democratic in one way. It was not so democratic in another. I grew into manhood thoroughly imbued with the feeling that a man must be respected for what he made of himself. But I had also, consciously or unconsciously, been taught that socially and industrially pretty much the whole duty of the man lay in thus making the best of himself; that he should be honest in his dealings with others and charitable in the old-fashioned way to the unfortunate; but that it was no part of his business to join with others in trying to make things better for the many by curbing the abnormal and excessive development of individualism in a few. Now I do not mean that this training was by any means all bad. On the contrary, the insistence upon individual responsibility was, and is, and always will be, a prime necessity. Teaching of the kind I absorbed from both my textbooks and my surroundings is a healthy antiscorbutic to the sentimentality which by complacently excusing the individual for all his shortcomings would finally hopelessly weaken the spring of moral purpose. It also keeps alive that virile vigor for the lack of which in the average individual no possible perfection of law or of community action can ever atone. But such teaching, if not corrected by other teaching, means acquiescence in a riot of lawless business individualism which would be quite as destructive to real civilization as the lawless military individualism of the Dark Ages. I left college and entered the big world owing more than I can express to the training I had received, especially in my own home; but with much else also to learn if I were to become really fitted to do my part in the work that lay ahead for the generation of Americans to which I belonged.

TR was only telling the truth when he recalled in his autobiography his childhood passion for playing naturalist. When not ten years old, he wrote his mother and his sister Corinne (Conie):

My Dear Mamma I have just received your letter! What an excitement. How nice to read it What long letters you do write. I don't see how you can write them. My mouth opened wide with astonish when I heard how many flowers were sent in to you. I could revel in the buggie ones. I jumped with delight when I found you heard the mock-ing-bird, get some of its feathers if you can. Thank Johnny for the feathers of the soldier's cap, give him my love also. We cried when you wrote about Grand-Mamma. Give my love to the good natured (to use your own expression) handsome, lion, Conie, Johnny, Maud and Aunt Lucy. I am sorry the trees have been cut down. Aunt Annie, Edith, and Ellie send their love to you and all I sent mine to. I send this picture to Conie. In the letter you write to me tell me how many curiosities and living things you have got for me. I miss Conie very much. I wish I were with you and Johnny for I could hunt for myself. Here is Conie's letter

My dear Conie As I wrote so much in Mamma's letter I can not write so much in yours I have got four mice two white-skined, red eyed, velvety cretures very tame for I let them run all over me they trie to get down the back of my neck and under my vest and two brown-skined, black-eyed soft as the others but wilder. Lordy and Rosa are the names of the white mice which are male and female. I keep them in different cages

TR *worshipped his father, who died in 1878, when the future President was not yet 20. From Harvard TR wrote his father in the fall of 1876:*

I do not think there is a fellow in College who has a family that love him as much as you all do me, and I am *sure* that there is no one who has a Father who is also his best and most intimate friend, as you are mine. I have kept the first letter you wrote me and shall do my best to deserve your trust. I do not find it nearly so hard as I expected not to drink and smoke, many of the fellows backing me up. For example, out of the eleven other boys at the table where I am, no less than seven do not smoke and four drink nothing stronger than beer.

In his autobiography TR made no mention of his first wife Alice Lee. That he was deeply in love with her is evident in this memorial he wrote on her death. (The baby girl was the future Alice Roosevelt Longworth.)

She was born at Chestnut Hill, Massachusetts, on July 29, 1861; I first saw her on October 18, 1878, and loved her as soon as I saw her sweet, fair young face; we were betrothed on January 25, 1880, and married on October 27th, of the same year; we spent three years of happiness such as rarely comes to man or woman; on February 12, 1884, her baby girl was born; she kissed it, and seemed perfectly well; some hours afterward she, not knowing that she was in the slightest danger, but thinking only that she was falling into a sleep, became insensible, and died at two o'clock on Thursday afternoon, February 14, 1884, at 6 West Fifty-seventh Street, in New York; she was buried two days afterward, in Greenwood Cemetery.

She was beauitful in face and form, and lovelier still in spirit; as a flower she grew, and as a fair young flower she died. Her life had been always in the sunshine; there had never come to her a single great sorrow; and none ever knew her who did not love and revere her for her bright, sunny temper and her saintly unselfishness. Fair, pure, and joyous as a maiden; loving, tender, and happy as a young wife; when she had just become a mother, when her life seemed to be but just begun, and when the years seemed so bright before her—then, by a strange and terrible fate, death came to her.

And when my heart's dearest died, the light went from my life for ever.

CHAPTER 2

The Vigor of Life

HAVING BEEN a sickly boy, with no natural bodily prowess, and having lived much at home, I was at first quite unable to hold my own when thrown into contact with other boys of rougher antecedents. I was nervous and timid. Yet from reading of the people I admired—ranging from the soldiers of Valley Forge, and Morgan's riflemen, to the heroes of my favorite stories—and from hearing of the feats performed by my Southern forefathers and kinsfolk, and from knowing my father, I felt a great admiration for men who were fearless and who could hold their own in the world, and I had a great desire to be like them. Until I was nearly fourteen I let this desire take no more definite shape than day-dreams. Then an incident happened that did me real good. Having an attack of asthma, I was sent off by myself to Moosehead Lake. On the stage-coach ride thither I encountered a couple of other boys who were about my own age, but very much more competent and also much more mischievous. I have no doubt they were goodhearted boys, but they were boys! They found that

I was a foreordained and predestined victim, and industriously proceeded to make life miserable for me. The worst feature was that when I finally tried to fight them I discovered that either one singly could not only handle me with easy contempt, but handle me so as not to hurt me much and yet to prevent my doing any damage whatever in return.

The experience taught me what probably no amount of good advice could have taught me. I made up my mind that I must try to learn so that I would not again be put in such a helpless position; and having become quickly and bitterly conscious that I did not have the natural prowess to hold my own, I decided that I would try to supply its place by training. Accordingly, with my father's hearty approval, I started to learn to box. I was a painfully slow and awkward pupil, and certainly worked two or three years before I made any perceptible improvement whatever. My first boxing-master was John Long, an ex-prize-fighter. I can see his rooms now, with colored pictures of the fights between Tom Hyer and Yankee Sullivan, and Heenan and Sayers, and other great events in the annals of the squared circle. On one occasion, to excite interest among his patrons, he held a series of "championship" matches for the different weights, the prizes being, at least in my own class, pewter mugs of a value, I should suppose, approximating fifty cents. Neither he nor I had any idea that I could do anything, but I was entered in the lightweight contest, in which it happened that I was pitted in succession against a couple of reedy striplings who were even worse than I was. Equally to their surprise and to my own, and to John Long's, I won, and the pewter mug became one of my most prized possessions.

I kept it, and alluded to it, and I fear bragged about it,

for a number of years, and I only wish I knew where it was now. Years later I read an account of a little man who once in a fifth-rate handicap race won a worthless pewter medal and joyed in it ever after. Well, as soon as I read that story I felt that that little man and I were brothers.

This was, as far as I remember, the only one of my exceedingly rare athletic triumphs which would be worth relating. I did a good deal of boxing and wrestling in Harvard, but never attained to the first rank in either, even at my own weight. Once, in the big contests in the Gym, I got either into the finals or semi-finals, I forget which; but aside from this the chief part I played was to act as trial horse for some friend or classmate who did have a chance of distinguishing himself in the championship contests.

I was fond of horseback-riding, but I took to it slowly and with difficulty, exactly as with boxing. It was a long time before I became even a respectable rider, and I never got much higher. I mean by this that I never became a first-flight man in the hunting-field, and never even approached the bronco-busting class in the West. Any man, if he chooses, can gradually school himself to the requisite nerve, and gradually learn the requisite seat and hands, that will enable him to do respectably across country, or to perform the average work on a ranch. . . .

I was fond of walking and climbing. As a lad I used to go to the north woods, in Maine, both in fall and winter. There I made life friends of two men, Will Dow and Bill Sewall; I canoed with them, and tramped through the woods with them, visiting the winter logging camps on snow-shoes. Afterward they were with me in the West. . . . Bill Sewall was collector of customs under me, on the Aroostook border. Except when hunting I never did any mountaineering save for a couple of conventional trips up the Matterhorn and the Jungfrau on one occasion when I was in Switzerland.

I never did much with the shotgun, but I practised a good deal with the rifle. I had a rifle-range at Sagamore Hill, where I often took friends to shoot. Once or twice when I was visited by parties of released Boer prisoners, after the close of the South African War, they and I held shooting-matches together. The best man with both pistol and rifle who ever shot there was Stewart Edward White. Among the many other good men was a stanch friend, Baron Speck von Sternberg, afterward German Ambassador at Washington during my presidency. He was a capital shot, rider, and walker, a devoted and most efficient servant of Germany, who had fought with distinction in the Franco-German War when barely more than a boy; he was the hero of the story of "the pig dog" in Archibald Forbes's volume of reminiscences. It was he who first talked over with me the raising of a regiment of horse riflemen from among the ranchmen and cowboys of the plains. When Ambassador, the poor, gallant, tender-hearted fellow was dying of a slow and painful disease, so that he could not play with the rest of us, but the agony of his mortal illness never in the slightest degree interfered with his work. Among the other men who shot and rode and walked with me was Cecil Spring-Rice, . . . [later] British ambassador to the United States. He was my groomsman, my best man, when I was married—at St. George's, Hanover Square, which made me feel as if I were living in one of Thackeray's novels. . . .*

* In London, December 2, 1886, Theodore Roosevelt was married to Edith Carow of New York whom he had known since his boyhood. [*Editor's note*]

When obliged to live in cities, I for a long time found that boxing and wrestling enabled me to get a good deal of exercise in condensed and attractive form. I was reluctantly obliged to abandon both as I grew older. I dropped the wrestling earliest. When I became Governor, the champion middle-weight wrestler of America happened to be in Albany, and I got him to come round three or four afternoons a week. Incidentally I may mention that his presence caused me a difficulty with the comptroller, who refused to audit a bill I put in for a wrestling-mat, explaining that I could have a billiard-table, billiards being recognized as a proper gubernatorial amusement, but that a wrestling-mat symbolized something unusual and unheard of and could not be permitted. The middle-weight champion was of course so much better than I was that he could not only take care of himself but of me too and see that I was not hurt—for wrestling is a much more violent amusement than boxing. But after a couple of months he had to go away, and he left as a substitute a good-humored, stalwart professional oarsman. The oarsman turned out to know very little about wrestling. He could not even take care of himself, not to speak of me. By the end of our second afternoon one of his long ribs had been caved in and two of my short ribs badly damaged, and my left shoulder-blade so nearly shoved out of place that it creaked. He was nearly as pleased as I was when I told him I thought we would "vote the war a failure" and abandon wrestling. After that I took up boxing again. While President I used to box with some of the aides, as well as play single-stick with General Wood. After a few years I had to abandon boxing as well as wrestling, for in one bout a young captain of artillery cross-countered me on the eye, and the blow smashed the little blood-vessels. Fortunately it was my left eye, but the sight has been dim ever since, and if it had been the right eye I should have been entirely unable to shoot. Accordingly I thought it better to acknowledge that I had become an elderly man and would have to stop boxing. I then took up jiu-jitsu for a year or two.

When I was in the legislature and was working very hard, with little chance of getting out-of-doors, all the exercise I got was boxing and wrestling. A young fellow turned up who was a second-rate prize-fighter, the son of one of my old boxing teachers. For several weeks I had him come round to my rooms in the morning to put on the gloves with me for half an hour. Then he suddenly stopped, and some days later I received a letter of woe from him from the jail. I found that he was by profession a burglar, and merely followed boxing as the amusement of his lighter moments, or when business was slack. . . .

On one occasion one of my prize-fighting friends called on me at the White House on business. He explained that he wished to see me alone, sat down opposite me, and put a very expensive cigar on the desk, saying: "Have a cigar." I thanked him and said I did not smoke, to which he responded: "Put it in your pocket." He then added: "Take another; put both in your pocket." This I accordingly did. Having thus shown at the outset the necessary formal courtesy, my visitor, an old and valued friend, proceeded to explain that a nephew of his had enlisted in the Marine Corps, but had been absent without leave, and was threatened with dishonorable discharge on the ground of desertion. My visitor, a good citizen and a patriotic American, was stung to the quick at the thought of such an incident occurring in his family, and he explained to me that it must not occur, that there must not be the disgrace to the

family, although he would be delighted to have the offender "handled rough" to teach him a needed lesson; he
added that he wished I would take him and handle him
myself, for he knew that I would see that he "got all that
was coming to him." Then a look of pathos came into his
eyes, and he explained: "That boy I just cannot understand. He was my sister's favorite son, and I always took
a special interest in him myself. I did my best to bring him
up the way he ought to go. But there was just nothing to
be done with him. His tastes were naturally low. He took
to music!" What form this debasing taste for music assumed I did not inquire; and I was able to grant my friend's
wish.

While in the White House I always tried to get a couple
of hours' exercise in the afternoons—sometimes tennis,
more often riding, or else a rough cross-country walk,
perhaps down Rock Creek, which was then as wild as a
stream in the White Mountains, or on the Virginia side
along the Potomac. My companions at tennis or on these
rides and walks we gradually grew to style the Tennis
Cabinet; and then we extended the term to take in many of
my old-time Western friends. . . . and others who had taken
part with me in more serious outdoor adventures than
walking and riding for pleasure. Most of the men who were
oftenest with me on these trips . . . were better men
physically than I was; but I could ride and walk well
enough for us all thoroughly to enjoy it. Often, especially
in the winters and early springs, we would arrange for a
point-to-point walk, not turning aside for anything—for
instance, swimming Rock Creek or even the Potomac if
it came in our way. Of course under such circumstances
we had to arrange that our return to Washington should
be when it was dark, so that our appearance might scandal-

ize no one. On several occasions we thus swam Rock Creek in the early spring when the ice was floating thick upon it. If we swam the Potomac, we usually took off our clothes. I remember one such occasion when the French ambassador, Jusserand, who was a member of the Tennis Cabinet, was along; and, just as we were about to get in to swim, somebody said, "Mr. Ambassador, Mr. Ambassador, you haven't taken off your gloves," to which he promptly responded: "I think I will leave them on; we might meet ladies!"

We liked Rock Creek for these walks because we could do so much scrambling and climbing along the cliffs; there was almost as much climbing when we walked down the Potomac to Washington from the Virginia end of the Chain Bridge. I would occasionally take some big-game friend from abroad . . . on these walks. Once I invited an entire class of officers who were attending lectures at the War College to come on one of these walks; I chose a route which gave us the hardest climbing along the rocks and the deepest crossings of the creek; and my army friends enjoyed it hugely—being the right sort, to a man.

On March 1, 1909, three days before leaving the presidency, various members of the Tennis Cabinet lunched with me at the White House. "Tennis Cabinet" was an elastic term, and of course many who ought to have been at the lunch were, for one reason or another, away from Washington; but, to make up for this, a goodly number of out-of-town honorary members, so to speak, were present—for instance, Seth Bullock; Luther Kelly, better known as Yellowstone Kelly in the days when he was an army scout against the Sioux; and Abernathy, the wolf-hunter. At the end of the lunch Seth Bullock suddenly reached forward, swept aside a mass of flowers which made a centerpiece on the table, and revealed a bronze cougar by Proctor, which was a parting gift to me. The lunch-party and the cougar were then photographed on the lawn.

Some of the younger officers who were my constant companions on these walks and rides pointed out to me the condition of utter physical worthlessness into which certain of the elder ones had permitted themselves to lapse, and the very bad effect this would certainly have if ever the army were called into service. I then looked into the matter for myself, and was really shocked at what I found Many of the older officers were so unfit physically that their condition would have excited laughter, had it not been so serious, to think that they belonged to the military arm of the government. A cavalry colonel proved unable to keep his horse at a smart trot for even half a mile, when I visited his post; a major-general proved afraid even to let his horse canter, when he went on a ride with us; and certain otherwise good men proved as unable to walk as if they had been sedentary brokers. I consulted with men like Major-Generals Wood and Bell, who were themselves of fine physique, with bodies fit to meet any demand. It was late in my administration; and we deemed it best only to make a beginning—experience teaches the most inveterate reformer how hard it is to get a totally non-military nation to accept seriously any military improvement. Accordingly, I merely issued directions that each officer should prove his ability to walk fifty miles, or ride one hundred, in three days.

This is, of course, a test which many a healthy middle-aged woman would be able to meet. But a large portion of the press adopted the view that it was a bit of capricious tyranny on my part; and a considerable number of elderly officers, with desk rather than field experience, intrigued with their friends in Congress to have the order annulled. So one day I took a ride of a little over one hundred miles myself, in company with Surgeon-General Rixey and two other officers. The Virginia roads were frozen and in ruts, and in the afternoon and evening there was a storm of snow and sleet; and when it had been thus experimentally shown, under unfavorable conditions, how easy it was to do in one day the task for which the army officers were allowed three days, all open objection ceased. . . .

CHAPTER 3

Practical Politics

WHEN I LEFT HARVARD, I took up the study of law. If I had been sufficiently fortunate to come under Professor Thayer, of the Harvard Law School, it may well be that I would have realized that the lawyer can do a great work for justice and against legalism.

But, doubtless chiefly through my own fault, some of the teaching of the law-books and of the classroom seemed to me to be against justice. The *caveat emptor* side of the law, like the *caveat emptor* side of business, seemed to me repellent; it did not make for social fair dealing. The "let the buyer beware" maxim, when translated into actual practice, whether in law or business, tends to translate itself further into the seller making his profit at the expense of the buyer, instead of by a bargain which shall be to the profit of both. It did not seem to me that the law was framed to discourage as it should sharp practice, and all other kinds of bargains except those which are fair and of benefit to both sides. I was young; there was much in the judgment which I then formed on this matter which I should now revise; but, then as now, many of the big corporation lawyers, to whom the ordinary members of the bar then as now looked up, held certain standards which were difficult to recognize as compatible with the idealism I suppose every high-minded young man is apt to feel. . . .

Almost immediately after leaving Harvard in 1880 I began to take an interest in politics. I did not then believe, and I do not now believe, that any man should ever attempt to make politics his only career. It is a dreadful misfortune for a man to grow to feel that his whole livelihood and whole happiness depend upon his staying in office. Such a feeling prevents him from being of real service to the people while in office, and always puts him under the heaviest strain of pressure to barter his convictions for the sake of holding office. A man should have some other oc-cupation—I had several other occupations—to which he can resort if at any time he is thrown out of office, or if at any time he finds it necessary to choose a course which will probably result in his being thrown out, unless he is willing to stay in at cost to his conscience.

At that day, in 1880, a young man of my bringing-up and convictions could join only the Republican party, and join it I accordingly did. It was no simple thing to join it then. That was long before the era of ballot reform and the control of primaries; long before the era when we realized that the government must take official notice of the deeds and acts of party organizations. The party was still treated as a private corporation, and in each district the organization formed a kind of social and political club. A man had to be regularly proposed for and elected into this club, just as into any other club. As a friend of mine picturesquely phrased it, I "had to break into the organization with a jimmy." . . .

It was over thirty-three years ago that I thus became a member of the Twenty-first District Republican Association in the city of New York. The men I knew best were the men in the clubs of social pretension and the men of cultivated taste and easy life. When I began to make inquiries as to the whereabouts of the local Republican association and the means of joining it, these men—and the big business men and lawyers also—laughed at me, and told me that politics were "low"; that the organizations were not controlled by "gentlemen"; that I would find them run by saloon-keepers, horse-car conductors, and the like, and not by men with any of whom I would come in contact outside; and, moreover, they assured me that the men I met would be rough and brutal and unpleasant to deal with. I answered that if this were so it merely meant that the people I knew did not belong to the governing class, and that the other people did—and that I intended to be one of the governing class; that if they proved too hard-bit for me I supposed I would have to quit, but that I certainly would not quit until I had made the effort and found out whether I really was too weak to hold my own in the rough and tumble. . . .

I soon became on good terms with a number of the ordinary "heelers" and even some of the minor leaders. The big leader was Jake Hess, who treated me with rather distant affability. There were prominent lawyers and business men who belonged, but they took little part in the actual meetings. What they did was done elsewhere. The running of the machine was left to Jake Hess and his captains of tens and of hundreds.

Among these lesser captains I soon struck up a friendship with Joe Murray, a friendship which is as strong now as it was thirty-three years ago. He had been born in Ireland, but brought to New York by his parents when he was three or four years old, and, as he expressed it, "raised as a barefooted boy on First Avenue." When not eighteen he had enlisted in the Army of the Potomac and taken part in the campaign that closed the Civil War. Then he came back to First Avenue, and, being a fearless, powerful, energetic young fellow, careless and reckless, speedily grew to some prominence as leader of a gang. In that district, and at that time, politics was a rough business, and Tammany Hall held unquestioned sway. The district was overwhelmingly Democratic, and Joe and his friends were Democrats who on election day performed the usual gang work for the local Democratic leader, whose business it was to favor and reward them in return. This same local leader, like many other greater leaders, became puffed up by prosperity, and forgot the instruments through which he had achieved prosperity. After one election he showed a callous indifference to the hard work of the gang and complete disregard of his before-election promises. He counted upon the resentment wearing itself out, as usual, in threats and bluster.

But Joe Murray was not a man who forgot. He explained to his gang his purposes and the necessity of being quiet. Accordingly they waited for their revenge until the next election day. They then, as Joe expressed it, decided "to vote furdest away from the leader"—I am using the language of Joe's youth—and the best way to do this was to vote the Republican ticket. In those days each party had a booth near the polling-place in each election district, where the party representative dispensed the party ballots.

This had been a district in which, as a rule, very early in the day the Republican election leader had his hat knocked over his eyes and his booth kicked over and his ballots scattered; and then the size of the Democratic majority depended on an elastic appreciation of exactly how much was demanded from headquarters. But on this day things went differently. The gang, with a Roman sense of duty, took an active interest in seeing that the Republican was given his full rights. Moreover, they made the most energetic reprisals on their opponents, and as they were distinctly the tough and fighting element, justice came to her own with a whoop. Would-be repeaters were thrown out on their heads. Every person who could be cajoled or, I fear, intimidated, was given the Republican ticket, and the upshot was that at the end of the day a district which had never hitherto polled more than two or three per cent of its vote Republican broke about even between the two parties.

To Joe it had been merely an act of retribution in so far as it was not simply a spree. But the leaders at the Republican headquarters did not know this, and when they got over their paralyzed astonishment at the returns, they investigated to find out what it meant. Somebody told them that it represented the work of a young man named Joseph Murray. Accordingly they sent for him. . . . He was received and patted on the back by a man who was a great man to the world in which he lived. He was introduced to the audience as a young man whose achievement was such as to promise much for the future, and moreover he was given a place in the post-office—as I have said, this was long before the day of civil service reform.

Now, to the wrong kind of man all this might have meant nothing at all. But in Joe Murray's case it meant everything. He was by nature as straight a man, as fearless and as stanchly loyal, as any one whom I have ever met, a man to be trusted in any position demanding courage, integrity, and good faith. He did his duty in the public service, and became devotedly attached to the organization which he felt had given him his chance in life. . . .

Next fall, as the elections drew near, Joe thought he would like to make a drive at Jake Hess, and after considerable planning decided that his best chance lay in the fight for the nomination to the Assembly, the Lower House of the legislature. He picked me as the candidate with whom he would be most likely to win; and win he did. It was not my fight, it was Joe's; and it was to him that I owe my entry into politics. I had at that time neither the reputation nor the ability to have won the nomination for myself, and indeed never would have thought of trying for it.

Jake Hess was entirely good-humored about it. In spite of my being antimachine, my relations with him had been friendly and human, and when he was beaten he turned in to help Joe elect me. At first they thought they would take me on a personal canvass through the saloons along Sixth Avenue. The canvass, however, did not last beyond the first saloon. I was introduced with proper solemnity to the saloon-keeper—a very important personage, for this was before the days when saloon-keepers became merely the mortgaged chattels of the brewers—and he began to cross-examine me, a little too much in the tone of one who was dealing with a suppliant for his favor. He said he expected that I would of course treat the liquor business fairly; to which I answered, none too cordially, that I hoped I should treat all interests fairly. He then said that he regarded the licenses as to high; to which I responded that I believed they were really not high enough, and that I should try to have them made higher. The conversation threatened to become stormy. Messrs. Murray and Hess, on some hastily improvised plea, took me out into the street, and then Joe explained to me that it was not worth my while staying in Sixth Avenue any longer, that I had better go right back to Fifth Avenue and attend to my friends there, and that he would look after my interests on Sixth Avenue. I was triumphantly elected.

Once before Joe had interfered in similar fashion and secured the nomination of an assemblyman; and shortly after election he had grown to feel toward this assemblyman that he must have fed on the meat which rendered Caesar proud, as he became inaccessible to the ordinary mortals whose place of resort was Morton Hall. He eyed me warily for a short time to see if I was likely in this respect to follow in my predecessor's footsteps. Finding that I did not, he and all my other friends and supporters assumed toward me the very pleasantest attitude that it was possible to assume. They did not ask me for a thing. They accepted as a matter of course the view that I was absolutely straight and was trying to do the best I could in the legislature. They desired nothing except that I should make a success, and they supported me with hearty enthusiasm. . . .

My first days in the legislature were much like those of a boy in a strange school. My fellow legislators and I eyed one another with mutual distrust. Each of us chose his seat, each began by following the lead of some veteran in the first routine matters, and then, in a week or two, we began to drift into groups according to our several affinities. The legislature was Democratic. I was a Republican from the "silk-stocking" district, the wealthiest district in New York, and I was put, as one of the minority members, on the Committee of Cities. It was a coveted position. I did not make any effort to get on, and, as far as I know, was put there merely because it was felt to be in accordance with the fitness of things. . . .

My closest friend for the three years I was there was Billy O'Neill, from the Adirondacks. He kept a small crossroads store. He was a young man, although a few years older than I was, and, like myself, had won his position without regard to the machine. He had thought he would like to be assemblyman, so he had taken his buggy and had driven around Franklin County visiting everybody, had upset the local ring, and came to the legislature as his own master. There is surely something in American traditions that does tend toward real democracy in spite of our faults and shortcomings. In most other countries two men of as different antecedents, ancestry, and surroundings as Billy O'Neill and I would have had far more difficulty in coming together. I came from the biggest city in America and from the wealthiest ward of that city, and he from a backwoods county where he kept a store at a crossroads. In all the unimportant things we seemed far apart. But in all the important things we were close together. We looked at all questions from substantially the same view-point, and we stood shoulder to shoulder in every legislative fight during those three years. He abhorred demagogy just as he abhorred corruption. He had thought much on political problems; he admired Alexander Hamilton as much as I did, being a strong believer in a powerful national government; and we both of us differed from Alexander Hamilton in being stout adherents of Abraham Lincoln's views wherever the rights of the people were concerned. Any man who has met with success, if he will be frank with himself, must admit that there has been a big element of fortune in the success. Fortune favored me, whereas her hand was heavy against Billy O'Neill. All his life he had to strive hard to wring his bread from harsh surroundings and a reluctant fate; if fate had been but a little kinder, I believe he would have had a great political career; and he would have done good service for the country in any position in which he might have been put. . . .

Among the Democrats . . . [was] Tom Welch, of Niagara, who did a great service in getting the State to set aside Niagara Falls Park . . . Then there were a couple of members from New York and Brooklyn, Mike Costello and Pete Kelly.

Mike Costello had been elected as a Tammany man. He was as fearless as he was honest. He came from Ireland, and had accepted the Tammany Fourth of July orations as indicating the real attitude of that organization toward the rights of the people. A month or two in Albany converted him to a profound distrust of applied Tammany methods. He and I worked hand in hand with equal indifference to our local machines. His machine leaders warned him fairly that they would throw him out at the next election, which they did; but he possessed a seasoned-hickory toughness of ability to contend with adverse circumstances, and kept his head well above water. A better citizen does not exist; and our friendship has never faltered.

Peter Kelly's fate was a tragedy. He was a bright, well-educated young fellow, an ardent believer in Henry George. At the beginning he and I failed to understand each other or to get on together, for our theories of government were radically opposed. After a couple of months spent in active contests with men whose theories had nothing whatever to do with their practices, Kelly and I found in our turn that it really did not make much difference what our abstract theories were on questions that were not before the legislature, in view of the fact that on the actual matters before the legislature, the most important of which involved questions of elementary morality, we were heartily at one. We began to vote together and act together, and by the end of the session found that in all practical matters that were up for action we thought together. Indeed, each of us was beginning to change his theories, so that even in theory we were coming closer together. He was ardent and generous; he was a young lawyer, with a wife and children, whose ambition had tempted him into politics, and who had been befriended by the local bosses under the belief that they could count upon him for anything they really wished. Unfortunately, what they really wished was often corrupt. Kelly defied them, fought the battles of the people with ardor and good faith, and when the bosses refused him a renomination, he appealed from them to the people. when we both came up for re-election, I won easily in my district, where circumstances conspired to favor me; and Kelly, with exactly the same record that I had, except that it was more creditable because he took his stand against greater odds, was beaten in his district. Defeat to me would have meant merely chagrin; to Kelly it meant terrible material disaster. He had no money. Like every rigidly honest man, he had found that going into politics was expensive and that his salary as assemblyman did not cover the financial outgo. He had lost his practice and he had incurred the ill-will of the powerful, so that it was impossible at the moment to pick up his practice again; and the worry and disappointment affected him so much that shortly after election he was struck down by sickness. Just before Christmas some of us were informed that Kelly was in such financial straits that he and his family would be put out into the street before New Year. This was prevented by the action of some of his friends who had served with him in the legislature, and he recovered, at least to a degree, and took up the practice of his profession. But he was a broken man. . . .

When I went into politics, New York City was under the control of Tammany, which was from time to time opposed by some other—and evanescent—city Democratic organization. The up-country Democrats had not yet fallen under Tammany sway, and were on the point of developing a big country political boss in the shape of David B. Hill. The Republican party was split into the Stalwart and Half-Breed factions. Accordingly neither party had one dominant boss, or one dominant machine, each being controlled by jarring and warring bosses and machines. . . .

Of course I never had anything in the nature of legal proof of corruption, and the figures I am about to give are merely approximate. But three years' experience convinced me, in the first place, that there were a great many thoroughly corrupt men in the legislature, perhaps a third of the whole number; and, in the next place, that the honest men outnumbered the corrupt men, and that, if it were ever possible to get an issue of right and wrong put vividly and unmistakably before them in a way that would arrest their attention and that would arrest the attention of their constituents, we could count on the triumph of the right. The trouble was that in most cases the issue was confused. To read some kinds of literature one would come to the conclusion that the only corruption in legislative circles was in the form of bribery by corporations, and that the line was sharp between the honest man who was always voting against corporations and the dishonest man who was always bribed to vote for them. My experience was the direct contrary of this. For every one bill introduced (not passed) corruptly to favor a corporation, there were at least ten introduced (not passed, and in this case not intended to be passed) to blackmail corporations. . . .

The effective fight against [the] bill for the revision of the Elevated Railway taxes—perhaps the most openly crooked measure which during my time was pushed at Albany—was waged by Mike Costello and myself. We used to spend a good deal of time in industrious research into the various bills introduced, so as to find out what their authors really had in mind; this research, by the way, being highly unappreciated and much resented by the authors. In the course of his researches Mike had been puzzled by an unimportant bill, seemingly related to a constitutional amendment, introduced by a local saloon-keeper, whose interests, as far as we knew, were wholly remote from the Constitution, or from any form of abstract legal betterment. However, the measure seemed harmless; we did not interfere; and it passed the house. Mike, however, followed its career in the Senate, and at the last moment, almost by accident, discovered that it had been "amended" by the simple process of striking out everything after the enacting clause and unobtrusively substituting the proposal to remit the Elevated Railway taxes! . . .

[Now] this was the great bill of the session for the lobby; and the lobby was keenly alive to the need of quick, wise action. No public attention whatever had so far been excited. Every measure was taken to secure immediate and silent action. A powerful leader, whom the beneficiaries of the bill trusted, a fearless and unscrupulous man, of much force and great knowledge of parliamentary law, was put in the chair. Costello and I were watched; and when for a moment we were out of the house, the bill was brought over from the Senate, and the clerk began to read it, all the black horse cavalry, in expectant mood, being in their seats. But Mike Costello, who was in the clerk's room, happened to catch a few words of what was being read. In he rushed, dispatched a messenger for me, and began a single-handed filibuster. The Speaker pro tem called him to order. Mike continued to speak and protest; the Speaker hammered him down; Mike continued his protests; the sergeant-at-arms was sent to arrest and remove him; and then I bounced in, and continued the protest, and refused to sit down or be silent. Amid wild confusion the amendment was declared adopted, and the bill was ordered engrossed and sent to the governor. But we had carried our point. The next morning the whole press rang with what had happened; every detail of the bill, and every detail of the way it had been slipped through the legislature, were made public. All the slow and cautious men in the House, who had been afraid of taking sides, now came forward in support of us. Another debate was held on the proposal to rescind the vote; the city authorities waked up to protest; the governor refused to sign the bill. . . .

One of the stand-by "strikes" was a bill for reducing the Elevated Railway fare, which at that time was ten cents, to five cents. In one legislature the men responsible for the introduction of the bill suffered such an extraordinary change of heart that when the bill came up—being pushed by zealous radicals who really were honest—the introducers actually voted against it! A number of us who had been very doubtful about the principle of the bill voted for it simply because we were convinced that money was being used to stop it, and we hated to seem to side with the corruptionists. Then there came a wave of popular feeling in its favor, the bill was reintroduced at the next session, the railways very wisely decided that they would simply fight it on its merits, and the entire black-horse-cavalry contingent, together with all the former friends of the measure, voted against it. Some of us, who in our anger at the methods formerly resorted to for killing the bill had voted for it the previous year, with much heart-searching again voted for it, as I now think unwisely; and the bill was vetoed by the then governor, Grover Cleveland. I believe the veto was proper, and those who felt as I did supported the veto; for although it was entirely right that the fare should be reduced to five cents, which was soon afterward done, the method was unwise, and would have set a mischievous precedent. . . .

Except as above mentioned, I was not brought in contact with big business, save in the effort to impeach a certain judge.* This judge had been used as an instrument in their business by certain of the men connected with the Elevated Railways and other great corporations at that time. We got hold of his correspondence with one of these men, and it showed a shocking willingness to use the judicial office in any way that one of the kings of finance of that day desired. He had actually held court in one of that financier's rooms. One expression in one of the judge's letters to this financier I shall always remember: "I am willing to go to the very verge of judicial discretion to serve your vast interests." The curious thing was that I was by no means certain that the judge himself was corrupt. He may have been; but I am inclined to think that, aside from his being

* T. R. Westbrook—an ally of Jay Gould. [*Editor's note*]

a man of coarse moral fibre, the trouble lay chiefly in the fact that he had a genuine—if I had not so often seen it, I would say a wholly inexplicable—reverence for the possessor of a great fortune as such. He sincerely believed that business was the end of existence, and that judge and legislator alike should do whatever was necessary to favor it; and the bigger the business the more he desired to favor it. Big business of the kind that is allied with politics thoroughly appreciated the usefulness of such a judge, and every effort was strained to protect him. We fought hard—by "we" I mean some thirty or forty legislators, both Republicans and Democrats—but the "black-horse cavalry," and the timid good men, and the dull conservative men, were all against us; and the vote in the legislature was heavily against impeachment. The minority of the committee that investigated him, with Chapin at its head, recommended impeachment. . . .

It was my first experience of the kind. Various men whom I had known well socially and had been taught to look up to, prominent business men and lawyers, acted in a way which not only astounded me, but which I was quite unable to reconcile with the theories I had formed as to their high standing. . . .

One member of a prominent law firm, an old family friend, did, however, take me out to lunch one day, evidently for the purpose of seeing just what it was that I wished and intended to do. I believe he had a genuine personal liking for me. He explained that I had done well in the legislature; that it was a good thing to have made the "reform play," that I had shown that I possessed ability such as would make me useful in the right kind of law office or business concern; but that I must not overplay my hand; that I had gone far enough, and that now was the time to leave politics and identify myself with the right kind of people, the people who would always in the long run control others and obtain the real rewards which were worth having. I asked him if that meant that I was to yield to the ring in politics. He answered somewhat impatiently that I was entirely mistaken (as in fact I was) about there being merely a political ring, of the kind of which the papers were fond of talking; that the "ring," if it could be called such—that is, the inner circle—included certain big business men, and the politicians, lawyers, and judges who were in alliance with and to a certain extent dependent upon them, and that the successful man had to win his success by the backing of the same forces, whether in law, business, or politics.

This conversation not only interested me, but made such an impression that I always remembered it, for it was the first glimpse I had of that combination between business and politics which I was in after-years so often to oppose. . . .

The only kinds of courage and honesty which are permanently useful to good institutions anywhere are those shown by men who decide all cases with impartial justice on grounds of conduct and not on grounds of class. We found that in the long run the men who in public blatantly insisted that labor was never wrong were the very men who in private could not be trusted to stand for labor when it was right. We grew heartily to distrust the reformer who never denounced wickedness unless it was embodied in a rich man. Human nature does not change; and that type of "reformer" is as noxious now as he ever was. The loud-mouthed upholder of popular rights who attacks wickedness only when it is allied with wealth, and who never publicly assails any misdeed, no matter how flagrant, if committed nominally in the interest of labor, has either a warped mind or a tainted soul, and should be trusted by no honest man. It was largely the indignant and contemptuous dislike aroused in our minds by the demagogues of this class which then prevented those of us whose instincts at bottom were sound from going as far as we ought to have gone along the lines of governmental control of corporations and governmental interference on behalf of labor.

I did, however, have one exceedingly useful experience. A bill was introduced by the Cigarmakers' Union to prohibit the manufacture of cigars in tenement-houses. I was appointed one of a committee of three to investigate conditions in the tenement-houses and see if legislation should be had. Of my two colleagues on the committee, one took no interest in the measure and privately said he did not think it was right, but that he had to vote for it because the labor-unions were strong in his district and he was pledged to support the bill. The other, a sporting Tammany man who afterward abandoned politics for the race-track, was a very good fellow. He told me frankly that he had to be against the bill because certain interests which were all-powerful and with which he had dealings required him to be against it, but that I was a free agent, and that if I would look into the matter he believed I would favor the legislation. As a matter of fact, I had supposed I would be against the legislation, and I rather think that I was put on the committee with that idea, for the respectable people I knew were against it; it was contrary to the principles of political economy of the *laissez-faire* kind; and the business men who spoke to me about it shook their heads and said that it was designed to prevent a man doing as he wished and as he had a right to do with what was his own.

However, my first visits to the tenement-house districts in question made me feel that, whatever the theories might be, as a matter of practical common sense I could not conscientiously vote for the continuance of the conditions which I saw. These conditions rendered it impossible for the families of the tenement-house workers to live so that the children might grow up fitted for the exacting duties of American citizenship. I visited the tenement-houses once with my colleagues of the committee, once with some of the labor-union representatives, and once or twice by myself. In a few of the tenement-houses there were suites of rooms ample in number where the work on the tobaccoo was done in rooms not occupied for cooking or sleeping or living. In the overwhelming majority of cases, however, there were one, two, or three room apartments, and the work of manufacturing the tobacco by men, women, and children went on day and night in the eating, living, and sleeping rooms—sometimes in one room. I have always remembered one room in which two families were living. On my inquiry as to who the third adult male was I was told that he was a boarder with one of the families. There were several children, three men, and two women in this room. The tobacco was stowed about everywhere, alongside the foul bedding, and in a corner where there were scraps of food. The men, women, and children in this room worked by day and far on into the evening, and they slept and ate there. They were Bohemians, unable to speak English, except that one of the children knew enough to act as interpreter.

Instead of opposing the bill I ardently championed it.

It was a poorly drawn measure, and the governor, Grover Cleveland, was at first doubtful about signing it. The Cigar-makers' Union then asked me to appear before the governor and argue for it. I accordingly did so, acting as spokesman for the battered, undersized foreigners who represented the Union and the workers. The governor signed the bill. Afterward this tenement-house cigar legislation was declared invalid by the court of appeals in the Jacobs decision. Jacobs was one of the rare tenement-house manufacturers of cigars who occupied quite a suite of rooms, so that in his case the living conditions were altogether exceptional. What the reason was which influenced those bringing the suit to select the exceptional instead of the average worker I do not know; of course such action was precisely the action which those most interested in having the law broken down were anxious to see taken. The court of appeals declared the law unconstitutional, and in their decision the judges reprobated the law as an assault upon the "hallowed" influences of "home." It was this case which first waked me to a dim and partial understanding of the fact that the courts were not necessarily the best judges of what should be done to better social and industrial conditions. The judges who rendered this decision were well-meaning men. They knew nothing whatever of tenement-house conditions; they knew nothing whatever of the needs, or of the life and labor, of three-fourths of their fellow citizens in great cities. They knew legalism, but not life. . . .

Like most young men in politics, I went through various oscillations of feeling before I "found myself." At one period I became so impressed with the virtue of complete independence that I proceeded to act on each case purely as I personally viewed it, without paying any heed to the principles and prejudices of others. The result was that I speedily and deservedly lost all power of accomplishing anything at all; and I thereby learned the invaluable lesson that in the practical activities of life no man can render the highest service unless he can act in combination with his fellows, which means a certain amount of give and take between him and them. Again, I at one period began to believe that I had a future before me, and that it behooved me to be very far-sighted and scan each action carefully with a view to its possible effect on that future. This speedily made me useless to the public and an object of aversion to myself; and I then made up my mind that I would try not to think of the future at all, but would proceed on the assumption that each office I held would be the last I ever should hold, and that I would confine myself to trying to do my work as well as possible while I held that office. I found that for me personally this was the only way in which I could either enjoy myself or render good service to the country, and I never afterward deviated from this plan.

As regards political advancement the bosses could of course do a good deal. . . . The third year the Republicans carried the legislature, and the bosses at once took a hand in the Speakership contest. I made a stout fight for the nomination, but the bosses of the two factions, the Stalwarts and the Half-Breeds, combined and I was beaten. I was much chagrined for the moment. But the fact that I had fought hard and efficiently, even though defeated, and that I had made the fight single-handed, with no machine back of me, assured my standing as floor leader. . . . After the session closed four of us who looked at politics from the same standpoint and were known as Independent or Antimachine Republicans, were sent by the State convention as delegates-at-large to the Republican National Convention of 1884, where I advocated, as vigorously as I knew how, the nomination of Senator George F. Edmunds. Mr. Edmunds was defeated and Mr. Blaine nominated. Mr. Blaine was clearly the choice of the rank and file of the party; his nomination was won in fair and above-board fashion, because the rank and file of the party stood back of him; and I supported him to the best of my ability in the ensuing campaign.

The Speakership contest enlightened me as regards more things than the attitude of the bosses. I had already had some exasperating experiences with the "silk-stocking" reformer type, as Abraham Lincoln called it, the gentlemen who were very nice, very refined, who shook their heads over political corruption and discussed it in drawing-rooms and parlors, but who were wholly unable to grapple with real men in real life. They were apt vociferously to demand "reform" as if it were some concrete substance, like cake, which could be handed out at will, in tangible masses, if only the demand were urgent enough. These parlor reformers made up for inefficiency in action by zeal in criticising; and they delighted in criticising the men who really were doing the things which they said ought to be done, but which they lacked the sinewy power to do. They often upheld ideals which were not merely impossible but highly undesirable, and thereby played into the hands of the very politicians to whom they professed to be most hostile. Moreover, if they believed that their own interests, individually or as a class, were jeoparded, they were apt to show no higher standards than did the men they usually denounced. . . .

When Blaine secured the Republican nomination for President in 1884, TR dutifully supported him—but with many more misgivings than a reader of his autobiography would guess. To his sister Anna TR made plain that his heart was not in the race:

Well, the fight has been fought and lost, and moreover our defeat is an overwhelming rout. Of all the men presented to the convention as presidential candidates, I consider Blaine as by far the most objectionable, because his personal honesty, as well as his faithfulness as a public servant, are both open to question; yet beyond a doubt he was opposed by many, if not most, of the politicians and was the free choice of the great majority of the Republican voters of the northern states. That such should be the fact speaks badly for the intelligence of the mass of my party, as well as for their sensitiveness to the honesty and uprightness of a public official, and bodes no good for the future of the nation—though I am far from thinking that any very serious harm can result even from either of the two evils to which our choice is now limited viz:—a democratic administration or four years of Blaine in the White House. The country has stood a great deal in the past and can stand a great deal more in the future. It is by no means the first time that a vast popular majority has been on the side of wrong. It may be that "the voice of the people is the voice of God" in fifty one cases out of a hundred; but in the remaining forty nine it is quite as likely to be the voice of the devil, or, what is still worse, the voice of a fool.

While ranching in the Badlands, TR recovered, quickly, from the shock of Cleveland's election.

CHAPTER 4

In Cowboy Land

THOUGH I HAD PREVIOUSLY made a trip into the then Territory of Dakota, beyond the Red River, it was not until 1883 that I went to the Little Missouri, and there took hold of two cattle-ranches, the Chimney Butte and the Elkhorn.

It was still the Wild West in those days, the far West, the West of Owen Wister's stories and Frederic Remington's drawings, the West of the Indian and the buffalo-hunter, the soldier and the cow-puncher. That land of the West has gone now, "gone, gone with lost Atlantis," gone to the isle of ghosts and of strange dead memories. It was a land of vast silent spaces, of lonely rivers, and of plains where the wild game stared at the passing horseman. It was a land of scattered ranches, of herds of long-horned cattle, and of reckless riders who unmoved looked in the eyes of life or of death. In that land we led a free and hardy life, with horse and with rifle. We worked under the scorching midsummer sun, when the wide plains shimmered and wavered in the heat; and we knew the freezing

58

misery of riding night guard round the cattle in the late
fall round-up. In the soft springtime the stars were glorious
in our eyes each night before we fell asleep; and in the
winter we rode through blinding blizzards, when the
driven snow-dust burned our faces. There were monotonous days, as we guided the trail cattle or the beef herds,
hour after hour, at the slowest of walks; and minutes or
hours teeming with excitement as we stopped stampedes
or swam the herds across rivers treacherous with quick-
sands or brimmed with running ice. We knew toil and
hardship and hunger and thirst; and we saw men die violent
deaths as they worked among the horses and cattle, or
fought in evil feuds with one another; but we felt the beat
of hardy life in our veins, and ours was the glory of work
and the joy of living.

It was right and necessary that this life should pass, for
the safety of our country lies in its being made the country
of the small home-maker. The great unfenced ranches, in
the days of "free grass," necessarily represented a temporary stage in our history. The large migratory flocks of
sheep, each guarded by the hired shepherds of absentee
owners, were the first enemies of the cattlemen; and owing
to the way they ate out the grass and destroyed all other
vegetation, these roving sheep bands represented little of
permanent good to the country. But the homesteaders, the
permanent settlers, the men who took up each his own
farm on which he lived and brought up his family, these
represented from the national standpoint the most desirable
of all possible users of, and dwellers on, the soil. Their
advent meant the breaking up of the big ranches; and the
change was a national gain, although to some of us an
individual loss.

I first reached the Little Missouri on a Northern Pacific

train about three in the morning of a cool September day in 1883. Aside from the station, the only building was a ramshackle structure called the Pyramid Park Hotel. I dragged my duffle-bag thither, and hammered at the door until the frowsy proprietor appeared, muttering oaths. He ushered me up-stairs, where I was given one of the fourteen beds in the room which by itself constituted the entire upper floor. Next day I walked over to the abandoned army post, and, after some hours among the gray log shacks, a ranchman who had driven into the station agreed to take me out to his ranch, the Chimney Butte ranch, where he was living with his brother and their partner.

The ranch was a log structure with a dirt roof, a corral for the horses near by, and a chicken-house jabbed against the rear of the ranch-house. Inside there was only one room, with a table, three or four chairs, a cooking-stove, and three bunks. The owners were Sylvane and Joe Ferris and William J. Merrifield. Later all three of them held my commissions while I was President. . . .

After a buffalo-hunt with my original friend, Joe Ferris, I entered into partnership with Merrifield and Sylvane Ferris, and we started a cow-ranch, with the maltese-cross brand—always known as "maltee-cross" by the way, as the general impression along the Little Missouri was that "maltese" must be a plural. . . .

I do not believe there ever was any life more attractive to a vigorous young fellow than life on a cattle-ranch in those days. It was a fine, healthy life, too; it taught a man self-reliance, hardihood, and the value of instant decision —in short, the virtues that ought to come from life in the open country. I enjoyed the life to the full. After the first year I built on the Elkhorn ranch a long, low ranch-house of hewn logs, with a veranda, and with, in addition to the

other rooms, a bedroom for myself, and a sitting-room
with a big fireplace. I got out a rocking-chair—I am very
fond of rocking-chairs—and enough books to fill two or
three shelves, and a rubber bathtub so that I could get a
bath. And then I do not see how any one could have lived
more comfortably. We had buffalo-robes and bearskins
of our own killing. We always kept the house clean—
using the word in a rather large sense. There were at least
two rooms that were always warm, even in the bitterest
weather; and we had plenty to eat. Commonly the main-
stay of every meal was game of our own killing, usually
antelope or deer, sometimes grouse or ducks, and occasionally, in the earlier days, buffalo or elk. We also had flour
and bacon, sugar, salt, and canned tomatoes. And later,
when some of the men married and brought out their
wives, we had all kinds of good things, such as jams and
jellies made from the wild plums and the buffalo-berries,
and potatoes from the forlorn little garden patch. Moreover, we had milk. Most ranchmen at that time never had
milk. I knew more than one ranch with ten thousand head
of cattle where there was not a cow that could be milked.
We made up our minds that we would be more enterprising. Accordingly, we started to domesticate some of
the cows. Our first effort was not successful, chiefly because we did not devote the needed time and patience to
the matter. And we found that to race a cow two miles at
full speed on horseback, then rope her, throw her, and
turn her upside down to milk her, while exhilarating as a
pastime, was not productive of results. Gradually we accumulated tame cows, and, after we had thinned out the
bobcats and coyotes, more chickens.

The ranch-house stood on the brink of a low bluff over-
looking the broad, shallow bed of the Little Missouri,

through which at most seasons there ran only a trickle of water, while in times of freshet it was filled brimful with the boiling, foaming, muddy torrent. There was no neighbor for ten or fifteen miles on either side of me. The river twisted down in long curves between narrow bottoms bordered by sheer cliff walls, for the Bad Lands, a chaos of peaks, plateaus, and ridges, rose abruptly from the edges of the level, tree-clad, or grassy, alluvial meadows. In front of the ranch-house veranda was a row of cottonwood-trees with gray-green leaves which quivered all day long if there was a breath of air. From these trees came the far-away, melancholy cooing of mourning-doves, and little owls perched in them and called tremulously at night. In the long summer afternoons we would sometimes sit on the piazza, when there was no work to be done, for an hour or two at a time, watching the cattle on the sand-bars, and the sharply channelled and strangely carved amphitheatre of cliffs across the bottom opposite; while the vultures wheeled overhead, their black shadows gliding across the glaring white of the dry river-bed. Sometimes from the ranch we saw deer, and once when we needed meat I shot one across the river as I stood on the piazza. In the winter, in the days of iron cold, when everything was white under the snow, the river lay in its bed fixed and immovable as a bar of bent steel, and then at night wolves and lynxes travelled up and down it as if it had been a highway passing in front of the ranch-house. Often in the late fall or early winter, after a hard day's hunting, or when returning from one of the winter line camps, we did not reach the ranch until hours after sunset; and after the weary tramping in the cold it was keen pleasure to catch the first red gleam of the firelit windows across the snowy wastes.

The Elkhorn ranch-house was built mainly by Sewall and Dow, who, like most men from the Maine woods, were mighty with the axe. I could chop fairly well for an amateur, but I could not do one-third the work they could. One day when we were cutting down the cottonwood-trees, to begin our building operations, I heard some one ask Dow what the total cut had been, and Dow, not realizing that I was within hearing, answered: "Well, Bill cut down fifty-three, I cut down forty-nine, and the boss he beavered down seventeen." Those who have seen the stump of a tree which has been gnawed down by a beaver will understand the exact force of the comparison.

In those days on a cow-ranch the men were apt to be away on the various round-ups at least half the time. It was interesting and exciting work, and except for the lack of sleep on the spring and summer round-ups it was not exhausting work; compared to lumbering or mining or blacksmithing, to sit in the saddle is an easy form of labor. The ponies were of course grass-fed and unshod. Each man had his own string of nine or ten. One pony would be used for the morning work, one for the afternoon, and neither would again be used for the next three days. A separate pony was kept for night riding.

The spring and early summer round-ups were especially for the branding of calves. There was much hard work and some risk on a round-up, but also much fun. The meeting-place was appointed weeks beforehand, and all the ranch-men of the territory to be covered by the round-up sent their representatives. There were no fences in the West that I knew, and their place was taken by the cowboy and the branding-iron. The cattle wandered free. Each calf was branded with the brand of the cow it was following. Sometimes in winter there was what we called line riding;

that is, camps were established and the line riders travelled a definite beat across the desolate waste of snow, to and fro from one camp to another, to prevent the cattle from drifting. But as a rule nothing was done to keep the cattle in any one place. In the spring there was a general round-up in each locality. Each outfit took part in its own round-up and all the outfits of a given region combined to send representatives to the two or three round-ups that covered the neighborhoods near by into which their cattle might drift. For example, our Little Missouri round-up generally worked down the river from a distance of some fifty or sixty miles above my ranch toward the Kildeer Mountains, about the same distance below. In addition we would usually send representatives to the Yellowstone round-up, and to the round-up along the upper Little Missouri, and, moreover, if we heard that cattle had drifted, perhaps toward the Indian reservation southeast of us, we would send a wagon and rider after them.

At the meeting-point, which might be in the valley of a half-dry stream, or in some broad bottom of the river itself, or perchance by a couple of ponds under some queerly shaped butte that was a landmark for the region roundabout, we would all gather on the appointed day. The chuck-wagons, containing the bedding and food, each drawn by four horses and driven by the teamster-cook, would come jolting and rattling over the uneven sward. Accompanying each wagon were eight or ten riders, the cow-punchers, while their horses, a band of a hundred or so, were driven by the two herders, one of whom was known as the day wrangler and one as the night wrangler. The men were lean, sinewy fellows, accustomed to riding half-broken horses at any speed over any country by day or by night. They wore flannel shirts, with loose handkerchiefs knotted round their necks, broad hats, high-heeled boots with jingling spurs, and sometimes leather chaps, although often they merely had their trousers tucked into the tops of their high boots. There was a good deal of rough horse-play, and, as with any other gathering of men or boys of high animal spirits, the horse-play sometimes became very rough indeed; and as the men usually carried revolvers, and as there were occasionally one or two noted gun-fighters among them, there was now and then a shooting affray. A man who was a coward or who shirked his work had a bad time, of course; a man could not afford to let himself be bullied or treated as a butt; and, on the other hand, if he was "looking for a fight," he was certain to find it. But my own experience was that if a man did not talk until his associates knew him well and liked him, and if he did his work, he never had any difficulty in getting on. In my own round-up district I speedily grew to be friends with most of the men. When I went among strangers I always had to spend twenty-four hours in living down the fact that I wore spectacles, remaining as long as I could judiciously deaf to any side-remarks about "four-eyes," unless it became evident that my being quiet was misconstrued and that it was better to bring matters to a head at once.

If, for instance, I was sent off to represent the Little Missouri brands on some neighboring round-up, such as the Yellowstone, I usually showed that kind of diplomacy which consists in not uttering one word that can be avoided. I would probably have a couple of days' solitary ride, mounted on one horse and driving eight or ten others before me, one of them carrying my bedding. Loose horses drive best at a trot, or canter, and if a man is travelling alone in this fashion it is a good thing to have them reach the camp-ground sufficiently late to make them desire to feed and sleep where they are until morning. In consequence I never spent more than two days on the journey from whatever the point was at which I left the Little Missouri, sleeping the one night for as limited a number of hours as possible.

As soon as I reached the meeting-place I would find out the wagon to which I was assigned. Riding to it, I turned my horses into the saddle-band and reported to the wagon boss, or, in his absence, to the cook—always a privileged character, who was allowed and expected to order men around. He would usually grumble savagely and profanely about my having been put with his wagon, but this was merely conventional on his part; and if I sat down and said nothing he would probably soon ask me if I wanted anything to eat, to which the correct answer was that I was not hungry and would wait until meal-time. The bedding-rolls of the riders would be strewn round the grass, and I would put mine down a little outside the ring, where I would not be in any one's way, with my six or eight branding-irons beside it. The men would ride in, laughing and talking with one another, and perhaps nodding to me. One of their number, usually the wagon foreman, might put some question to me as to what brands I represented, but no other word would be addressed to me, nor would I be expected to volunteer any conversation. Supper would consist of bacon, Dutch oven bread, and possibly beef; once I won the good graces of my companions at the outset by appearing with two antelope which I had shot. After supper I would roll up in my bedding as soon as possible, and the others would follow suit at their pleasure.

At three in the morning or thereabouts, at a yell from the cook, all hands would turn hurriedly out. Dressing was a simple affair. Then each man rolled and corded his bedding—if he did not, the cook would leave it behind and he would go without any for the rest of the trip—and came to the fire, where he picked out a tin cup, tin plate, and knife and fork, helped himself to coffee and to whatever food there was, and ate it standing or squatting as best suited him. Dawn was probably breaking by this time, and the trampling of unshod hoofs showed that the night wrangler was bringing in the pony-herd. Two of the men would then run ropes from the wagon at right angles to one another, and into this as a corral the horses would be driven. Each man might rope one of his own horses, or more often point it out to the most skilful roper of the outfit, who would rope it for him—for if the man was an unskilful roper and roped the wrong horse or roped the horse in the wrong place there was a chance of the whole herd stampeding. Each man then saddled and bridled his horse. This was usually followed by some resolute bucking on the part of two or three of the horses, especially in the early days of each round-up. The bucking was always a source of amusement to all the men whose horses did not buck, and these fortunate ones would gather round giving ironical advice, and especially adjuring the rider not to "go to leather"—that is, not to steady himself in the saddle by catching hold of the saddle-horn.

As soon as the men had mounted, the whole outfit started on the long circle, the morning circle. Usually the ranch foreman who bossed a given wagon was put in charge of the men of one group by the round-up foreman; he might keep his men together until they had gone some ten or fifteen miles from camp, and then drop them in couples at different points. Each couple made its way toward the wagon, gathering all the cattle it could find. The morning's ride might last six or eight hours, and it was still longer before some of the men got in. Singly and in twos and threes they appeared from every quarter of the horizon, the dust rising from the hoofs of the steers and bulls, the cows and calves, they had collected. Two or three of the men were left to take care of the herd while the others changed horses, ate a hasty dinner, and then came out to the afternoon work. This consisted of each man in succession being sent into the herd, usually with a companion, to cut out the cows of his brand or brands which were followed by unbranded calves, and also to cut out any mavericks or unbranded yearlings. We worked each animal gently out to the edge of the herd, and then with a sudden dash took it off at a run. It was always desperately anxious to break back and rejoin the herd. There was much breakneck galloping and twisting and turning before its desire was thwarted and it was driven to join the rest of the cut—that is, the other animals which had been cut out, and which were being held by one or two other men. Cattle hate being alone, and it was no easy matter to hold the first one or two that were cut out; but soon they got a little herd of their own, and then they were contented. When the cutting out had all been done, the calves were branded, and all misadventures of the "calf wrestlers," the men who seized, threw, and held each calf when roped by the mounted roper, were hailed with yelling laughter. Then the animals which for one reason or another it was desired to drive along with the round-up were put into one herd and left in charge of a couple of night guards, and the rest of us would loaf back to the wagon for supper and bed.

By this time I would have been accepted as one of the rest of the outfit, and all strangeness would have passed off, the attitude of my fellow cow-punchers being one of friendly forgiveness even toward my spectacles. Night guards for the cattle-herd were then assigned by the captain of the wagon, or perhaps by the round-up foreman, according to the needs of the case, the guards standing for two hours at a time from eight in the evening till four in the morning. The first and last watches were preferable, because sleep was not broken as in both of the other two. If things went well, the cattle would soon bed down and nothing further would occur until morning, when there was a repetition of the work, the wagon moving each day eight or ten miles to some appointed camping-place.

Each man would picket his night horse near the wagon, usually choosing the quietest animal in his string for that purpose, because to saddle and mount a "mean" horse at night is not pleasant. When utterly tired, it was hard to have to get up for one's trick at night herd. Nevertheless, on ordinary nights the two hours round the cattle in the still darkness were pleasant. The loneliness, under the vast empty sky, and the silence, in which the breathing of the cattle sounded loud, and the alert readiness to meet any emergency which might suddenly arise out of the formless night, all combined to give one a sense of subdued interest. Then, one soon got to know the cattle of marked individuality, the ones that led the others into mischief; and one also grew to recognize the traits they all possessed in common, and the impulses which, for instance, made a whole herd get up toward midnight, each beast turning round and then lying down again. But by the end of the watch each rider had studied the cattle until it grew monotonous, and heartily welcomed his relief guard. A newcomer, of course, had any amount to learn, and sometimes the simplest things were those which brought him to grief.

One night early in my career I failed satisfactorily to identify the direction in which I was to go in order to reach the night herd. It was a pitch-dark night. I managed to get started wrong, and I never found either the herd or the wagon again until sunrise, when I was greeted with withering scorn by the injured cow-puncher, who had been obliged to stand double guard because I failed to relieve him.

There were other misadventures that I met with where the excuse was greater. The punchers on night guard usually rode round the cattle in reverse directions; calling and singing to them if the beasts seemed restless, to keep them quiet. On rare occasions something happened that made the cattle stampede, and then the duty of the riders was to keep with them as long as possible and try gradually to get control of them.

One night there was a heavy storm, and all of us who were at the wagons were obliged to turn out hastily to help the night herders. After a while there was a terrific peal of thunder, the lightning struck right by the herd, and away all the beasts went, heads and horns and tails in the air. For a minute or two I could make out nothing except the dark forms of the beasts running on every side of me, and I should have been very sorry if my horse had stumbled, for those behind would have trodden me down. Then the herd split, part going to one side, while the other part seemingly kept straight ahead, and I galloped as hard as ever beside them. I was trying to reach the point—the leading animals—in order to turn them, when suddenly there was a tremendous splashing in front. I could dimly make out that the cattle immediately ahead and to one side of me were disappearing, and the next moment the horse and I went off a cut bank into the Little Missouri. I bent away back in the saddle, and though the horse almost went down he just recovered himself, and, plunging and struggling through water and quicksand, we made the other side. Here I discovered that there was another cowboy with the same part of the herd that I was with; but almost immediately we separated. I galloped hard through a bottom covered with big cottonwood-trees, and stopped the part of the herd that I was with, but very soon they broke on me again, and repeated this twice. Finally toward morning the few I had left came to a halt.

It had been raining hard for some time. I got off my horse and leaned against a tree, but before long the infernal cattle started on again, and I had to ride after them. Dawn came soon after this, and I was able to make out where I was and head the cattle back, collecting other little bunches as I went. After a while I came on a cowboy on foot carrying his saddle on his head. He was my companion of the previous night. His horse had gone full speed into a tree and killed itself, the man, however, not being hurt. I could not help him, as I had all I could do to handle the cattle. When I got them to the wagon, most of the other men had already come in and the riders were just starting on the long circle. One of the men changed my horse for me while I ate a hasty breakfast and then we were off for the day's work.

As only about half of the night herd had been brought back, the circle riding was particularly heavy, and it was ten hours before we were back at the wagon. We then changed horses again and worked the whole herd until after sunset, finishing just as it grew too dark to do anything more. By this time I had been nearly forty hours in the saddle, changing horses five times, and my clothes had thoroughly dried on me, and I fell asleep as soon as I touched the bedding. Fortunately some men who had gotten in late in the morning had had their sleep during the daytime, so that the rest of us escaped night guard and were not called until four next morning. Nobody ever gets enough sleep on a round-up.

The above was the longest number of consecutive hours I ever had to be in the saddle. But, as I have said, I changed horses five times, and it is a great lightening of labor for a rider to have a fresh horse. Once when with Sylvane Ferris I spent about sixteen hours on one horse, riding seventy or eighty miles. The round-up had reached a place called the ox-bow of the Little Missouri, and we had to ride there, do some work around the cattle, and ride back.

Another time I was twenty-four hours on horseback in company with Merrifield without changing horses. On this occasion we did not travel fast. We had been coming back with the wagon from a hunting trip in the Big Horn Mountains. The team was fagged out, and we were tired of walking at a snail's pace beside it. When we reached country that the driver thoroughly knew, we thought it safe to leave him, and we loped in one night across a distance which it took the wagon the three following days to cover. It was a beautiful moonlight night, and the ride was delightful. All day long we had plodded at a walk, weary and hot. At suppertime we had rested two or three hours, and the tough little riding-horses seemed as fresh as ever. It was in September. As we rode out of the circle of the firelight, the air was cool in our faces. Under the bright moonlight, and then under the starlight, we loped and cantered mile after mile over the high prairie. We passed bands of antelope and herds of long-horn Texas cattle, and at last, just as the first red beams of the sun flamed over the bluffs in front of us, we rode down into the valley of the Little Missouri, where our ranch-house stood.

I never became a good roper, nor more than an average rider, according to ranch standards. Of course a man on a ranch has to ride a good many bad horses, and is bound to encounter a certain number of accidents, and of these I had my share, at one time cracking a rib, and on another occasion the point of my shoulder. We were hundreds of miles from a doctor, and each time, as I was on the round-up, I had to get through my work for the next few weeks as best I could, until the injury healed of itself. When I had the opportunity I broke my own horses, doing it gently and gradually and spending much time over it, and choosing the horses that seemed gentle to begin with. With these horses I never had any difficulty. But frequently there was neither time nor opportunity to handle our mounts so elaborately. We might get a band of horses, each having been bridled and saddled two or three times, but none of them having been broken beyond the extent implied in this bridling and saddling. Then each of us in succession would choose a horse (for his string), I as owner of the ranch being given the first choice on each round, so to speak. The first time I was ever on a round-up Sylvane Ferris, Merrifield, Meyer, and I each chose his string in this fashion. Three or four of the animals I got were not easy to ride. The effort both to ride them and to look as if I enjoyed doing so, on some cool morning when my grinning cowboy friends had gathered round "to see whether the high-headed bay could buck the boss off," doubtless was of benefit to me, but lacked much of being enjoyable. The time I smashed my rib I was bucked off on a stone. The time I hurt the point of my shoulder I was riding a big, sulky horse named Ben Butler, which went over backward with me. When we got up it still refused to go anywhere; so while I sat it, Sylvane Ferris and George Meyer got their ropes on its neck and dragged it a few hundred yards, choking but stubborn, all four feet firmly planted and ploughing the ground. When they released the ropes it lay down and wouldn't get up. The round-up had started; so Sylvane gave me his horse, Baldy, which sometimes bucked but never went over backward, and he got on the now re-arisen Ben Butler. To my discomfiture Ben started quietly beside us, while Sylvane remarked: "Why, there's nothing the matter with this horse, he's a plumb gentle horse." Then Ben fell slightly behind and I heard Sylvane again: "That's all right! Come along! Here, you! Go on, you! Hi, hi, fellows, help me out! he's lying on me!" Sure enough, he was; and when we dragged Sylvane from under him the first thing the rescued Sylvane did was to execute a war-dance, spurs and all, on the iniquitous Ben. We could do nothing with him that day; subsequently we got him so that we could ride him; but he never became a nice saddle-horse.

As with all other forms of work, so on the round-up, a man of ordinary power, who nevertheless does not shirk things merely because they are disagreeable or irksome, soon earns his place. There were crack riders and ropers who, just because they felt such overweening pride in their own prowess, were not really very valuable men. Continually on the circles a cow or a calf would get into some thick patch of bullberry-bush and refuse to come out; or when it was getting late we would pass some Bad Lands that would probably not contain cattle, but might, or a steer would turn fighting mad, or a calf grow tired and want to lie down. If in such a case the man steadily persists in doing the unattractive thing, and after two hours of exasperation and harassment does finally get the cow out, and keep her out, of the bullberry-bushes, and drives her to the wagon, or finds some animals that have been passed by in the fourth or fifth patch of Bad Lands he hunts through, or gets the calf up on his saddle and takes it in anyhow, the foreman soon grows to treat him as having his uses and as being an asset of worth in the round-up, even though neither a fancy roper nor a fancy rider. . . .

In addition to my private duties, I sometimes served as deputy sheriff for the northern end of our county. The sheriff and I crisscrossed in our public and private relations. He often worked for me as a hired hand at the same time that I was his deputy. His name, or at least the name he went by, was Bill Jones, and as there were in the neighborhood several Bill Joneses—Three Seven Bill Jones, Texas Bill Jones, and the like—the sheriff was known as Hell Roaring Bill Jones. He was a thorough frontiersman, excellent in all kinds of emergencies, and a very game man. I became much attached to him. He was a thoroughly good citizen when sober, but he was a little wild when drunk. . . .

Bill Jones was a gun-fighter and also a good man with his fists. On one occasion there was an election in town. There had been many threats that the party of disorder would import section-hands from the neighboring railway-stations to down our side. I did not reach Medora, the forlorn little cattle-town which was our county-seat, until the election was well under way. I then asked one of my friends if there had been any disorder. Bill Jones was standing by. "Disorder, hell!" said my friend. "Bill Jones just stood there with one hand on his gun and the other pointing over toward the new jail whenever any man who didn't have a right to vote came near the polls. There was only one of them tried to vote, and Bill knocked him down. Lord!" added my friend, meditatively, "the way that man fell!" "Well," struck in Bill Jones, "if he hadn't fell I'd have walked round behind him to see what was propping him up!" . . .

Bill Jones had been unconventional in other relations besides that of sheriff. He once casually mentioned to me that he had served on the police force of Bismarck, but he had left because he "beat the mayor over the head with his gun one day." He added: "The mayor, he didn't mind it, but the superintendent of police said he guessed I'd better resign." His feeling, obviously, was that the superintendent of police was a martinet, unfit to take large views of life. . . .

I owe more than I can ever express to the West, which of course means to the men and women I met in the West. There were a few people of bad type in my neighborhood —that would be true of every group of men, even in a theological seminary—but I could not speak with too great affection and respect of the great majority of my friends, the hard-working men and women who dwelt for a space of perhaps a hundred and fifty miles along the Little Missouri. I was always as welcome at their houses as they were at mine. Everybody worked, everybody was willing to help everybody else, and yet nobody asked any favors. The same thing was true of the people whom I got to know fifty miles east and fifty miles west of my own range, and of the men I met on the round-ups. They soon accepted me as a friend and fellow worker who stood on an equal footing with them, and I believe the most of them have kept their feeling for me ever since. No guests were ever more welcome at the White House than these old friends of the cattle-ranches and the cow camps—the men with whom I had ridden the long circle and eaten at the tail-board of a chuck-wagon—whenever they turned up at Washington during my presidency. I remember one of them who appeared at Washington one day just before lunch, a huge, powerful man who, when I knew him, had been distinctly a fighting character. It happened that on that day another old friend, the British ambassador, Mr. Bryce, was among those coming to lunch. Just before we went in I turned to my cow-puncher friend and said to him with great solemnity: "Remember, Jim, that if you shot at the feet of the British ambassador to make him dance, it would be likely to cause international complications"; to which Jim responded with unaffected horror: "Why, Colonel, I shouldn't think of it, I shouldn't think of it!"

Not only did the men and women whom I met in the cow country quite unconsciously help me, by the insight which working and living with them enabled me to get into the mind and soul of the average American of the right type, but they helped me in another way. I made up my mind that the men were of just the kind whom it would be well to have with me if ever it became necessary to go to war. When the Spanish War came, I gave this thought practical realization. . . .

There were bad characters in the Western country at that time, of course, and under the conditions of life they were probably more dangerous than they would have been elsewhere. I hardly ever had any difficulty, however. I never went into a saloon, and in the little hotels I kept out of the barroom unless, as sometimes happened, the barroom was the only room on the lower floor except the dining-room. I always endeavored to keep out of a quarrel until self-respect forbade my making any further effort to avoid it, and I very rarely had even the semblance of trouble.

Of course amusing incidents occurred now and then. Usually these took place when I was hunting lost horses, for in hunting lost horses I was ordinarily alone, and occasionally had to travel a hundred or a hundred and fifty miles away from my own country. On one such occasion I reached a little cow-town long after dark, stabled my horse in an empty outbuilding, and when I reached the hotel was informed in response to my request for a bed that I could have the last one left, as there was only one other man in it. The room to which I was shown contained two double beds; one contained two men fast asleep, and the other only one man, also asleep. This man proved to be a friend, one of the Bill Joneses whom I have previously mentioned. I undressed according to the fashion of the day and place, that is, I put my trousers, boots, chaps, and gun down beside the bed and turned in. A couple of hours later I was awakened by the door being thrown open and a lantern flashed in my face, the light gleaming on the muzzle of a cocked .45. Another man said to the lantern-bearer, "It ain't him"; the next moment my bedfellow was covered with two guns, and addressed: "Now, Bill, don't make a fuss, but come along quiet." "I'm not thinking of making a fuss," said Bill. "That's right," was the answer; "we're your friends; we don't want to hurt you; we just want you to come along, you know why." And Bill pulled on his trousers and boots and walked out with them. Up to this time there had not been a sound from the other bed. Now a match was scratched, a candle lit, and one of the men in the other bed looked round the room. At this point I committed the breach of etiquette of asking questions. "I wonder why they took Bill," I said. There was no answer, and I repeated: "I wonder why they took Bill." "Well," said the man with the candle dryly, "I reckon they wanted him," and with that he blew out the candle and conversation ceased. Later I discovered that Bill in a fit of playfulness had held up the Northern Pacific train at a near-by station by shooting at the feet of the conductor to make him dance. . . .

The only time I ever had serious trouble was at an even more primitive little hotel than the one in question. It was also on an occasion when I was out after lost horses. Below the hotel had merely a barroom, a dining-room, and a lean-to kitchen; above was a loft with fifteen or twenty beds in it. It was late in the evening when I reached the place. I heard one or two shots in the barroom as I came up, and I disliked going in. But there was nowhere else to go, and it was a cold night. Inside the room were several men, who, including the bartender, were wearing the kind of smile worn by men who are making believe to like what they don't like. A shabby individual in a broad hat with a cocked gun in each hand was walking up and down the floor talking with strident profanity. He had evidently been shooting at the clock, which had two or three holes in its face.

He was not a "bad man" of the really dangerous type, the true man-killer type, but he was an objectionable creature, a would-be bad man, a bully who for the moment was having things all his own way. As soon as he saw me he hailed me as "Four-eyes," in reference to my spectacles, and said: "Four-eyes is going to treat." I joined in the laugh and got behind the stove and sat down, thinking to escape notice. He followed me, however, and though I tried to pass it off as a jest this merely made him more offensive, and he stood leaning over me, a gun in each hand, using very foul language. He was foolish to stand so near, and, moreover, his heels were close together, so that his position was unstable. Accordingly, in response to his reiterated command that I should set up the drinks, I said: "Well, if I've got to, I've got to," and rose, looking past him.

As I rose, I struck quick and hard with my right just to one side of the point of his jaw, hitting with my left as I straightened out, and then again with my right. He fired the guns, but I do not know whether this was merely a convulsive action of his hands or whether he was trying to shoot at me. When he went down he struck the corner of the bar with his head. It was not a case in which one could afford to take chances, and if he had moved I was about to drop on his ribs with my knees; but he was senseless. I took away his guns, and the other people in the room, who were now loud in their denunciation of him, hustled him out and put him in a shed. I got dinner as soon as possible, sitting in a corner of the dining-room away from the windows, and then went up-stairs to bed where it was dark so that there would be no chance of any one shooting at me from the outside. However, nothing happened. When my assailant came to, he went down to the station and left on a freight.

As I have said, most of the men in my regiment were just such men as those I knew in the ranch country . . . After the regiment was disbanded the careers of certain of the men were diversified by odd incidents. Our relations were of the friendliest, and, as they explained, they felt "as if I was a father" to them. The manifestations of this feeling were sometimes less attractive than the phrase sounded, as it was chiefly used by the few who were behaving like very bad children indeed. The great majority of the men when the regiment disbanded took up the business of their lives where they had dropped it a few months previously, and these men merely tried to help me or help one another as the occasion arose; no man ever had more cause to be proud of his regiment than I had of mine, both in war and in peace. But there was a minority among them who in certain ways were unsuited for a life of peaceful regularity, although often enough they had been first-class soldiers. . . .

While I was President, a member of the regiment, Major Llewellyn, who was Federal district attorney under me in New Mexico, wrote me a letter filled, as his letters usually were, with bits of interesting gossip about the comrades. It ran in part as follows: "Since I last wrote you Comrade Ritchie has killed a man in Colorado. I understand that the comrade was playing a poker game, and the man sat into the game and used such language that Comrade Ritchie had to shoot. Comrade Webb has killed two men in Beaver, Arizona. Comrade Webb is in the Forest Service, and the killing was in the line of professional duty. I was out at the penitentiary the other day and saw Comrade Gritto, who, you may remember, was put there for shooting his sister-in-law [this was the first information I had had as to the identity of the lady who was shot in the eye]. Since he was in there Comrade Boyne has run off to old Mexico with his (Gritto's) wife, and the people of Grant County think he ought to be let out." Evidently the sporting instincts of the people of Grant County had been roused, and they felt that, as Comrade Boyne had had a fair start, the other comrade should be let out in order to see what would happen.

The men of the regiment always enthusiastically helped me when I was running for office. On one occasion Buck

Taylor, of Texas, accompanied me on a trip and made a speech for me. The crowd took to his speech from the beginning and so did I, until the peroration, which ran as follows: "My fellow citizens, vote for my Colonel! vote for my Colonel! *and he will lead you, as he led us, like sheep to the slaughter!*" This hardly seemed a tribute to my military skill; but it delighted the crowd, and as far as I could tell did me nothing but good. . . .

There was one bit of frontier philosophy which I should like to see imitated in more advanced communities. Certain crimes of revolting baseness and cruelty were never forgiven. But in the case of ordinary offenses, the man who had served his term and who then tried to make good was given a fair chance; and of course this was equally true of the women. Every one who has studied the subject at all is only too well aware that the world offsets the readiness with which it condones a crime for which a man escapes punishment by its unforgiving relentlessness to the often far less guilty man who *is* punished, and who therefore has made his atonement. On the frontier, if the man honestly tried to behave himself there was generally a disposition to give him fair play and a decent show. Several of the men I knew and whom I particularly liked came in this class. There was one such man in my regiment, a man who had served a term for robbery under arms, and who had atoned for it by many years of fine performance of duty. I put him in a high official position, and no man under me rendered better service to the State, nor was there any man whom, as soldier, as civil officer, as citizen, and as friend, I valued and respected—and now value and respect —more.

Now I suppose some good people will gather from this that I favor men who commit crimes. I certainly do **not** favor them. I have not a particle of sympathy with the sentimentality—as I deem it, the mawkishness—which overflows with foolish pity for the criminal and cares not at all for the victim of the criminal. I am glad to see wrong-doers punished. The punishment is an absolute necessity from the standpoint of society; and I put the reformation of the criminal second to the welfare of society. But I do desire to see the man or woman who has paid the penalty and who wishes to reform given a helping hand—surely every one of us who knows his own heart must know that he too may stumble, and should be anxious to help his brother or sister who has stumbled. When the criminal has been punished, if he then shows a sincere desire to lead a decent and upright life, he should be given the chance, he should be helped and not hindered; and if he makes good, he should receive that respect from others which so often aids in creating self-respect—the most invaluable of all possessions.

While out in the Badlands TR could not help thinking of what he might be missing in New York. In the spring of 1886 he wrote his sister Anna of his longing for

. . . that far distant salon wherein we are to gather society men who take part in politics, literature and art and poli-ticians, authors and artists whose bringing up and personal habits do not disqualify them for society; where the clever women will neither dress too prismatically nor yet have committed the still graver crime of marrying dull husbands and where the pretty women who know how to dress and dance will not have brains of the type of Gussie Drayton and Mamie Astor.

TR's reaction to the Haymarket Riot of May 4, 1886 was automatic. In spite of the fact that no one was able to discover the identity of the person who threw the bomb killing seven and injuring many more at this mass meeting of Chicago workers, he was in favor of retaliation that could only be described as indiscriminate. Like many other Americans in public life, he was as yet unaware of the social conditions of which so perverse an advantage was taken. To his sister Anna he wrote:

My men here are hardworking, labouring men, who work longer hours for no greater wages than many of the strikers; but they are Americans through and through; I believe nothing would give them greater pleasure than a chance with their rifles at one of the mobs. When we get the papers, especially in relation to the dynamite business they become more furiously angry and excited than I do. I wish I had them with me, and a fair show at ten times our number of rioters; my men shoot well and fear very little.

Meantime he had reached the conclusion that Tolstoi's moral code left much to be desired. As he put it in a letter to Anna:

La Guerre et La Paix, [*War and Peace*] like all Tolstoi's work, is very strong and very interesting. The descriptions of the battles are excellent, but though with one or two good ideas underneath them, the criticisms of the commanders, especially of Napoléon, and of wars in general, are absurd. Moreover when he criticises battles (and the iniquity of war) in his capacity of author, he deprives himself of all excuse for the failure to criticise the various other immoralities he portrays. In *Anna Karénine* he let each character, good or bad, speak for itself; and while he might better have shown some reprobation of evil, at least it could be alleged in answer that he simply narrated, putting the facts before us that we ourselves might judge them. But when he again and again spends pages in descanting on the wickedness and folly of war, and passes over other vices without a word of reproach he certainly in so far acts as the apologist for the latter, and the general tone of the book does not seem to me to be in the least conducive to morality.

CHAPTER 5

Applied Idealism

IN THE SPRING of 1889 I was appointed . . . Civil Service Commissioner. For nearly five years I had not been very active in political life; although I had done some routine work in the organization and had made campaign speeches, and in 1886 had run for mayor of New York against Abram S. Hewitt, Democrat, and Henry George, Independent, and had been defeated.

I served six years as Civil Service Commissioner—four years under President Harrison and then two years under President Cleveland. I was treated by both Presidents with the utmost consideration. . . .

Civil service reform had two sides. There was, first, the effort to secure a more efficient administration of the public service; and, second, the even more important effort to withdraw the administrative offices of the government from the domain of spoils politics, and thereby cut out of American political life a fruitful source of corruption and degradation. . . .

Such being the case, it would seem at first sight extraordinary that it should be so difficult to uproot the system. Unfortunately, it was permitted to become habitual and traditional in American life, so that the conception of public office as something to be used primarily for the good of the dominant political party became ingrained in the mind of the average American, and he grew so accustomed to the whole process that it seemed part of the order of nature. . . .

Patronage does not really help a party. It helps the bosses to get control of the machinery of the party—as in 1912 was true of the Republican party—but it does not help the party. On the average, the most sweeping party victories in our history have been won when the patronage was against the victors. All that the patronage does is to help the worst element in the party retain control of the party organization. Two of the evil elements in our government against which good citizens have to contend are, 1, the lack of continuous activity on the part of these good citizens themselves, and, 2, the ever-present activity of those who have only an evil self-interest in political life. It is difficult to interest the average citizen in any particular movement to the degree of getting him to take an efficient part in it. He wishes the movement well, but he will not, or often cannot, take the time and the trouble to serve it efficiently; and this whether he happens to be a mechanic or a banker, a telegraph-operator or a storekeeper. . . .

On the other hand, the spoils system breeds a class of men whose financial interest it is to take this necessary time and trouble. They are paid for so doing, and they are paid out of the public chest. . . .

During my six years' service as Commissioner the field of the merit system was extended at the expense of the spoils system so as to include several times the number of offices that had originally been included. Generally this was done by the introduction of competitive entrance examinations; sometimes, as in the navy-yards, by a system of registration. This of itself was good work. . . .

The first effort of myself and my colleagues was to secure the genuine enforcement of the law. In this we succeeded after a number of lively fights. But of course in these fights we were obliged to strike a large number of influential politicians, some of them in Congress, some of them the supporters and backers of men who were in Congress. . . .

Occasionally we would bring to terms these senators or congressmen who fought the commission by the simple expedient of not holding examinations in their districts. This always brought frantic appeals from their constituents, and we would explain that unfortunately the appropriations had been cut, so that we could not hold examinations in every district, and that obviously we could not neglect the districts of those congressmen who believed in the reform and therefore in the examinations. The constituents then turned their attention to the congressman, and the result was that in the long run we obtained sufficient money to enable us to do our work. . . .

One opponent with whom we had a rather lively tilt was a Republican congressman from Ohio, Mr. Grosvenor, one of the floor leaders. Mr. Grosvenor made his attack in the House, and enumerated our sins in picturesque rather than accurate fashion. There was a congressional committee investigating us at the time, and on my next appearance before them I asked that Mr. Grosvenor be requested to meet me before the committee. Mr. Grosvenor did not take up the challenge for several weeks, until it was announced that I was leaving for my ranch in Dakota; whereupon, deeming it safe, he wrote me a letter expressing his ardent wish that I should appear before the committee to meet him. I promptly cancelled my ticket, waited, and met him. He proved to be a person of happily treacherous memory, so that the simple expedient of arranging his statements in pairs was sufficient to reduce him to confusion. For instance, he had been trapped into making the unwary remark: "I do not want to repeal the civil service law, and I never said so." I produced the following extract from one of his speeches: "I will vote not only to strike out this provision, but I will vote to repeal the whole law." To this he merely replied that there was "no inconsistency between those two statements." He asserted that "Rufus P. Putnam, fraudulently credited to Washington County, Ohio, never lived in Washington County, Ohio, or in my congressional district, or in Ohio as far as I know." We produced a letter which, thanks to a beneficent Providence, he had himself written about Mr. Rufus P. Putnam, in which he said: "Mr. Rufus P. Putnam is a legal resident of my district and has relatives living there now." He explained, first, that he had not written the letter; second, that he had forgotten he had written the letter; and, third that he was grossly deceived when he wrote it. . . . When I started further to question him, he accused me of a lack of humor in not appreciating that his statements were made "in a jesting way," and then announced that "a congressman making a speech on the floor of the House of Representatives was perhaps in a little different position from a witness on the witness stand"— a frank admission that he did not consider exactitude of statement necessary when he was speaking as a congressman. Finally he rose with great dignity and said that it was his "constitutional right" not to be questioned elsewhere as to what he said on the floor of the House of Representatives; and accordingly he left the delighted committee to pursue its investigations without further aid from him. . . .

Most of the newspapers which regarded themselves as the especial champions of civil service reform and as the highest exponents of civic virtue, and which distrusted the average citizen and shuddered over the "coarseness" of the professional politicians, were, nevertheless, given to vices even more contemptible than, although not so gross as, those they denounced and derided. Their editors were refined men of cultivated tastes, whose pet temptations were backbiting, mean slander, and the snobbish worship of anything clothed in wealth and the outward appearances of conventional repectability. They were not robust or powerful men; they felt ill at ease in the company of rough, strong men; often they had in them a vein of physical timidity. They avenged themselves to themselves for an uneasy subconsciousness of their own short-comings by sitting in cloistered—or, rather, pleasantly upholstered—seclusion, and sneering at and lying about men who made them feel uncomfortable. . . .

One of the reasons why the boss so often keeps his hold, especially in municipal matters, is, or at least has been in the past, because so many of the men who claim to be reformers have been blind to the need of working in human fashion for social and industrial betterment. . . . If these bosses were responsible for nothing but pure wickedness, they would probably last but a short time in any community. And, in any event, if the men who are horrified by their wickedness were themselves as practical and as thoroughly in touch with human nature, the bosses would have a short shrift. The trouble is that the boss does understand human nature, and that he fills a place which the reformer cannot fill unless he likewise understands human nature. . . .

There is often much good in the type of boss, especially common in big cities, who fulfils toward the people of his district in rough and ready fashion the position of friend and protector. He uses his influence to get jobs for young men who need them. He goes into court for a wild young fellow who has gotten into trouble. He helps out with cash or credit the widow who is in straits, or the bread-winner who is crippled or for some other cause temporarily out of work. He organizes clambakes and chowder parties and picnics, and is consulted by the local labor leaders when a cut in wages is threatened. For some of his constituents he does proper favors, and for others wholly improper favors; but he preserves human relations with all. He may be a very bad and very corrupt man, a man whose action in blackmailing and protecting vice is of far-reaching damage to his constituents. But these constituents are for the most part men and women who struggle hard against poverty and with whom the problem of living is very real and very close. They would prefer clean and honest government, if this clean and honest government is accompanied by human sympathy, human understanding. But an appeal made to them for virtue in the abstract, an appeal made by good men who do not really understand their needs, will often pass quite unheeded, if on the other side stands the boss, the friend and benefactor, who may have been guilty of much wrong-doing in things that they are hardly aware concern them, but who appeals to them, not only for the sake of favors to come, but in the name of gratitude and loyalty, and above all of understanding and fellow-feeling. They have a feeling of clan-loyalty to him; his and their relations may be substantially those which are right and proper among primitive people still in the clan stage of moral development. The successful fight against this type of vicious boss, and the type of vicious politics which produces it, can be made only by men who have a genuine fellow-feeling for and understanding of the people for and with whom they are to work, and who in practical fashion seek their social and industrial benefit. . . .

My duty was to stand with every one while he was right, and to stand against him when he went wrong; and this I have tried to do as regards individuals and as regards groups of individuals. When a business man or labor leader, politician or reformer, is right, I support him; when he goes wrong, I leave him. . . . The principles or methods which the Socialists advocate and which I believe to be in the interest of the people I support, and those which I believe to be against the interest of the people I oppose. Moreover, when a man has done evil, but changes, and works for decency and righteousness, and when, as far as I can see, the change is real and the man's conduct sincere, then I welcome him and work heartily with him, as an equal with an equal. . . .

Every man who has been in practical politics grows to realize that politicians, big and little, are no more all of them bad than they are all of them good. Many of these men are very bad men indeed, but there are others among them—and some among those held up to special obloquy, too—who, even although they may have done much that is evil, also show traits of sterling worth which many of their critics wholly lack. There are few men for whom I have ever felt a more cordial and contemptuous dislike than for some of the bosses and big professional politicians with whom I have been brought into contact. On the other hand, in the case of some political leaders who were most bitterly attacked as bosses, I grew to know certain sides of their characters which inspired in me a very genuine regard and respect.

To read much of the assault on Senator Hanna, one would have thought that he was a man incapable of patriotism or of far-sighted devotion to the country's good. I was brought into intimate contact with him only during the two and a half years immediately preceding his death. I was then President, and perforce watched all his actions at close range. During that time he showed himself to be a man of rugged sincerity of purpose, of great courage and loyalty, and of unswerving devotion to the interests of the nation and the people as he saw those interests. He was as sincerely desirous of helping laboring men as of helping capitalists. His ideals were in many ways not my ideals, and there were points where both by temperament and by conviction we were far apart. Before this time he had always been unfriendly to me; and I do not think he ever grew to like me, at any rate not until the very end of his life. Moreover, I came to the presidency under circumstances which, if he had been a smaller, man would inevitably have thrown him into violent antagonism to me. He was the close and intimate friend of President McKinley. He was McKinley's devoted ally and follower, and his trusted adviser, who was in complete sympathy with him. Partly because of this friendship, his position in the Senate and in the country was unique.

With McKinley's sudden death Senator Hanna found himself bereft of his dearest friend, while I, who had just come to the presidency, was in his view an untried man, whose trustworthiness on many public questions was at least doubtful. . . . Within a few days of my accession he called on me, and with entire friendliness and obvious sincerity, but also with entire self-respect, explained that he mourned McKinley as probably no other man did; that he had not been especially my friend, but that he wished me to understand that henceforward, on every question where he could conscientiously support me, I could count upon his giving me as loyal aid as it was in his power to render. He added that this must not be understood as committing him to favor me for nomination and election, because that matter must be left to take care of itself as events should decide; but that, aside from this, what he said was to be taken literally; in other words, he would do his best to make my administration a success by supporting me heartily on every point on which he conscientiously could, and that this I could count upon. He kept his word absolutely. . . .

My experience with Senator Quay was similar. I had no personal relations with him before I was President, and knew nothing of him save by hearsay. Soon after I became President, Senator Quay called upon me, told me he had known me very slightly, that he thought most men who claimed to be reformers were hypocrites, but that he deemed me sincere, that he thought conditions had become such that aggressive courage and honesty were necessary in order to remedy them, that he believed I intended to be a good and efficient President, and that to the best of his ability he would support me in making my administration a success. He kept his word with absolute good faith. He had been in the Civil War, and was a medal of honor man; and I think my having been in the Spanish War gave him at the outset a kindly feeling toward me. He was also a very well-read man—I owe to him, for instance, my acquaintance with the writings of the Finnish novelist Topelius. . . .

Quay was descended from a French voyageur who had

some Indian blood in him. He was proud of this Indian blood, took an especial interest in Indians, and whenever Indians came to Washington they always called on him. Once during my administration a delegation of Iroquois came over from Canada to call on me at the White House. Their visit had in it something that was pathetic as well as amusing. They represented the descendants of the Six Nations, who fled to Canada after Sullivan harried their towns in the Revolutionary War. Now, a century and a quarter later, their people thought that they would like to come back into the United States; and these representatives had called upon me with the dim hope that perhaps I could give their tribes land on which they could settle. As soon as they reached Washington they asked Quay to bring them to call on me, which he did, telling me that of course their errand was hopeless and that he had explained as much to them, but that they would like me to extend the courtesy of an interview. At the close of the interview, which had been conducted with all the solemnities of calumet and wampum, the Indians filed out. Quay, before following them, turned to me with his usual emotionless face and said, "Good-by, Mr. President; this reminds one of the Flight of a Tartar Tribe, doesn't it?" I answered, "So you're fond of De Quincey, senator?" to which Quay rseponded, "Yes; always liked De Quincey; good-by." And away he went with the tribesmen, who seemed to have walked out of a remote past.

Quay had become particularly concerned about the Delawares in the Indian Territory. He felt that the Interior Department did not do them justice. He also felt that his colleagues of the Senate took no interest in them. When in the spring of 1904 he lay in his house mortally sick, he sent me word that he had something important to say to me, and would have himself carried round to see me. I sent back word not to think of doing so, and that on my way back from church next Sunday I would stop in and call on him. This I accordingly did. He was lying in his bed, death written on his face. He thanked me for coming, and then explained that, as he was on the point of death and knew he would never return to Washington—it was late spring and he was about to leave—he wished to see me to get my personal promise that, after he died, I would myself look after the interests of the Delaware Indians. He added that he did not trust the Interior Department—although he knew that I did not share his views on this point —and that still less did he believe that any of his colleagues in the Senate would exert themselves in the interests of the Delawares, and that therefore he wished my personal assurance that I would personally see that no injustice was done them. I told him I would do so, and then added, in rather perfunctory in fashion, that he must not take such a gloomy view of himself, that when he got away for the summer I hoped he would recover and be back all right when Congress opened. A gleam came into the old fighter's eyes and he answered: "No, I am dying, and you know it. I don't mind dying; but I do wish it were possible for me to get off into the great north woods and crawl out on a rock in the sun and die like a wolf!"

I never saw him again. When he died I sent a telegram of sympathy to his wife. A paper which constantly preached reform, and which kept up its circulation by the no less constant practice of slander, a paper which in theory condemned all public men who violated the eighth commandment, and in practice subsisted by incessant violation of the ninth, assailed me for sending my message to the dead man's wife. I knew the editors of this paper, and the editor who was their predecessor. They had led lives of bodily ease and the avoidance of bodily risk; they earned their livelihood by the practice of mendacity for profit; and they delivered malignant judgment on a dead man who, whatever his faults, had in his youth freely risked his life for a great ideal, and who when death was already clutching his breast had spent almost his last breath on behalf of humble and friendless people whom he had served with disinterested loyalty. . . .

Though TR made a most conscientious Civil Service Commissioner, he would have been the first to confess that civil service reform was only one of many topics on which he spent his energy. A much more fascinating field for speculation was the foreign policy of the United States. He was not appalled by the prospect of a war with Germany over Samoa, as he made plain to his English friend Spring-Rice in the spring of 1889:

Just at present our statesmen seem inclined to abandon the tail of the lion, and instead are plucking vigorously at the caudal feathers of that delightful war-fowl, the German eagle—a cousin of our own bald-headed bird of prey. Frankly, I don't know that I should be sorry to see a bit of a spar with Germany; the burning of New York and a few other seacoast cities would be a good object lesson on the need of an adequate system of coast defences; and I think it would have a good effect on our large German population to force them to an ostentatiously patriotic display of anger against Germany; besides, while we would have to take some awful blows at first, I think in the end we would worry the Kaiser a little.

All this while TR was bent on making his contribution to our knowledge of American history. The biographer of Thomas Hart Benton and of Gouverneur Morris, he launched in 1889 the first two volumes of The Winning of the West.

He also made a point of re-reading the English classics. Although he felt there was much that was improper in the poetry of Chaucer, he complimented Professor Thomas Raynesford Lounsbury of Yale on the publication in 1892 of the latter's Studies in Chaucer.

The praise of a layman can count but little in relation to a book on a subject requiring special and peculiar knowledge. Still, I cannot refrain from writing you to tell you how much I have enjoyed your "Chaucer." Of course there were parts that would appeal most to the professed scholar of Chaucer's works, but much the greater part of each of your three volumes cannot but please even the multitude like myself, not only because of the extremely interesting matter which they contain, but because of the delightful style in which they are written. But having just reread Chaucer in consequence of your book, I must protest a little against some of his tales, on the score of cleanliness. It seems to me that the (Friar's Tale and) prologue to the Sompnour's tale, and the tale itself, for instance, are very nearly indefensible. There are parts of them which will be valuable to the student of the manners of the age simply from the historical standpoint, but as literature I don't think they have a redeeming feature. On the other hand, I must confess that it was only on account of what you had said that I ever cared for the prologue to the tale of the wife of Bath and the tale itself. I have always regarded them with extreme disfavor, knowing that, as a matter of fact, among the men I knew, of every ten who had read them nine had done so for improper reasons; but after reading what you said I took them up and read them from a changed point of view, and am now a convert to your ideas.

The vulgarity of Chaucer was offensive to TR. Equally objectionable in his eyes was the preoccupation of our expatriate novelist Henry James with the life led by the British aristocracy. Writing to Professor Brander Matthews of Columbia in the summer of 1894, he could scarcely contain himself:

By the way, have you seen that London *Yellow Book?* I think it represents the last stage of degradation. What a miserable little snob Henry James is. His polished, pointless, uninteresting stories about the upper social classes of England make one blush to think that he was once an American. The rest of the book is simply diseased. I turned to a story of Kipling's with the feeling of getting into fresh, healthy, out-of-doors life.

CHAPTER 6

The New York Police

In the spring of 1895 I was appointed by Mayor Strong Police Commissioner, and I served as president of the Police Commission of New York for the two following years. Mayor Strong had been elected mayor the preceding fall, when the general anti-Democratic wave of that year coincided with one of the city's occasional insurrections of virtue and consequent turning out of Tammany from municipal control. He had been elected on a non-partisan ticket—usually (although not always) the right kind of ticket in municipal affairs, provided it represents not a bargain among factions but genuine non-partisanship with the genuine purpose to get the right men in control of the city government on a platform which deals with the needs of the average men and women, the men and women who work hard and who too often live hard. I was appointed with the distinct understanding that I was to administer the Police Department with entire disregard of partisan politics, and only from the standpoint of a good citizen interested in promoting the welfare of all good citizens.

My task, therefore, was really simple. Mayor Strong had already offered me the Street-Cleaning Department. For this work I did not feel that I had any especial fitness. . . .

The man who was closest to me throughout my two years in the Police Department was Jacob Riis. By this time, as I have said, I was getting our social, industrial, and political needs into pretty fair perspective. I was still ignorant of the extent to which big men of great wealth played a mischievous part in our industrial and social life, but I was well awake to the need of making ours in good faith both an economic and an industrial as well as a political democracy. I already knew Jake Riis, because his book "How the Other Half Lives" had been to me both an enlightenment and an inspiration for which I felt I could never be too grateful. Soon after it was written I had called at his office to tell him how deeply impressed I was by the book, and that I wished to help him in any practical way to try to make things a little better. I have always had a horror of words that are not translated into deeds, of speech that does not result in action—in other words, I believe in realizable ideals and in realizing them, in preaching what can be practised and then in practising it. Jacob Riis had drawn an indictment of the things that were wrong, pitifully and dreadfully wrong, with the tenement homes and the tenement lives of our wage-workers. In his book he had pointed out how the city government, and especially those connected with the departments of police and health, could aid in remedying some of the wrongs.

As president of the Police Board I was also a member of the Health Board. In both positions I felt that with Jacob Riis's guidance I would be able to put a goodly number of his principles into actual effect. He and I looked at life and its problems from substantially the same standpoint. Our ideals and principles and purposes, and our beliefs as to the methods necessary to realize them, were alike. . . .

As I viewed it, there were two sides to the work: first, the actual handling of the Police Department; second, using my position to help in making the city a better place in which to live and work for those to whom the conditions of life and labor were hardest. The two problems were closely connected; for one thing never to be forgotten in striving to better the conditions of the New York police force is the connection between the standard of morals and behavior in that force and the general standard of morals and behavior in the city at large. The form of government of the Police Department at that time was such as to make it a matter of extreme difficulty to get good results. It represented that device of old-school American political thought, the desire to establish checks and balances so elaborate that no man shall have power enough to do anything very bad. In practice this always means that no man has power enough to do anything good, and that what is bad is done anyhow.

In most positions the "division of powers" theory works unmitigated mischief. The only way to get good service is to give somebody power to render it, facing the fact that power which will enable a man to do a job well will also necessarily enable him to do it ill if he is the wrong kind of man. What is normally needed is the concentration in the hands of one man, or of a very small body of men, of ample power to enable him or them to do the work that is necessary; and then the devising of means to hold these men fully responsible for the exercise of that power by the people. This of course means that, if the people are willing to see power misused, it will be misused. But it also means

that if, as we hold, the people are fit for self-government—
if, in other words, our talk and our institutions are not
shams—we will get good government. I do not contend
that my theory will automatically bring good government.
I do contend that it will enable us to get as good government as we deserve, and that the other way will not. . . .

The first fight I made was to keep politics absolutely out
of the force; and not only politics, but every kind of improper favoritism. Doubtless in making thousands of appointments and hundreds of promotions there were men
who contrived to use influence of which I was ignorant.
But these cases must have been few and far between. As
far as was humanly possible, the appointments and promotions were made without regard to any question except the
fitness of the man and the needs of the service. As Civil
Service Commissioner I had been instructing heads of departments and bureaus how to get men appointed without
regard to politics, and assuring them that by following
our methods they would obtain first-class results. As police
commissioner I was able practically to apply my own
teachings. . . . We paid not the slightest attention to a
man's politics or creed, or where he was born, so long as
he was an American citizen; and on an average we obtained
far and away the best men that had ever come into the
Police Department. . . .

The many-sided ethnic character of the force now and
then gives rise to, or affords opportunity for, queer hap-
penings. Occasionally it enables one to meet emergencies
in the best possible fashion. While I was Police Commissioner an anti-Semitic preacher from Berlin, Rector Ahlwardt, came over to New York to preach a crusade against
the Jews. Many of the New York Jews were much excited
and asked me to prevent him from speaking and not to

give him police protection. This, I told them, was impossible; and if possible would have been undesirable because it would have made him a martyr. The proper thing to do was to make him ridiculous. Accordingly I detailed for his protection a Jew sergeant and a score or two of Jew policemen. He made his harangue against the Jews under the active protection of some forty policemen, every one of them a Jew! It was the most effective possible answer; and incidentally it was an object-lesson to our people, whose greatest need it is to learn that there must be no division by class hatred, whether this hatred be that of creed against creed, nationality against nationality, section against section, or men of one social or industrial condition against men of another social or industrial condition. We must ever judge each individual on his own conduct and merits, and not on his membership in any class, whether that class be based on theological, social, or industrial considerations. . . .

There was in New York City a strong sentiment in favor of honesty in politics; there was also a strong sentiment in favor of opening the saloons on Sundays; and, finally, there was a strong sentiment in favor of keeping the saloons closed on Sunday. Unfortunately, many of the men who favored honest government nevertheless preferred keeping the saloons open to having honest government; and many others among the men who favored honest government put it second to keeping the saloons closed. Moreover, among the people who wished the law obeyed and the saloons closed there were plenty who objected strongly to every step necessary to accomplish the result, although they also insisted that the result should be accomplished. . . .

This was the situation that confronted me when I came to Mulberry Street. The saloon was the chief source of mischief. It was with the saloon that I had to deal, and there was only one way to deal with it. That was to enforce the law. The howl that rose was deafening. The professional politicians raved. The yellow press surpassed themselves in clamor and mendacity. A favorite assertion was that I was enforcing a "blue" law, an obsolete law that had never before been enforced. As a matter of fact, I was only enforcing honestly a law that had hitherto been enforced dishonestly. There was very little increase in the number of arrests made for violating the Sunday law. Indeed, there were weeks when the number of arrests went down. The only difference was that there was no protected class. Everybody was arrested alike, and I took especial pains to see that there was no discrimination, and that the big men and the men with political influence were treated like every one else. The immediate effect was wholly good. I had been told that it was not possible to close the saloons on Sunday and that I could not succeed. However, I did succeed. The warden of Bellevue Hospital reported, two or three weeks after we had begun, that for the first time in its existence there had not been a case due to a drunken brawl in the hospital all Monday. The police courts gave the same testimony, while savings-banks recorded increased deposits and pawn-shops hard times. The most touching of all things was the fact that we received letters, literally by the hundred, from mothers in tenement-houses who had never been allowed to take their children to the country in the wide-open days, and who now found their husbands willing to take them and their families for an outing on Sunday. Jake Riis and I spent one Sunday from morning till night in the tenement districts, seeing for ourselves what had happened.

During the two years that we were in office things never

slipped back to anything like what they had been before. But we did not succeed in keeping them quite as highly keyed as during these first weeks. As regards the Sunday-closing law, this was partly because public sentiment was not really with us. The people who had demanded honesty, but who did not like to pay for it by the loss of illegal pleasure, joined the openly dishonest in attacking us. Moreover, all kinds of ways of evading the law were tried, and some of them were successful. The statute, for instance, permitted any man to take liquor with meals. After two or three months a magistrate was found who decided judicially that seventeen beers and one pretzel made a meal—after which decision joy again became unconfined in at least some of the saloons, and the yellow press glee-fully announced that my "tyranny" had been curbed. But my prime object, that of stopping blackmail, was largely attained. . . .

In company with Jacob Riis, I did much work that was not connected with the actual discipline of the force or indeed with the actual work of the force. There was one thing which he and I abolished—police lodging-houses, which were simply tramp lodging-houses, and a fruitful encouragement to vagrancy. Those who read Mr. Riis's story of his own life will remember the incidents that gave him from actual personal experience his horror of these tramp lodging-houses. As member of the Health Board I was brought into very close relations with the conditions of life in the tenement-house districts. Here again I used to visit the different tenement-house regions, usually in company with Riis, to see for myself what the conditions were. It was largely this personal experience that enabled me while on the Health Board to struggle not only zeal-ously, but with reasonable efficiency and success, to improve conditions. We did our share in making forward strides in the matter of housing the working people of the city with some regard to decency and comfort.

The midnight trips that Riis and I took enabled me to see what the Police Department was doing, and also gave me personal insight into some of the problems of city life. It is one thing to listen in perfunctory fashion to tales of overcrowded tenements, and it is quite another actually to see what that overcrowding means, some hot summer night, by even a single inspection during the hours of darkness. There was a very hot spell one midsummer while I was police commissioner, and most of each night I spent walking through the tenement-house districts and visiting police stations to see what was being done. It was a tragic week. We did everything possible to alleviate the suffering. Much of it was heart-breaking, especially the gasping misery of the little children and of the worn-out mothers. Every resource of the Health Department, of the Police Department, and even the Fire Department (which flooded the hot streets) was taxed in the effort to render service. The heat killed such multitudes of horses that the means at our disposal for removing the poor dead beasts proved quite inadequate, although every nerve was strained to the limit. In consequence we received scores of complaints from persons before whose doors dead horses had remained, festering in the heat, for two or three days. One irascible man sent us furious denunciations, until we were at last able to send a big dray to drag away the horse that lay dead before his shop-door. The huge dray already contained eleven other dead horses, and when it reached this particular door it broke down, and it was hours before it could be moved. The unfortunate man who had thus been cursed with a granted wish closed his doors in despair and wrote us a final pathetic letter in which he requested us to remove either the horses or his shop, he didn't care which.

I have spoken before of my experience with the tenement-house cigar factory law which the highest court of New York State declared unconstitutional. My experience in the Police Department taught me that not a few of the worst tenement-houses were owned by wealthy individuals, who hired the best and most expensive lawyers to persuade the courts that it was "unconstitutional" to insist on the betterment of conditions. These business men and lawyers were very adroit in using a word with fine and noble associations to cloak their opposition to vitally necessary movements for industrial fair play and decency. They made it evident that they valued the Constitution, not as a help to righteousness, but as a means for thwarting movements against unrighteousness. After my experience with them I became more set than ever in my distrust of those men, whether business men or lawyers, judges, legislators, or executive officers, who seek to make of the Constitution a fetich for the prevention of the work of social reform, or the prevention of work in the interest of those men, women, and children on whose behalf we should be at liberty to employ freely every governmental agency.

Occasionally during the two years we had to put a stop to riotous violence, and now and then on these occasions some of the labor-union leaders protested against the actions of the police. By this time I was becoming a strong believer in labor-unions, a strong believer in the rights of labor. For that very reason I was all the more bound to see that lawlessness and disorder were put down, and that no rioter was permitted to masquerade under the guise of being a friend of labor or a sympathizer with labor. I was scrupulous to see that the labor men had fair play; that, for instance, they were allowed to picket just so far as under the law picketing could be permitted, so that the strikers had ample opportunity peacefully to persuade other labor men not to take their places. But I made it clearly and definitely understood that under no circumstances would I permit violence or fail to insist upon the keeping of order. If there were wrongs, I would join with a full heart in striving to have them corrected. But where there was violence all other questions had to drop until order was restored. This is a democracy, and the people have the power, if they choose to exercise it, to make conditions as they ought to be made, and to do this strictly within the law; and therefore the first duty of the true democrat, of the man really loyal to the principles of popular government, is to see that law is enforced and order upheld. It was a peculiar gratification to me that so many of the labor leaders with whom I was thrown in contact grew cordially to accept this view. . . .

A big police force was needed in New York City, of that TR was well aware. But a big navy was needed by the United States, of that he was equally certain, and he was disappointed to find that President Eliot of Harvard failed to see the wisdom of his stand on national defense. To Henry Cabot Lodge he wrote in the spring of 1896:

I see that President Eliot attacked you and myself as "degenerated sons of Harvard." It is a fine alliance, that between the anglo-maniac mugwumps, the socialist working men, and corrupt politicians like Gorman, to prevent the increase of our Navy and coast defenses. The moneyed and semi-cultivated classes, especially of the Northeast, are doing their best to bring this country down to the Chinese level. If we ever come to nothing as a nation it will be because the teaching of Carl Schurz, President Eliot, the *Evening Post* and the futile sentimentalists of the international arbitration type, bears its legitimate fruit in producing a flabby, timid type of character, which eats away the great fighting features of our race. Hand in hand with the Chinese timidity and inefficiency of such a character would go the Chinese corruption; for men of such a stamp are utterly unable to war against the Tammany stripe of politicians. There is nothing that provokes me more than the unintelligent, cowardly chatter for "peace at any price" in which all of those gentlemen indulge.

Preaching a big navy was, of course, only one way of annoying Eliot of Harvard. In 1905 TR turned up in Cambridge for the twenty-fifth anniversary of his class. "As he was President," said Eliot, "I invited him to stay at my house. . . . He said he was dirty, and he looked dirty. I showed him to his room. The first thing he did was to pull off his coat, roll it up with his hands, and fling it across the bed so violently it sent a pillow to the floor beyond. The next thing he did was to take a great pistol from his trouser's pocket and slam it down on the dresser. After awhile he came rushing downstairs, as if his life depended on it."

"Now, you are taking breakfast with me?" asked Eliot.

"Oh, no," said TR, "I promised Bishop Lawrence I would breakfast with him,—and good gracious! . . . I've forgotten my gun!"

The sense of humor that TR displayed in this encounter with Eliot was unfortunately missing from his speeches in the presidential campaign of 1896. Dismayed by the thought that Bryan might enter the White House, he made no secret of his apprehensions in the following address before the American Republican League of Chicago. Governor John Peter Altgeld of Illinois, then running for re-election (he was defeated), had made the mistake (TR would have used a harsher word) of pardoning three prisoners involved in the Haymarket Riot, judging that their trial had not been without prejudice.

It is not merely schoolgirls that have hysterics; very vicious mob-leaders have them at times and so do well-meaning demagogues when their heads are turned by the applause of men of little intelligence and their minds inflated with the possibility of acquiring solid leadership in the country. The dominant note in Mr. Bryan's utterances and in the campaign waged in his behalf is the note of hysteria. Messrs. Bryan, Altgeld, Tillman, Debs, Coxey, and the rest have not the power to rival the deeds of Marat, Barrère, and Robespierre, but they are strikingly like the leaders of the Terror of France in mental and moral attitudes, plus an added touch of the grotesque rising from the utter folly as well as the base dishonesty of their trying to play such a rôle in such a country as ours. For Mr. Bryan we can feel the contemptuous pity always felt for the small man unexpectedly thrust into a big place. He does not look well in a lion's skin, but that is chiefly the fault of those who put the skin on him. But in Mr. Altgeld's case we see all too clearly the jaws and hide of the wolf through the fleecy covering. Mr. Altgeld is a much more dangerous man than Mr. Bryan. He is much slyer, much more intelligent, much less silly, much more free from all the restraints of some public morality. The one is unscrupulous from vanity, the other from calculation. The one plans wholesale repudiation with a light heart and bubbling eloquence, because he lacks intelligence and is intoxicated by hope of power; the other would connive at wholesale murder and would justify it by elaborate and cunning sophistry for reasons known only to his own tortuous soul. For America to put men like this in control of her destinies would be such a dishonor, as it is scarcely bearable to think of. . . .

TR was moving on a higher plane when he came to review Brooks Adams' The Law of Civilization and Decay *for the January, 1897 issue of* The Forum. *There was much with which he sympathized in Adams' indictment of the modern world—and much of which he disapproved.*

Few more melancholy books have been written than Mr. Brooks Adams' "Law of Civilization and Decay." It is a marvel of compressed statement. In a volume of less than four hundred pages Mr. Adams singles out some of the vital factors in the growth and evolution of civilized life during the last two thousand years; and so brilliant is his discussion of these factors as to give, though but a glimpse, yet one of the most vivid glimpses ever given, of some of the most important features in the world life of Christendom. Of some of the features only; for a fundamentally defective point in Mr. Adams' brilliant book is his failure to present certain phases of the life of the nations—phases which are just as important as those which he discusses with such vigorous ability. Furthermore, he disregards not a few facts which would throw light on others, the weight of which he fully recognizes. Both these shortcomings are very natural in a writer who possesses an entirely original point of view, who is the first man to see clearly certain things that to his predecessors have been nebulous, and who writes with a fervent intensity of conviction, even in his bitterest cynicism, such as we are apt to associate rather with the prophet and reformer than with a historian to whom prophet and reformer alike appeal no more than do their antitypes. It is a rare thing for a historian to make a distinct contribution to the philosophy of history; and this Mr. Adams has done. Naturally enough, he, like other men who break new ground, tends here and there to draw a devious furrow.

That there is grave reason for some of Mr. Adams' melancholy forebodings, no serious student of the times, no sociologist or reformer, and no practical politician who is interested in more than momentary success, will deny. A foolish optimist is only less noxious than an utter pessimist; and the prerequisite for any effort, whether hopeful or hopeless, to better our conditions is an accurate knowledge of what these conditions are. There is no use in blinding ourselves to certain of the tendencies and results of our high-pressure civilization. Some very omnious facts have become more and more apparent during the present century, in which the social movement of the white race has gone on with such unexampled and ever-accelerating rapidity. The rich have undoubtedly grown richer; and, while the most careful students are inclined to answer with an emphatic negative the proposition that the poor have grown poorer, it is nevertheless certain that there has been a large absolute, though not relative, increase of poverty, and that the very poor tend to huddle in immense masses in the cities. Even though these masses are, relatively to the rest of the population, smaller than they formerly were, they constitute a standing menace, not merely to our prosperity, but to our existence. The improvement in the means of communication, moreover, has so far immensely increased the tendency of the urban population to grow at the expense of the rural; and philosophers have usually been inclined to regard the ultimate safety of a nation as resting upon its peasantry. The improvement in machinery, the very perfection of scientific processes, cause great, even though temporary, suffering to unskilled laborers. Moreover, there is a certain softness of fibre in civilized nations which, if it were to prove progressive, might mean the development of a cultured and refined people quite unable to hold its own in those conflicts through which alone any great race can ultimately march to victory. . . .

From many of the statements in Mr. Adams' very interesting concluding chapter I should . . . differ; and yet this chapter is one which is not merely interesting but soul-stirring, and it contains much with which most of us would heartily agree. Through the cold impartiality with which he strives to work merely as a recorder of facts, there break now and then flashes of pent-up wrath and vehement scorn for all that is mean and petty in a purely materialistic, purely capitalistic, civilization. With his scorn of what is ignoble and base in our development, his impatient contempt of the deification of the stock-market, the trading-counter, and the factory, all generous souls must agree. When we see prominent men deprecating the assertion of national honor because it "has a bad effect upon business," or because it "impairs the value of securities"; when we see men seriously accepting Mr. Edward Atkinson's pleasant theory that patriotism is of no consequence when compared with the price of cotton sheeting or the capacity to undersell our competitors in foreign markets, it is no wonder that a man who has in him the stuff of ancestors who helped to found our government and helped to bring it safely through the Civil War, should think blackly of the future. But Mr. Adams should remember that there always have been men of this merely huckstering type, or of other types not much higher. It is not a nice thing that Mr. Eliot, the president of one of the greatest educational institutions of the land, should reflect discredit upon the educated men of the country by his attitude on the Venezuela affair, carrying his desertion of American principles so far as to find himself left in the lurch by the very English statesman whose cause he was championing; but Mr. Adams by turning to the "History" of the administration of Madison, by his brother, Henry Adams, would find that Mr. Eliot had plenty of intellectual ancestors among the "blue lights" federalists of that day. . . .

This applies also to what Mr. Adams says of the fall of the soldier and the rise of the usurer. He quite overstates his case in asserting that in Europe the soldier has lost his importance since 1871, and that the administration of society since then has fallen into the hands of the "economic man," thereby making a change "more radical than any that happened at Rome or even at Byzantium." In the first place, a period of a quarter of a century is altogether too short to admit of such a generalization. In the next place, the facts do not support this particular generalization. The Germans are quite as military in type as ever they were, and very much more so than they were at any period during the two centuries preceding Bismarck and Moltke.

Nor is it true to say that "the ruler of the French people has passed for the first time from the martial to the moneyed type." Louis XV and Louis Philippe can hardly be held to belong to any recognized martial type; and the reason of the comparative sinking of the military man in France is due not in the least to the rise of his economic fellow countryman, but to the rise of the other military man in Germany. Mr. Adams says that since the capitulation of Paris the soldier has tended to sink more and more, until he merely receives his orders from financiers (which term when used by Mr. Adams includes all business and working men) with his salary, without being allowed a voice, even in the questions which involve peace and war. Now this is precisely the position which the soldier has occupied for two centuries among English-speaking races; and it is during these very centuries that the English-speaking race has produecd its greatest soldiers. . . .

CHAPTER 7

The War of America
the Unready

... In the spring of 1897 President McKinley appointed me Assistant Secretary of the Navy. I owed the appointment chiefly to the efforts of Senator H. C. Lodge, of Massachusetts, who doubtless was actuated mainly by his long and close friendship for me, but also—I like to believe—by his keen interest in the Navy. ... I have always taken the interest in the Navy which every good American ought to take. . . . In the early eighties, the Navy had reached its nadir, and we were then utterly incompetent to fight Spain or any other power that had a navy at all. Shortly afterward we began timidly and hesitatingly to build up a fleet. It is amusing to recall the roundabout steps we took to accomplish our purpose. In the reaction after the colossal struggle of the Civil War our strongest and most capable men had thrown their whole energy into business, into money-making, into the development, and above all the exploitation and exhaustion at the most rapid rate possible, of our natural resources—

mines, forests, soil, and rivers. These men were not weak men, but they permitted themselves to grow short-sighted and selfish; and while many of them down at the bottom possessed the fundamental virtues, including the fighting virtues, others were purely of the glorified huckster or glorified pawnbroker type—which when developed to the exclusion of everything else makes about as poor a national type as the world has seen. This unadulterated huckster or pawnbroker type is rarely keenly sympathetic in matters of social and industrial justice, and is usually physically timid and likes to cover an unworthy fear of the most just war under high-sounding names.

It was reinforced by the large mollycoddle vote—the people who are soft physically and morally, or who have a twist in them which makes them acidly cantankerous and unpleasant as long as they can be so with safety to their bodies. In addition there are the good people with no imagination and no foresight, who think war will not come, but that if it does come armies and navies can be improvised. . . . Then, among the wise and high-minded people who in self-respecting and genuine fashion strive earnestly for peace, there are the foolish fanatics always to be found in such a movement and always discrediting it— the men who form the lunatic fringe in all reform movements. . . .

We did not at the time of which I write take our foreign duties seriously, and as we combined bluster in speech with refusal to make any preparation whatsoever for action, we were not taken seriously in return. Gradually a slight change for the better occurred, the writings of Captain Mahan playing no small part therein. We built some modern cruisers to start with; the people who felt that battleships were wicked compromising with their misguided consciences by saying that the cruisers could be used "to protect our commerce"—which they could not be, unless they had battleships to back them. Then we attempted to build more powerful fighting vessels, and as there was a section of the public which regarded battleships as possessing a name immorally suggestive of violence, we compromised by calling the new ships armored cruisers, and making them combine with exquisite nicety all the defects and none of the virtues of both types. Then we got to the point of building battleships. . . .

Soon after I began work as Assistant Secretary of the Navy I became convinced that the war would come. The revolt in Cuba had dragged its weary length until conditions in the island had become so dreadful as to be a standing disgrace to us for permitting them to exist. There is much that I sincerely admire about the Spanish character; and there are few men for whom I have felt greater respect than for certain gentlemen of Spain whom I have known. But Spain attempted to govern her colonies on archaic principles which rendered her control of them incompatible with the advance of humanity and intolerable to the conscience of mankind. In 1898 the so-called war in Cuba had dragged along for years with unspeakable horror, degradation, and misery. It was not "war" at all, but murderous oppression. Cuba was devastated. . . .

The big financiers and the men generally who were susceptible to touch on the money nerve, and who cared nothing for national honor if it conflicted even temporarily with business prosperity, were against the war. The more fatuous type of philanthropist agreed with them. The newspapers controlled by, or run in the interests of, these two classes deprecated war, and did everything in their power to prevent any preparation for war. As a whole the people in Congress were at that time (and are now) a short-sighted set as regards international matters. . . .

However, in the Navy Department we were able to do a good deal, thanks to the energy and ability of some of the bureau chiefs, and to the general good tone of the service. . . .

Sound naval opinion was overwhelmingly in favor of Dewey to command one squadron. . . . Accordingly I did my best to get him put in command of the Asiatic fleet, the fleet where it was most essential to have a man who would act without referring things back to the home authorities. An officer senior to him, of the respectable commonplace type, was being pushed by certain politicians who I knew had influence with the Navy Department and with the President. I would have preferred to see Dewey get the appointment without appealing to any politician at all. But while this was my preference, the essential thing was to get him the appointment. . . . In a fortunate hour for the nation, Dewey was given command of the Asiatic squadron.

When the *Maine* was blown up in Havana Harbor, war became inevitable. A number of the peace-at-any-price men of course promptly assumed the position that she had blown herself up; but investigation showed that the explosion was from outside. And, in any event, it would have been impossible to prevent war. The enlisted men of the navy, who often grew bored to the point of desertion in peace, became keyed up to a high pitch of efficiency, and crowds of fine young fellows, from the interior as well as from the seacoast, thronged to enlist. The navy officers showed alert ability and unwearied industry in getting things ready. There was one deficiency, however, which there was no time to remedy, and of the very existence of which, strange to say, most of our best men were ignorant. Our navy had no idea how low our standard of marksmanship was. We had not realized that the modern battleship had become such a complicated piece of mechanism that the old methods of training in marksmanship were as obsolete as the old muzzle-loading broadside guns themselves. . . .

Like the people, the government was for a long time unwilling to prepare for war, because so many honest but misguided men believed that the preparation itself tended to bring on the war. I did not in the least share this feeling, and whenever I was left as acting secretary I did everything in my power to put us in readiness. I knew that in the event of war Dewey could be slipped like a wolfhound from a leash; I was sure that if he were given half a chance he would strike instantly and with telling effect; and I made up my mind that all I could do to give him that half-chance should be done. I was in the closest touch with Senator Lodge throughout this period, and either consulted him about or notified him of all moves I was taking. By the end of February I felt it was vital to send Dewey (as well as each of our other commanders who were not in home waters) instructions that would enable him to be in readiness for immediate action. On the afternoon of Saturday, February 25, when I was acting secretary, Lodge called on me just as I was preparing the order, which (as it was addressed to a man of the right stamp) was of much importance to the subsequent operations. . . .

WASHINGTON, February 25, '98.

DEWEY, HONG KONG:

Order the squadron, except the *Monocacy*, to Hong Kong. Keep full of coal. In the event of declaration of war

Spain, your duty will be to see that the Spanish squadron does not leave the Asiatic coast, and then offensive operations in Philipine Islands. Keep *Olympia* until further orders.

ROOSEVELT.

... It would be instructive to remember, if only we were willing to do so, the fairly comic panic which swept in waves over our seacoast, first when it became evident that war was about to be declared, and then when it was declared. ... The governor of one State actually announced that he would not permit the National Guard of that State to leave its borders, the idea being to retain it against a possible Spanish invasion. So many of the business men of the city of Boston took their securities inland to Worcester that the safe-deposit companies of Worcester proved unable to take care of them. In my own neighborhood on Long Island clauses were gravely put into leases to the effect that if the property were destroyed by the Spaniards the lease should lapse. ...

This was one side of the picture. The other side was that the crisis at once brought to the front any amount of latent fighting strength. There were plenty of congressmen who showed cool-headed wisdom and resolution. The plain people, the men and women back of the persons who lost their heads, set seriously to work to see that we did whatever was necessary, and made the job a thorough one. The young men swarmed to enlist. In time of peace it had been difficult to fill the scanty Regular Army and Navy, and there were innumerable desertions; now the ships and regiments were overenlisted, and so many deserters returned in order to fight that it became difficult to decide what to do with them. ...

Among my friends was the then army surgeon Leonard Wood. He was a surgeon. Not having an income, he had to earn his own living. He had gone through the Harvard Medical School, and had then joined the Army in the Southwest as a contract doctor. He had every physical, moral, and mental quality which fitted him for a soldier's life and for the exercise of command. In the inconceivably wearing and harassing campaigns against the Apaches he had served nominally as a surgeon, really in command of troops, on more than one expedition. He was as anxious as I was that if there were war we should both have our part in it. I had always felt that if there were a serious war I wished to be in a position to explain to my children why I did take part in it, and not why I did not take part in it. Moreover, I had very deeply felt that it was our duty to free Cuba, and I had publicly expressed this feeling; and when a man takes such a position, he ought to be willing to make his words good by his deeds unless there is some very strong reason to the contrary. He should pay with his body.

As soon as war was upon us, Wood and I began to try for a chance to go to the front. Congress had authorized the raising of three National Volunteer Cavalry regiments, wholly apart from the State contingents. Secretary Alger of the War Department was fond of me personally, and Wood was his family doctor. Alger had been a gallant soldier in the Civil War, and was almost the only member of the Administration who felt all along that we would have to go to war with Spain over Cuba. He liked my attitude in the matter, and because of his remembrance of his own experiences he sympathized with my desire to go to the front. Accordingly he offered me the command of one of the regiments. I told him that after six weeks' service in the field I would feel competent to handle the regiment, but that I would not know how to equip it or how to get it into the first action; but that Wood was entirely competent at once to take command, and that if he would make Wood colonel I would accept the lieutenant-colonelcy. General Alger though this an act of foolish self-abnegation on my part—instead of its being, what it was, the wisest act I could have performed. He told me to accept the colonelcy, and that he would make Wood lieutenant-colonel, and that Wood would do the work anyway; but I answered that I did not wish to rise on any man's shoulders; that I hoped to be given every chance that my deeds and abilities warranted; but that I did not wish what I did not earn, and that above all I did not wish to hold any position where any one else did the work. He laughed at me a little and said I was foolish, but I do not think he really minded, and he promised to do as I wished. True to his word, he secured the appointment of Wood as colonel and of myself as lieutenant-colonel of the First United States Volunteer Cavalry. This was soon nicknamed, both by the public and by the rest of the army, the Rough Riders, doubtless because the bulk of the men were from the southwestern ranch country and were skilled in the wild horsemanship of the great plains.

Wood instantly began the work of raising the regiment. He first assembled several old non-commissioned officers of experience, put them in office, and gave them blanks for requisitions for the full equipment of a cavalry regiment. He selected San Antonio as the gathering-place, as it was in a good horse country, near the Gulf from some port on which we would have to embark, and near an old arsenal and an old army post from which we got a good deal of stuff—some of it practically condemned, but which we found serviceable at a pinch, and much better than nothing. . . .

For several weeks before I joined the regiment, to which Wood went ahead of me, I continued as Assistant Secretary of the Navy, trying to get some coherence of plan between the War Department and the Navy Department; and also being used by Wood to finish getting the equipment for the regiment. As regards finding out what the plans of the War Department were, the task was simple. They had no plans. . . .

I suppose every man tends to brag about his regiment; but it does seem to me that there never was a regiment better worth bragging about than ours. Wood was an exceptional commander, of great power, with a remarkable gift for organization. The rank and file were as fine natural fighting men as ever carried a rifle or rode a horse in any country or any age. We had a number of first-class young fellows from the East, most of them from colleges like Harvard, Yale, and Princeton; but the great majority of the men were southwesterners, from the then Territories of Oklahoma, Indian Territory, Arizona, and New Mexico. They were accustomed to the use of firearms, accustomed to taking care of themselves in the open; they were intelligent and self-reliant; they possessed hardihood and endurance and physical prowess; and, above all, they had the fighting edge, the cool and resolute fighting temper. They went into the war with full knowledge, having deliberately counted the cost. . . .

Wood was so busy getting the regiment ready that when I reached San Antonio he turned most of the drilling of it over to me. This was a piece of great good fortune for me, and I drilled the men industriously, mounted and unmounted. I had plenty to learn, and the men and the officers

even more; but we went at our work with the heartiest
good-will. We speedily made it evident that there was no
room and no mercy for any man who shirked any duty,
and we accomplished good results. . . . My business was
to be where I could keep most command over the regiment,
and, in a rough-and-tumble, scrambling fight in thick
jungle, this had to depend upon the course of events, and
usually meant that I had to be at the front. . . .

At San Antonio we entrained for Tampa. In various
sociological books by authors of Continental Europe there
are jeremiads as to the way in which service in the great
European armies, with their minute and machine-like
efficiency and regularity tends to dwarf the capacity for individual initiative among the officers and men. There is
no such danger for any officer or man of a volunteer
organization in America when our country, with playful
light-heartedness, has pranced into war without making
any preparation for it. I know no larger or finer field for
the display of an advanced individualism than that which
opened before us as we went from San Antonio to Tampa,
camped there, and embarked on a transport for Cuba. Nobody ever had any definite information to give us, and
whatever information we unearthed on our own account
was usually wrong. Each of us had to show an alert and
not over-scrupulous self-reliance in order to obtain food
for his men, provender for his horses, or transportation of
any kind for any object. One lesson early impressed on me
was that if I wanted anything to eat it was wise to carry
it with me; and if any new war should arise, I would earnestly advise the men of every volunteer organization always to proceed upon the belief that their supplies will
not turn up, and to take every opportunity of getting food
for themselves.

Tampa was a scene of the wildest confusion. There were miles of tracks loaded with cars of the contents of which nobody seemed to have any definite knowledge. General Miles, who was supposed to have supervision over everything, and General Shafter, who had charge of the expedition, were both there. But, thanks to the fact that nobody had had any experience in handling even such a small force as ours—about seventeen thousand men—there was no semblance of order. Wood and I were bound that we should not be left behind when the expedition started. When we were finally informed that it was to leave next morning, we were ordered to go to a certain track to meet a train. We went to the track, but the train never came. Then we were sent to another track to meet another train. Again it never came. However, we found a coal train, of which we took possession, and the conductor, partly under duress and partly in a spirit of friendly helpfulness, took us down to the quay.

All kinds of other organizations, infantry and cavalry, Regular and volunteer, were arriving at the quay and wandering around it, and there was no place where we could get any specific information as to what transport we were to have. Finally Wood was told to "get any ship you can get which is not already assigned." He borrowed without leave a small motor-boat, and commandeered the transport *Yucatan*. . . .

We were kept several days on the transport, which was jammed with men, so that it was hard to move about on the deck. Then the fleet got under way, and we steamed slowly down to Santiago. Here we disembarked, higgledy-piggledy, just as we had embarked. Different parts of different outfits were jumbled together, and it was no light labor afterward to assemble the various batteries. For instance, one transport had guns, and another the locks for the guns; the two not getting together for several days after one of them had been landed. Soldiers went here, provisions there; and who got ashore first largely depended upon individual activity. Fortunately for us, my former naval aide, when I had been Assistant Secretary of the Navy, Lieutenant-Commander Sharp, a first-class fellow, was there in command of a little ship to which I had succeeded in getting him appointed before I left the Navy Department. He gave us a black pilot, who took our transport right in shore, the others following like a flock of sheep; and we disembarked with our rifles, ammunition belts, and not much else. In theory it was out of our turn, but if we had not disembarked then, Heaven only knows when our turn would have come, and we did not intend to be out of the fighting if we could help it. I carried some food in my pockets, and a light waterproof coat, which was my sole camp equipment for the next two or three days. Twenty-four hours after getting ashore we marched from Daiquiri, where we had landed, to Siboney, also on the coast, reaching it during a terrific downpour of rain. When this was over, we built a fire, dried our clothes, and ate whatever we had brought with us. . . .

It was a mountainous country covered with thick jungle, a most confusing country, and I had an awful time trying to get into the fight and trying to do what was right when in it; and all the while I was thinking that I was the only man who did not know what I was about, and that all the others did—whereas, as I found out later, pretty much everybody else was as much in the dark as I was. There was no surprise; we struck the Spaniards exactly where we had expected; then Wood halted us and put us into the fight deliberately and in order. He ordered us to deploy alternately by troops to the right and left of the trail, giving our senior major, Brodie, a West Pointer, and as good a soldier as ever wore a uniform, the left wing, while I took the right wing. I was told if possible to connect with the Regulars who were on the right. In theory this was excellent, but as the jungle was very dense the first troop that deployed to the right vanished forthwith, and I never saw it again until the fight was over—having a frightful feeling meanwhile that I might be court-martialled for losing it. The next troop deployed to the left under Brodie. Then the third came along, and I started to deploy it to the right as before.

By the time the first platoon had gotten into the jungle I realized that it likewise would disappear unless I kept hold of it. I managed to keep possession of the last platoon. One learns fast in a fight, and I marched this platoon and my next two troops in column through the jungle without any attempt to deploy until we got on the firing-line. This sounds simple. But it was not. I did not know when I had gotten on the firing-line! I could hear a good deal of firing, some over to my right at a good distance, and the rest to the left and ahead. I pushed on, expecting to strike the enemy somewhere between.

Soon we came to the brink of a deep valley. There was a good deal of cracking of rifles way off in front of us, but as they used smokeless powder we had no idea as to exactly where they were, or who they were shooting at. Then it dawned on us that we were the target. The bullets began to come overhead, making a sound like the ripping of a silk dress, with sometimes a kind of pop; a few of my men fell, and I deployed the rest, making them lie down and get behind trees. Richard Harding Davis was with us, and as we scanned the landscape with our glasses it was he who first pointed out to us some Spaniards in a trench some three-quarters of a mile off. It was difficult to make them out. There were not many of them. However, we finally did make them out, and we could see their conical hats, for the trench was a poor one. We advanced, firing at them, and drove them off.

What to do then I had not an idea. The country in front fell away into a very difficult jungle-filled valley. There was nothing but jungle all around, and if I advanced I was afraid I might get out of touch with everybody and not be going in the right direction. Moreover, as far as I could see, there was now nobody in front who was shooting at us, although some of the men on my left insisted that our own men had fired into us—an allegation which I soon found was almost always made in such a fight, and which in this case was not true. At this moment some of the Regulars appeared across the ravine on our right. The first thing they did was to fire a volley at us, but one of our first sergeants went up a tree and waved a guidon at them and they stopped. Firing was still going on to our left, however, and I was never more puzzled to know what to do. I did not wish to take my men out of their position without orders, for fear that I might thereby be leaving a gap if there was a Spanish force which meditated an offensive return. On the other hand, it did not seem to me that I had been doing enough fighting to justify my existence, and there was obviously fighting going on to the left. . . .

So I left my men where they were and started off at a trot toward where the firing was, with a couple of orderlies to send back for the men in case that proved advisable. Like most tyros, I was wearing my sword, which in thick jungle now and then got between my legs—from that day on it always went corded in the baggage. I struck the trail, and began to pass occasional dead men. Pretty soon I reached Wood and found, much to my pleasure, that I had done the right thing, for as I came up word was brought to him that Brodie had been shot, and he at once sent me to take charge of the left wing. It was more open country here, and at least I was able to get a glimpse of my own men and exercise some control over them. There was much firing going on, but for the life of me I could not see any Spaniards, and neither could any one else. Finally we made up our minds that they were shooting at us from a set of red-tiled ranch buildings a good way in front, and these I assaulted, finally charging them. Before we came anywhere near, the Spaniards, who, as it proved, really were inside and around them, abandoned them, leaving a few dead men.

By the time I had taken possession of these buildings all firing had ceased everywhere. I had not the faintest idea what had happened: whether the fight was over; or whether this was merely a lull in the fight; or where the Spaniards were; or whether we might be attacked again; or whether we ought ourselves to attack somebody somewhere else. I got my men in order and sent out small parties to explore the ground in front, who returned without finding any foe. (By this time, as a matter of fact, the Spaniards were in full retreat.) Meanwhile I was extending my line so as to get into touch with our people on the right. Word was brought to me that Wood had been shot —which fortunately proved not to be true—and as, if this were so, it meant that I must take charge of the regiment, I moved over personally to inquire. Soon I learned that he was all right, that the Spaniards had retreated along the main road, and that Colonel Wood and two or three other officers were a short distance away. Before I reached them I encountered a captain of the Ninth Cavalry, very glum because his troopers had not been up in time to take part in the fight, and he congratulated me—with visible effort! —upon my share in our first victory. I thanked him cordially, not confiding to him that till that moment I myself knew exceeding little about the victory; and proceeded to where Generals Wheeler, Lawton, and Chaffee, who had just come up, in company with Wood, were seated on a bank. They expressed appreciation of the way that I had handled my troops, first on the right wing and then on the left! As I was quite prepared to find I had committed some awful sin, I did my best to accept this in a nonchalant manner, and not to look as relieved as I felt. As throughout the morning I had preserved a specious aspect of wisdom, and had commanded first one and then the other wing, the fight was really a capital thing for me, for practically all the men had served under my actual command, and thenceforth felt an enthusiastic belief that I would lead them aright.

It was a week after this skirmish before the army made the advance on Santiago. Just before this occurred General Young was stricken down with fever. General Wheeler, who had commanded the cavalry division, was put in general charge of the left wing of the army, which fought before the city itself. Brigadier-General Sam Sumner, an excellent officer, who had the second cavalry brigade, took command of the cavalry division, and Wood took command of our brigade, while, to my intense delight, I got my regiment. I therefore had command of the regiment before the stiffest fighting occurred. Later, when Wood was put in command in Santiago, I became the brigade commander. . . .

Early in the morning our artillery began firing from the hill crest immediately in front of where our men were camped. Several of the regiment were killed and wounded by the shrapnel of the return fire of the Spaniards. One of the shrapnel bullets fell on my wrist and raised a bump as big as a hickory-nut, but did not even break the skin. Then we were marched down from the hill on a muddy road through thick jungle toward Santiago. The heat was great, and we strolled into the fight with no definite idea on the part of any one as to what we were to do or what would happen. There was no plan that our left wing was to make a serious fight that day; and as there were no plans, it was naturally exceedingly hard to get orders, and each of us had to act largely on his own responsibility.

Lawton's infantry division attacked the little village of El Caney, some miles to the right. Kent's infantry division and Sumner's dismounted cavalry division were supposed to detain the Spanish army in Santiago until Lawton had captured El Caney. Spanish towns and villages, however, with their massive buildings, are natural fortifications, as the French found in the Peninsular War, and as both the French and our people found in Mexico. The Spanish troops in El Caney fought very bravely, as did the Spanish troops in front of us, and it was late in the afternoon before Lawton accomplished his task.

Meanwhile we of the left wing had by degrees become involved in a fight which toward the end became not even a colonel's fight, but a squad leader's fight. The cavalry division was put at the head of the line. We were told to march forward, cross a little river in front, and then, turning to the right, march up alongside the stream until we connected with Lawton. Incidentally, this movement would not have brought us into touch with Lawton in any event. But we speedily had to abandon any thought of carrying it out. The manœuvre brought us within fair range of the Spanish intrenchments along the line of hills which we called the San Juan Hills, because on one of them was the San Juan blockhouse. On that day my regiment had the lead of the second brigade, and we marched down the trail following in trace behind the first brigade. Apparently the Spaniards could not make up their minds what to do as the three Regular regiments of the first brigade crossed and defiled along the other bank of the stream, but when our regiment was crossing they began to fire at us.

Under this flank fire it soon became impossible to continue the march. The first brigade halted, deployed, and finally began to fire back. Then our brigade was halted. From time to time some of our men would fall, and I sent repeated word to the rear to try to get authority to attack the hills in front. Finally General Sumner, who was fighting the division in fine shape, sent word to advance. The word was brought to me by Mills, who said that my orders were to support the Regulars in the assault on the hills, and that my objective would be the red-tiled ranch-house in front, on a hill which we afterward christened Kettle Hill. I mention Mills saying this because it was exactly the kind of definite order the giving of which does so much to insure success in a fight, as it prevents all obscurity as to what is to be done. The order to attack did not reach the first brigade until after we ourselves reached it, so that at first there was doubt on the part of their officers whether they were at liberty to join in the advance.

I had not enjoyed the Guasimas fight at all, because I had been so uncertain as to what I ought to do. But the

San Juan fight was entirely different. The Spaniards had a hard position to attack, it is true, but we could see them, and I knew exactly how to proceed. I kept on horseback, merely because I found it difficult to convey orders along the line, as the men were lying down; and it is always hard to get men to start when they cannot see whether their comrades are also going. So I rode up and down the lines, keeping them straightened out, and gradually worked through line after line until I found myself at the head of the regiment. By the time I had reached the lines of the Regulars of the first brigade I had come to the conclusion that it was silly to stay in the valley firing at the hills, because that was really where we were most exposed, and that the thing to do was to try to rush the intrenchments. Where I struck the Regulars there was no one of superior rank to mine, and after asking why they did not charge, and being answered that they had no orders, I said I would give the order. There was naturally a little reluctance shown by the elderly officer in command to accept my order, so I said, "Then let my men through, sir," and I marched through, followed by my grinning men. The younger officers and the enlisted men of the Regulars jumped up and joined us. I waved my hat, and we went up the hill with a rush. Having taken it, we looked across at the Spaniards in the trenches under the San Juan blockhouse to our left, which Hawkins's brigade was assaulting. I ordered our men to open fire on the Spaniards in the trenches. . . .

When Hawkins's soldiers captured the blockhouse, I, very much elated, ordered a charge on my own hook to a line of hills still farther on. Hardly anybody heard this order, however; only four men started with me, three of whom were shot. I gave one of them, who was wounded, my canteen of water, and ran back, much irritated that I had not been followed—which was quite unjustifiable, because I found that nobody had heard my orders. General Sumner had come up by this time, and I asked his permission to lead the charge. He ordered me to do so, and this time away we went, and stormed the Spanish intrenchments. There was some close fighting, and we took a few prisoners. We also captured the Spanish provisions, and ate them that night with great relish. One of the items was salted flying-fish, by the way. There were also bottles of wine, and jugs of fiery spirit, and as soon as possible I had these broken, although not before one or two of my men had taken too much liquor. Lieutenant Howze, of the Regulars, an aide of General Sumner's, brought me an order to halt where I was; he could not make up his mind to return until he had spent an hour or two with us under fire. The Spaniards attempted a counter-attack in the middle of the afternoon, but were driven back without effort, our men laughing and cheering as they rose to fire; because hitherto they had been assaulting breastworks, or lying still under artillery-fire, and they were glad to get a chance to shoot at the Spaniards in the open. We lay on our arms that night and as we were drenched with sweat, and had no blankets save a few we took from the dead Spaniards, we found even the tropical night chilly before morning came.

During the afternoon's fighting, while I was the highest officer at our immediate part of the front, Captains Boughton and Morton of the Regular cavalry, two as fine officers as any man could wish to have beside him in battle, came along the firing-line to tell me that they had heard a rumor that we might fall back, and that they wished to record their emphatic protest against any such course. I did not believe there was any truth in the rumor, for the Spaniards were utterly incapable of any effective counter-attack. However, late in the evening, after the fight, General Wheeler visited us at the front, and he told me to keep myself in readiness, as at any moment it might be decided to fall back. Jack Greenway was beside me when General Wheeler was speaking. I answered: "Well, General, I really don't know whether we would obey an order to fall back. We can take that city by a rush, and if we have to move out of here at all I should be inclined to make the rush in the right direction." Greenway nodded an eager assent. The old general, after a moment's pause, expressed his hearty agreement, and said that he would see that there was no falling back. He had been very sick for a couple of days, but, sick as he was, he managed to get into the fight. He was a game-cock if ever there was one, but he was in very bad physical shape on the day of the fight. If there had been any one in high command to supervise and press the attack that afternoon, we would have gone right into Santiago. In my part of the line the advance was halted only because we received orders not to move forward, but to stay on the crest of the captured hill and hold it.

We are always told that three-o'clock-in-the-morning courage is the most desirable kind. Well, my men and the Regulars of the cavalry had just that brand of courage. At about three o'clock on the morning after the first fight, shooting began in our front and there was an alarm of a Spanish advance. I was never more pleased than to see the way in which the hungry, tired, shabby men all jumped up and ran forward to the hill crest, so as to be ready for the attack; which, however, did not come. As soon as the sun rose the Spaniards again opened upon us with artillery.

A shell burst between Dave Goodrich and myself, black-ing us with powder, and killing and wounding several of the men immeditely behind us.

Next day the fight turned into a siege; there were some stirring incidents; but for the most part it was trench work. A fortnight later Santiago surrendered. Wood won his brigadier-generalship by the capital way in which he handled his brigade in the fight, and in the following siege. He was put in command of the captured city; and in a few days I succeeded to the command of the brigade.

The health of the troops was not good, and speedily became very bad. There was some dysentery, and a little yellow fever; but most of the trouble was from a severe form of malarial fever. The Washington authorities had behaved better than those in actual command of the ex-pedition at one crisis. Immediately after the first day's fighting around Santiago the latter had hinted by cable to Washington that they might like to withdraw, and Washington had emphatically vetoed the proposal. I record this all the more gladly because there were not too many gleams of good sense shown in the home management of the war; although I wish to repeat that the real blame for this rested primarily with us ourselves, the people of the United States, who had for years pursued in military mat-ters a policy that rendered it certain that there would be ineptitude and failure in high places if ever a crisis came. After the siege the people in Washington showed no knowledge whatever of the conditions around Santiago, and proposed to keep the army there. This would have meant that at least three-fourths of the men would either have died or have been permanently invalided, as a virulent form of malaria was wide-spread, and there was a steady growth of dysentery and other complaints. No object of any kind was to be gained by keeping the army in or near the captured city. General Shafter tried his best to get the Washington authorities to order the army home. As he failed to accomplish anything, he called a council of the division and brigade commanders and the chief medical officers to consult over the situation.

Although I had command of a brigade, I was only a colonel, and so I did not intend to attend, but the general informed me that I was particularly wanted, and accordingly I went. At the council General Shafter asked the medical authorities as to conditions, and they united in informing him that they were very bad, and were certain to grow much worse; and that in order to avoid frightful ravages from disease, chiefly due to malaria, the army should be sent back at once to some part of the northern United States. The general then explained that he could not get the War Department to understand the situation; that he could not get the attention of the public; and that he felt that there should be some authoritative publication which would make the War Department take action before it was too late to avert the ruin of the army. All who were in the room expressed their agreement.

Then the reason for my being present came out. It was explained to me by General Shafter, and by others, that as I was a volunteer officer and intended immediately to return to civil life, I could afford to take risks which the Regular Army men could not afford to take and ought not to be expected to take, and that therefore I ought to make the publication in question; because to incur the hostility of the War Department would not make any difference to me, whereas it would be destructive to the men in the Regular Army, or to those who hoped to get into the Regular Army. I thought this true, and said I would write a letter or make a statement which could then be published. Brigadier-General Ames, who was in the same position that I was, also announced that he would make a statement.

When I left the meeting it was understood that I was to make my statement as an interview in the press; but Wood, who was by that time brigadier-general commanding the city of Santiago, gave me a quiet hint to put my statement in the form of a letter to General Shafter, and this I accordingly did. When I had written my letter, the correspondent of the Associated Press, who had been informed by others of what had occurred, accompanied me to General Shafter. I presented the letter to General Shafter, who waved it away and said: "I don't want to take it; do whatever you wish with it." I, however, insisted on handing it to him, whereupon he shoved it toward the correspondent of the Associated Press, who took hold of it, and I released my hold. General Ames made a statement direct to the correspondent, and also sent a cable to the Assistant Secretary of the Navy at Washington, a copy of which he gave to the correspondent. By this time the other division and brigade commanders who were present felt that they had better take action themselves. They united in a round robin to General Shafter, which General Wood dictated, and which was signed by Generals Kent, Bates, Chaffee, Sumner, Ludlow, Ames, and Wood, and by myself. General Wood handed this to General Shafter, and it was made public by General Shafter, precisely as mine was made public. Later I was much amused when General Shafter stated that he could not imagine how my letter and the round robin got out! When I saw this statement, I appreciated how wise Wood had been in hinting to me not to act on the suggestion of the general that I should make a statement to the newspapers, but to put my statement in the form of a letter to him as my superior officer, a letter which I delivered to him. Both the letter and the round robin were written at General Shafter's wish, and at the unanimous suggestion of all the commanding and medical officers of the Fifth Army Corps, and both were published by General Shafter. . . .

We came back to Montauk Point and soon after were disbanded. We had been in the service only a little over four months. There are no four months of my life to which I look back with more pride and satisfaction. I believe most earnestly and sincerely in peace, but as things are yet in this world the nation that cannot fight, the people that have lost the fighting edge, that have lost the virile virtues, occupy a position as dangerous as it is ignoble. The future greatness of America in no small degree depends up on the possession by the average American citizen of the qualities which my men showed when they served under me at Santiago.

Moreover, there is one thing in connection with this war which it is well that our people should remember, our people who genuinely love the peace of righteousness, the peace of justice—and I would be ashamed to be other than a lover of the peace of righteousness and of justice. The true preachers of peace, who strive earnestly to bring nearer the day when peace shall obtain among all peoples, and who really do help forward the cause, are men who never hesitate to choose righteous war when it is the only alternative to unrighteous peace.

But there are other men who put peace ahead of righteousness, and who care so little for facts that they treat fantastic declarations for immediate universal arbitration as being valuable, instead of detrimental, to the cause they profess to champion, and who seek to make the United States impotent for international good under the pretense of making us impotent for international evil. All the men of this kind, and all of the organizations they have controlled, since we began our career as a nation, all put together, have not accomplished one-hundredth part as much for both peace and righteousness, have not done one-hundredth part as much either for ourselves or for other peoples, as was accomplished by the people of the United States when they fought the war with Spain and with resolute good faith and common sense worked out the solution of the problems which sprang from the war. . . .

TR took his duties as Assistant Secretary of the Navy seriously, even though he served so short a time. Deeply impressed by Captain Alfred Thayer Mahan's writings on the influence of sea power, he wrote him in the spring of 1897 concerning the grand design for the expansion of the United States.

I suppose I need not tell you that as regards Hawaii I take your views absolutely, as indeed I do on foreign policy generally. If I had my way we would annex those islands tomorrow. If that is impossible I would establish a protectorate over them. I believe we should build the Nicaraguan canal at once, and in the meantime that we should build a dozen new battleships, half of them on the Pacific Coast; and these battleships should have large coal capacity and a consequent increased radius of action. I am fully alive to the danger from Japan, and I know that it is idle to rely on any sentimental good will towards us. . . .

As regards Hawaii I am delighted to be able to tell you that Secretary Long shares our views. He believes we should take the islands, and I have just been preparing some memoranda for him to use at the Cabinet meeting tomorrow. If only we had some good man in the place of John Sherman as Secretary of State there would not be a hitch, and even as it is I hope for favorable action. I have been pressing upon the Secretary, and through him on the President, that we ought to act now without delay, before Japan gets her two new battleships which are now ready for delivery to her in England. Even a fortnight may make a difference. With Hawaii once in our hands most of the danger of friction with Japan would disappear.

At the same time TR was confiding to his English friend Cecil Spring-Rice his misgivings concerning the future of the Anglo-Saxon race:

I quite agree with you that the main cause of Rome's fall was a failure of population which was accompanied by a change in the population itself, caused by the immense importation of slaves, usually of inferior races. Our civilization is far more widely extended than the early civilizations, and in consequence, there is much less chance for evil tendencies to work universally through all its parts. The evils which afflict Russia are not the same as those which afflict Australia. There are very unhealthy sides to the concentration of power, at least of a certain kind of power, in the hands of the great capitalists; but in our country at any rate, I am convinced that there is no real oppression of the mass of the people by these capitalists. The condition of the workman and the man of small means has been improved. The diminishing rate of increase of the population is of course the feature fraught with most evil. In New England and France the population is decreasing; in Germany, England and the Southern United States it is increasing much less fast than formerly. Probably some time in the Twentieth Century the English-speaking peoples will become stationary, whereas the Slavs as yet show no signs of this tendency, and though they may show it, and doubtless will in the next century, it certainly seems as if they would beat us in the warfare of the cradle. However, there are still great waste spaces which the English-speaking peoples undoubtedly have the vigor to fill. America north of the Rio Grande, and Australia, and perhaps Africa south of the Zambesi, all possess a comparatively dense civilized population, English in law, tongue, government and culture, and with English the dominant strain in the blood. When the population becomes stationary I shall myself feel that evil days are probably at hand; but we need to remember that extreme fecundity does not itself imply any quality of social greatness. . . .

It certainly is extraordinary that just at this time there seems to be a gradual failure of vitality in the qualities, whatever they may be, that make men fight well and write well. I have a very uneasy feeling that this may mean some permanent deterioration.

Such was TR's mood on the eve of the Spanish-American War —and afterward.

CHAPTER 8

The New York Governorship

IN SEPTEMBER, 1898 the First Volunteer Cavalry, in company with most of the rest of the Fifth Army Corps, was disembarked at Montauk Point. Shortly after it was disbanded, and a few days later, I was nominated for Governor of New York by the Republican party. . . .

The previous year, the machine or standpat Republicans who were under the domination of Senator Platt, had come to a complete break with the antimachine element over the New York mayoralty. This had brought the Republican party to a smash, not only in New York City, but in the State, where the Democratic candidate for Chief Judge of the Court of Appeals, Alton B. Parker, was elected by sixty or eighty thousand majority. Mr. Parker was an able man, a lieutenant of Mr. Hill's, standing close to the conservative Democrats of the Wall Street type. These conservative Democrats were planning how to wrest the Democratic party from the control of Mr. Bryan. They hailed Judge Parker's victory as a godsend. The judge at once loomed up as a presidential possibility,

146

and was carefully groomed for the position by the New York Democratic machine and its financial allies in the New York business world.

The Republicans realized that the chances were very much against them. Accordingly the leaders were in a chastened mood and ready to nominate any candidate with whom they thought there was a chance of winning. I was the only possibility, and, accordingly, under pressure from certain of the leaders who recognized this fact, and who responded to popular pressure, Senator Platt picked me for the nomination. He was entirely frank in the matter. He made no pretense that he liked me personally; but he deferred to the judgment of those who insisted that I was the only man who could be elected, and that therefore I had to be nominated.

Foremost among the leaders who pressed me on Mr. Platt (who "pestered" him about me, to use his own words) were Mr. Quigg [and] Mr. Odell—then State chairman of the Republican organization, and afterward Governor. . . .

It was Mr. Quigg who called on me at Montauk Point to sound me about the Governorship; Mr. Platt being by no means enthusiastic over Mr. Quigg's mission, largely because he disapproved of the Spanish War and of my part in bringing it about. Mr. Quigg saw me in my tent, in which he spent a couple of hours with me, my brother-in-law, Douglas Robinson, being also present. Quigg spoke very frankly to me, stating that he earnestly desired to see me nominated and believed that the great body of Republican voters in the State so desired, but that the organization and the State convention would finally do what Senator Platt desired. He said that county leaders were already coming to Senator Platt, hinting at a close election, expressing doubt of Governor Black's availability for re-election, and asking why it would not be a good thing to nominate me; that now that I had returned to the United States this would go on more and more all the time, and that he (Quigg) did not wish that these men should be discouraged and be sent back to their localities to suppress a rising sentiment in my favor. For this reason he said that he wanted from me a plain statement as to whether or not I wanted the nomination, and as to what would be my attitude toward the organization in the event of my nomination and election, whether or not I would "make war" on Mr. Platt and his friends, or whether I would confer with them and with the organization leaders generally, and give fair consideration to their point of view as to party policy and public interest. He said he had not come to make me any offer of the nomination, and had no authority to do so, nor to get any pledges or promises. He simply wanted a frank definition of my attitude toward existing party conditions.

To this I replied that I should like to be nominated, and if nominated would promise to throw myself into the campaign with all possible energy. I said that I should not make war on Mr. Platt or anybody else if war could be avoided; that what I wanted was to be Governor and not a faction leader; that I certainly would confer with the organization men, as with everybody else who seemed to me to have knowledge of and interest in public affairs, and that as to Mr. Platt and the organization leaders, I would do so in the sincere hope that there might always result harmony of opinion and purpose; but that while I would try to get on well with the organization, the organization must with equal sincerity strive to do what I regarded as essential for the public good; and that in every case, after full consideration of what everybody had to say who might possess real knowledge of the matter, I should have to act finally as my own judgment and conscience dictated and administer the State government as I thought it ought to be administered. Quigg said that this was precisely what he supposed I would say, that it was all anybody could expect, and that he would state it to Senator Platt precisely as I had put it to him, which he accordingly did; and, throughout my term as governor, Quigg lived loyally up to our understanding.

After being nominated, I made a hard and aggressive campaign through the State. My opponent was a respectable man, a judge, behind whom stood Mr. Croker, the boss of Tammany Hall. My object was to make the people understand that it was Croker, and not the nominal candidate, who was my real opponent; that the choice lay between Crokerism and myself. Croker was a powerful and truculent man, the autocrat of his organization, and of a domineering nature. For his own reasons he insisted upon Tammany's turning down an excellent Democratic judge who was a candidate for reelection. This gave me my chance. Under my attack, Croker, who was a stalwart fighting man and who would not take an attack tamely, himself came to the front. I was able to fix the contest in the public mind as one between himself and myself; and, against all probabilities, I won by the rather narrow margin of eighteen thousand plurality.

As I have already said, there is a lunatic fringe to every reform movement. At least nine-tenths of all the sincere reformers supported me; but the ultrapacifists, the so-called anti-imperialists, or antimilitarists, or peace-at-any-price men, preferred Croker to me; and another knot of extremists who had at first ardently insisted that I must be "forced" on Platt, as soon as Platt supported me themselves opposed me *because* he supported me. . . .

At that time boss rule was at its very zenith. Mr. Bryan's candidacy in 1896 on a free-silver platform had threatened such frightful business disaster as to make the business men, the wage-workers, and the professional classes generally, turn eagerly to the Republican party. East of the Mississippi the Republican vote for Mr. McKinley was larger by far than it had been for Abraham Lincoln in the days when the life of the nation was at stake. Mr. Bryan championed many sorely needed reforms in the interest of the plain people; but many of his platform proposals, economic and otherwise, were of such a character that to have put them into practice would have meant to plunge all our people into conditions far worse than any of those for which he sought a remedy. The free-silver advocates included sincere and upright men who were able to make a strong case for their position; but with them and dominating them were all the believers in the complete or partial repudiation of national, state, and private debts; and not only the business men but the working men grew to feel that under these circumstances too heavy a price could not be paid to avert the Democratic triumph. . . .

The Republican bosses, who were already very powerful, and who were already in fairly close alliance with the privileged interests, now found everything working to their advantage. . . . In New York State, United States Senator Platt was the absolute boss of the Republican party. "Big business" was back of him; yet at the time this, the most important element in his strength, was only imperfectly understood. It was not until I was elected governor that I myself came to understand it. We were still accustomed to talking of the "machine" as if it were something merely political, with which business had nothing to do. Senator Platt did not use his political position to advance his private fortunes—therein differing absolutely from many other political bosses. He lived in hotels and had few extravagant tastes. Indeed, I could not find that he had any tastes at all except for politics, and on rare occasions for a very dry theology wholly divorced from moral implications. But big business men contributed to him large sums of money, which enabled him to keep his grip on the machine and secured for them the help of the machine if they were threatened with adverse legislation. The contributions were given in the guise of contributions for campaign purposes, of money for the good of the party; when the money was contributed there was rarely talk of specific favors in return. . . .

There had always been a good deal of opposition to Mr. Platt and the machine, but the leadership of this opposition was apt to be found only among those whom Abraham Lincoln called the "silk-stockings," and much of it excited almost as much derision among the plain people as the machine itself excited anger or dislike. . . . When reformers of this type attempted to oppose Mr. Platt, they usually put up either some rather inefficient, well-meaning person, who bathed every day, and didn't steal, but whose only good point was "respectability," and who knew nothing of the great fundamental questions looming before us; or else they put up some big business man or corporation lawyer who was wedded to the gross wrong and injustice of our economic system, and who neither by personality nor by programme gave the ordinary plain people any belief that there was promise of vital good to them in the change. The correctness of their view was proved by the fact that as soon as fundamental economic and social reforms were at stake the æsthetic, as distinguished from the genuinely moral, reformers, for the most part sided with the bosses against the people.

When I became Governor, the conscience of the people was in no way or shape aroused, as it has since become roused. The people accepted and practised in a matter-of-course way as quite proper things which they would not now tolerate. They had no definite and clearly outlined conception of what they wished in the way of reform. They on the whole tolerated, and indeed approved of, the machine. . . .

I had neither the training nor the capacity that would have enabled me to match Mr. Platt and his machine people on their own ground. Nor did I believe that the effort to build up a machine of my own under the then existing conditions would meet the needs of the situation so far as the people were concerned. I therefore made no effort to create a machine of my own, and consistently adopted the plan of going over the heads of the men holding public office and of the men in control of the organization, and appealing directly to the people behind them. . . .

I felt that I could count on their support wherever I could show them that the fight was not made just for the sake of the row, that it was not made merely as a factional contest against Senator Platt and the organization, but was waged from a sense of duty for real and tangible causes such as the promotion of governmental efficiency and honesty, and forcing powerful moneyed men to take the proper attitude toward the community at large. They stood by me when I insisted upon having the canal department, the insurance department, and the various departments of the State government run with efficiency and honesty; they stood by me when I insisted upon making wealthy

men who owned franchises pay the State what they properly ought to pay; they stood by me when, in connection
with the strikes on the Croton Aqueduct and in Buffalo,
I promptly used the military power of the State to put
a stop to rioting and violence.

In the latter case my chief opponents and critics were
local politicians who were truckling to the labor vote;
but in all cases coming under the first two categories I had
serious trouble with the State leaders of the machine. I
always did my best, in good faith, to get Mr. Platt and
the other heads of the machine to accept my views, and to
convince them, by repeated private conversations, that
I was right. I never wantonly antagonized or humiliated
them. I did not wish to humiliate them or to seem victorious over them; what I wished was to secure the things that
I thought it essential to the men and women of the State
to secure. If I could finally persuade them to support me,
well and good; in such case I continued to work with them
in the friendliest manner. . . .

Very soon after my victory in the race for governor I
had one or two experiences with Senator Platt which
showed in amusing fashion how absolute the rule of the
boss was in the politics of that day. Senator Platt, who
was always most kind and friendly in his personal relations
with me, asked me in one day to talk over what was to be
done at Albany. He had the two or three nominal heads
of the organization with him. They were his lieutenants,
who counselled and influenced him, whose advise he often
followed, but who, when he had finally made up his mind,
merely registered and carried out his decrees. After a little
conversation the Senator asked if I had any member of the
Assembly whom I wished to have put on any committee,
explaining that the committees were being arranged. I

answered no, and expressed my surprise at what he had said, because I had not understood the Speaker who appointed the committees had himself been agreed upon by the members-elect. "Oh!" responded the senator, with a tolerant smile; "he has not been chosen yet, but of course whomever we choose as Speaker will agree beforehand to make the appointments we wish." I made a mental note to the effect that if they attempted the same process with the Governor-Elect they would find themselves mistaken.

In a few days the opportunity to prove this arrived. Under the preceding Administration there had been grave scandals about the Erie Canal, the trans-State Canal, and these scandals had been one of the chief issues in the campaign for the governorship. The construction of this work was under the control of the superintendent of Public Works. In the actual state of affairs his office was by far the most important office under me, and I intended to appoint to it some man of high character and capacity who could be trusted to do the work not merely honestly and efficiently, but without regard to politics. A week or so after the Speakership incident Senator Platt asked me to come and see him (he was an old and physically feeble man, able to move about only with extreme difficulty).

On arrival I found the Lieutenant-Governor-Elect, Mr. Woodruff, who had also been asked to come. The Senator informed me that he was glad to say that I would have a most admirable man as Superintendent of Public Works, as he had just received a telegram from a certain gentleman, whom he named, saying that he would accept the position! He handed me the telegram. The man in question was a man I liked; later I appointed him to an important office in which he did well. But he came from a city along the line of the canal, so that I did not think it best that he should be appointed anyhow; and, moreover, what was far more important, it was necessary to have it understood at the very outset that the administration was my administration and was no one else's but mine. So I told the Senator very politely that I was sorry, but that I could not appoint his man. This produced an explosion, but I declined to lose my temper, merely repeating that I must decline to accept any man chosen for me, and that I must choose the man myself. Although I was very polite, I was also very firm, and Mr. Platt and his friends finally abandoned their position. . . .

My desire was to achieve results, and not merely to issue manifestoes of virtue. . . . My duty was to combine both idealism and efficiency. . . . My aim was persistently to refuse to be put in a position where what I did would seem to be a mere faction struggle against Senator Platt. . . .

In each case I did my best to persuade Mr. Platt not to oppose me. I endeavored to make it clear to him that I was not trying to wrest the organization from him; and I always gave him in detail the reasons why I felt I had to take the position I intended to adopt. It was only after I had exhausted all the resources of my patience that I would finally, if he still proved obstinate, tell him that I intended to make the fight anyhow. As I have said, the Senator was an old and feeble man in physique, and it was possible for him to go about very little. Until Friday evening he would be kept at his duties at Washington, while I was in Albany. If I wished to see him it generally had to be at his hotel in New York on Saturday, and usually I would go there to breakfast with him. The one thing I would not permit was anything in the nature of a secret or clandestine meeting. I always insisted on going openly. Solemn reformers of the tomfool variety, who, according to their custom, paid attention to the name and not the thing, were much exercised over my "breakfasting with Platt." Whenever I breakfasted with him they became sure that the fact carried with it some sinister significance. The worthy creatures never took the trouble to follow the sequence of facts and events for themselves. If they had done so they would have seen that any series of breakfasts with Platt always meant that I was going to do something he did not like, and that I was trying, courteously and frankly, to reconcile him to it. My object was to make it as easy as possible for him to come with me. As long as there was no clash between us there was no object in my seeing him; it was only when the clash came or was imminent that I had to see him. A series of breakfasts was always the prelude to some active warfare. In every instance I substantially carried my point, although in some cases not in exactly the way in which I had originally hoped.

There were various measures to which he gave a grudging and querulous assent without any break being threatened. I secured the re-enactment of the civil service law, which under my predecessor had very foolishly been repealed. I secured a mass of labor legislation, including the enactment of laws to increase the number of factory inspectors, to create a tenement-house commission (whose findings resulted in further and excellent legislation to improve housing conditions), to regulate and improve sweat-shop labor, to make the eight-hour and prevailing rate of wages law effective, to secure the genuine enforcement of the act relating to the hours of railway-workers, to compel railways to equip freight-trains with air-brakes, to regulate the working hours of women and protect both women and children from dangerous machinery, to enforce good scaffolding provisions for workmen on buildings, to provide seats for the use of waitresses in hotels and restaurants, to reduce the hours of labor for drug-store clerks, to provide for the registration of laborers for municipal employment. I tried hard but failed to secure an employers' liability law and the State control of employment offices. There was hard fighting over some of these bills, and, what was much more serious, there was effort to get round the law by trickery and by securing its inefficient enforcement. . . . In addition to labor legislation I was able to do a good deal for forest preservation and the protection of our wild life. All that later I strove for in the nation in connection with conservation was foreshadowed by what I strove to obtain for New York State when I was Governor; . . .

As regards most legislation, even that affecting labor and the forests, I got on fairly well with the machine. But on the two issues in which "big business" and the kind of politics which is allied to big business were most involved we clashed hard—and clashing with Senator Platt meant clashing with the entire Republican organization, and with the organized majority in each house of the legislature. One clash was in connection with the superintendent of insurance, a man whose office made him a factor of immense importance in the big business circles of New York. The then incumbent of the office was an efficient man, the boss of an up-State county, a veteran politician and one of Mr. Platt's right-hand men. Certain investigations which I made—in the course of the fight—showed that this superintendent of insurance had been engaged in large business operations in New York City. These operations had thrown him into a peculiarly intimate business contact of one sort and another with various financiers with whom I did not deem it expedient that the superintendent of insurance, while such, should have any intimate and secret money-making relations. Moreover, the gentleman in question represented the straitest sect of the old-time spoils politicians. I therefore determined not to reappoint him. Unless I could get his successor confirmed, however, he would stay in under the law, and the Republican machine, with the assistance of Tammany, expected to control far more than a majority of all the senators.

Mr. Platt issued an ultimatum to me that the incumbent must be reappointed or else that he would fight, and that if he chose to fight the man would stay in anyhow because I could not oust him—for under the New York constitution the assent of the Senate was necessary not only to appoint a man to office but to remove him from office. As always with Mr. Platt, I persistently refused to lose my temper, no matter what he said—he was much too old and physically feeble for there to be any point of honor in taking up any of his remarks—and I merely explained good-humoredly that I had made up my mind and that the gentleman in question would not be retained. As for not being able to get his successor confirmed, I pointed out that as soon as the legislature adjourned I could and would appoint another man temporarily. Mr. Platt then said that the incumbent would be put back as soon as the legislature reconvened; I admitted that this was possible, but added cheerfully that I would remove him again just as soon as that legislature adjourned, and that even though I had an uncomfortable time myself, I would guarantee to make my opponents more uncomfortable still. We parted without any sign of reaching an agreement.

There remained some weeks before final action could

be taken, and the Senator was confident that I would have to yield. His most efficient allies were the pretended reformers, most of them my open or covert enemies, who loudly insisted that I must make an open fight on the Senator himself and on the Republican organization. This was what he wished, for at that time there was no way of upsetting him within the Republican party; and, as I have said, if I had permitted the contest to assume the shape of a mere faction fight between the Governor and the United States Senator, I would have insured the victory of the machine. So I blandly refused to let the thing become a personal fight, explaining again and again that I was perfectly willing to appoint an organization man, and naming two or three whom I was willing to appoint, but also explaining that I would not retain the incumbent, and would not appoint any man of his type. Meanwhile pressure on behalf of the said incumbent began to come from the business men of New York.

The superintendent of insurance was not a man whose ill-will the big life-insurance companies cared to incur, and company after company passed resolutions asking me to reappoint him, although in private some of the men who signed these resolutions nervously explained that they did not mean what they had written, and hoped I would remove the man. . . .

Meanwhile Senator Platt declined to yield. I had picked out a man, a friend of his, who I believed would make an honest and competent official, and whose position in the organization was such that I did not believe the Senate would venture to reject him. However, up to the day before the appointment was to go to the Senate, Mr. Platt remained unyielding. I saw him that afternoon and tried to get him to yield, but he said no, that if I insisted, it would be war to the knife, and my destruction, and perhaps the destruction of the party. I said I was very sorry, that I could not yield, and if the war came it would have to come, and that next morning I should send in the name of the superintendent's successor. We parted, and soon afterward I received from the man who was at the moment Mr. Platt's right-hand lieutenant a request to know where he could see me that evening. I appointed the Union League Club. My visitor went over the old ground, explained that the Senator would under no circumstances yield, that he was certain to win in the fight, that my reputation would be destroyed, and that he wished to save me from such a lamentable smash-up as an ending to my career. I could only repeat what I had already said, and after half an hour of futile argument I rose and said that nothing was to be gained by further talk and that I might as well go. My visitor repeated that I had this last chance, and that ruin was ahead of me if I refused it; whereas, if I accepted it, everything would be made easy. I shook my head and answered: "There is nothing to add to what I have said." He responded, "You have made up your mind?" and I said, "I have." He then said, "You know it means your ruin?" and I answered, "Well, we will see about that," and walked toward the door. He said: "You understand, the fight will begin to-morrow and will be carried on to the bitter end." I said, "Yes," and added, as I reached the door, "Good night." Then, as the door opened, my opponent, or visitor, whichever one chooses to call him, whose face was . . . impassive and . . . inscrutable . . . said: "Hold on! We accept. Send in So-and-so [the man I had named]. The Senator is very sorry, but he will make no further opposition!" I never saw a bluff carried more resolutely through to the final limit. . . .

The case of most importance in which I clashed with Senator Platt related to a matter of fundamental governmental policy, and was the first step I ever took toward bringing big corporations under effective governmental control. In this case I had to fight the Democratic machine as well as the Republican machine, for Senator Hill and Senator Platt were equally opposed to my action, and the big corporation men, the big business men back of both of them, took precisely the same view of these matters without regard to their party feelings on other points. What I did convulsed people at that time, and marked the beginning of the effort, at least in the Eastern States, to make the great corporations really responsible to popular wish and governmental command. But we have gone so far past the stage in which we then were that now it seems well-nigh incredible that there should have been any opposition at all to what I at that time proposed.

The substitution of electric power for horse-power in the street-car lines of New York offered a fruitful chance for the most noxious type of dealing between business men and politicians. The franchises granted by New York were granted without any attempt to secure from the grantees returns, in the way of taxation or otherwise, for the value received. The fact that they were thus granted by improper favoritism, a favoritism which in many cases was unquestionably secured by down-right bribery, led to all kinds of trouble. In return for the continuance of these improper favors to the corporations the politicians expected improper favors in the way of excessive campaign contributions, often contributed by the same corporation at the same time to two opposing parties. Before I became Governor a bill had been introduced into the New York legislature to tax the franchises of these street-railways.

It affected a large number of corporations, but particularly those in New York and Buffalo. It had been suffered to slumber undisturbed, as none of the people in power dreamed of taking it seriously, and both the Republican and Democratic machines were hostile to it. . . .

After I was elected Governor I had my attention directed to the franchise-tax matter, looked into the subject, and came to the conclusion that it was a matter of plain decency and honesty that these companies should pay a tax on their franchises, inasmuch as they did nothing that could be considered as service rendered the public in lieu of a tax. This seemed to me so evidently the common-sense and decent thing to do that I was hardly prepared for the storm of protest and anger which my proposal aroused. Senator Platt and the other machine leaders did everything to get me to abandon my intention. As usual, I saw them, talked the matter all over with them, and did my best to convert them to my way of thinking. Senator Platt, I believe, was quite sincere in his opposition. He did not believe in popular rule, and he did believe that the big business men were entitled to have things their way. He profoundly distrusted the people—naturally enough, for the kind of human nature with which a boss comes in contact is not of an exalted type. He felt that anarchy would come if there was any interference with a system by which the people in mass were, under various necessary cloaks, controlled by the leaders in the political and business worlds. He wrote me a very strong letter of protest against my attitude, expressed in dignified, friendly, and temperate language, but using one word in a curious way. This was the word "altruistic." He stated in his letter that he had not objected to my being independent in politics, because he had been sure that I had the good of the party at heart, and meant to act fairly and honorably; but that he had been warned, before I became a candidate, by a number of his business friends that I was a dangerous man because I was "altruistic," and that he now feared that my conduct would justify the alarm thus expressed. I was interested in this, not only because Senator Platt was obviously sincere, but because of the way in which he used "altruistic" as a term of reproach, as if it was Communistic or Socialistic—the last being a word he did use to me when, as now and then happened, he thought that my proposals warranted fairly reckless vituperation. . . .

I had made up my mind that if I could get a show in the legislature the bill would pass, because the people had become interested and the representatives would scarcely dare to vote the wrong way. Accordingly, on April 27, 1899, I sent a special message to the Assembly, certifying that the emergency demanded the immediate passage of the bill. The machine leaders were bitterly angry, and the Speaker actually tore up the message without reading it to the Assembly. That night they were busy trying to arrange some device for the defeat of the bill—which was not difficult, as the session was about to close. At seven the next morning I was informed of what had occurred. At eight I was in the Capitol at the Executive chamber, and sent in another special message, which opened as follows: "I learn that the emergency message which I sent last evening to the Assembly on behalf of the Franchise-Tax Bill has not been read. I therefore send hereby another message on the subject. I need not impress upon the Assembly the need of passing this bill at once." I sent this message to the Assembly, by my secretary, . . . with an intimation that if this were not promptly read I should come up in person and read it. Then, as so often happens, the opposition collapsed and the bill went through both houses with a rush. . . .

The various clashes between myself and the machine, my triumph in them, and the fact that the people were getting more and more interested and aroused, brought on a curious situation in the Republican National Convention at Philadelphia in June, 1900. Senator Platt and the New York machine leaders had become very anxious to get me out of the Governorship, chiefly because of the hostility of the big corporation men toward me; but they had also become convinced that there was such popular feeling on my behalf that it would be difficult to refuse me a renomination if I demanded it. They accordingly decided to push me for Vice-President, taking advantage of the fact that there was at that time a good deal of feeling for me in the country at large. I myself did not appreciate that there was any such feeling, and as I greatly disliked the office of Vice-President and was much interested in the Governorship, I announced that I would not accept the Vice-Presidency. I was one of the delegates to Philadelphia. On reaching there I found that the situation was complicated. Senator Hanna appeared on the surface to have control of the convention. He was anxious that I should not be nominated as Vice-President. Senator Platt was anxious that I should be nominated as Vice-President, in order to get me out of the New York Governorship. Each took a position opposite to that of the other, but each at that time cordially sympathized with the other's feelings about me—it was the manifestations and not the feelings that differed. My supporters in New York State did not wish me nominated for Vice-President because they wished me to continue as Governor; but in every other State all the people who admired me were bound that I should be nominated as Vice-President. These people were almost all desirous of seeing Mr. McKinley renominated as President, but they became angry at Senator Hanna's opposition to me as Vice-President. He in his turn suddenly became aware that if he persisted he might find that in their anger these men would oppose Mr. McKinley's renomination, and although they could not have prevented the nomination, such opposition would have been a serious blow in the campaign which was to follow. Senator Hanna, therefore, began to waver.

Meanwhile a meeting of the New York delegation was called. Most of the delegates were under the control of Senator Platt. The Senator notified me that if I refused to accept the nomination for Vice-President I would be beaten for the nomination for Governor. I answered that I would accept the challenge, that we would have a straight-out fight on the proposition, and that I would begin it at once by telling the assembled delegates of the threat, and giving fair warning that I intended to fight for the Governorship nomination, and, moreover, that I intended to get it. This brought Senator Platt to terms. The effort to instruct the New York delegation for me was abandoned, and Lieutenant-Governor Woodruff was presented for nomination in my place.

I supposed that this closed the incident, and that no further effort would be made to nominate me for the Vice-Presidency. On the contrary, the effect was directly the reverse. The upset of the New York machine increased the feeling of the delegates from other States that it was necessary to draft me for the nomination. By next day Senator Hanna himself concluded that this was a necessity, and acquiesced in the movement. As New York was already committed against me, and as I was not willing that there should be any chance of supposing that the New Yorkers had nominated me to get rid of me, the result was that I was nominated and seconded from outside States. No other condidate was placed in the field. . . .

As Governor of New York, TR conceived that it was his duty to preach an occasional sermon to his fellow Americans. Coming before the Hamilton Club of Chicago in the spring of 1899, he announced that he was a man with a mission:

In speaking to you, men of the greatest city of the West, men of the State which gave to the country Lincoln and Grant, men who pre-eminently and distinctly embody all that is most American in the American character, I wish to preach, not the doctrine of ignoble ease, but the doctrine of the strenuous life, the life of toil and effort, of labor and strife; to preach that highest form of success which comes, not to the man who desires mere easy peace, but to the man who does not shrink from danger, from hardship, or from bitter toil, and who out of these wins the splendid ultimate triumph.

A life of slothful ease, a life of that peace which springs merely from lack either of desire or of power to strive after great things, is as little worthy of a nation as of an individual. I ask only that what every self-respecting American demands from himself and from his sons shall be demanded of the American nation as a whole. Who among you would teach your boys that ease, that peace, is to be the first consideration in their eyes—to be the ultimate goal after which they strive? You men of Chicago have made this city great, you men of Illinois have done your share, and more than your share, in making America great, because you neither preach nor practise such a doctrine. You work yourselves, and you bring up your sons to work. If you are rich and are worth your salt, you will teach your sons that though they may have leisure, it is not to be spent in idleness; for wisely used leisure merely means that those who possess it, being free from the necessity of working for their livelihood, are all the more bound to carry on some kind of non-remunerative work in science, in letters, in art, in exploration, in historical research—work of the type we most need in this country, the successful carrying out of which reflects most honor upon the nation. We do not admire the man of timid peace. We admire the man who embodies victorious effort; the man who never wrongs his neighbor, who is prompt to help a friend, but who has those virile qualities necessary to win in the stern strife of actual life. It is hard to fail, but it is worse never to have tried to succeed. In this life we get nothing save by effort. Freedom from effort in the present merely means that there has been stored up effort in the past. A man can be freed from the necessity of work only by the fact that he or his fathers before him have worked to good purpose. If the freedom thus purchased is used aright, and the man still does actual work, though of a different kind, whether as a writer or a general, whether in the field of politics or in the field of exploration and adventure, he shows he deserves his good fortune. But if he treats this period of freedom from the need of actual labor as a period, not of preparation, but of mere enjoyment, even though perhaps not of vicious enjoyment, he shows that he is simply a cumberer of the earth's surface, and he surely unfits himself to hold his own with his fellows if the need to do so should again arise. A mere life of ease is not in the end a very satisfactory life, and, above all, it is a life which ultimately unfits those who follow it for serious work in the world. . . .

I preach to you, then, my countrymen, that our country calls not for the life of ease but for the life of strenuous endeavor. The twentieth century looms before us big with the fate of many nations. If we stand idly by, if we seek merely swollen, slothful ease and ignoble peace, if we shrink from the hard contests where men must win at hazard of their lives and at the risk of all they hold dear, then the bolder and stronger peoples will pass us by, and will win for themselves the domination of the world. Let us therefore boldly face the life of strife, resolute to do our duty well and manfully; resolute to uphold righteousness by deed and by word; resolute to be both honest and brave, to serve high ideals, yet to use practical methods. Above all, let us shrink from no strife, moral or physical, within or without the nation, provided we are certain that the strife is justified, for it is only through strife, through hard and dangerous endeavor, that we shall ultimately win the goal of true national greatness.

If he were elected Vice-President of the United States, would he not be leading a life of slothful ease? He worried over this problem in a letter to Henry Cabot Lodge at the close of 1899:

The Vice-Presidency is a most honorable office, but for a young man there is not much to do. It is infinitely better than many other positions, but it hardly seems to me as good as being Governor of this State, which is a pretty important State. Then while it is very unlikely that I could be President, there is a chance of my being something else —Governor General of the Philippines, or a Cabinet Officer, or perchance in the remote future, Senator. Mind you, I do not think that any of these things are likely, but at least there is sufficient chance to warrant my taking them seriously, while I do not think the chance for the presidency *is* sufficient to warrant our taking it seriously. If I am Vice-President I am "planted" for four years. Here I can turn around. Platt told me definitely that of course he was for me for a renomination—that everybody was—and though we shall have a good deal of friction from time to time, I do not believe it very likely that he will come to a definite break with me, because I like him personally, I always tell him the truth, and I genuinely endeavor to help him, if I can, with proper regard for the interest of the State and party.

CHAPTER 9

Outdoors and Indoors

THERE ARE MEN who love out-of-doors who yet never open a book; and other men who love books but to whom the great book of nature is a sealed volume, and the lines written therein blurred and illegible. Nevertheless among those men whom I have known the love of books and the love of outdoors, in their highest expressions, have usually gone hand in hand. It is an affectation for the man who is praising outdoors to sneer at books. Usually the keenest appreciation of what is seen in nature is to be found in those who have also profited by the hoarded and recorded wisdom of their fellow men. Love of outdoor life, love of simple and hardy pastimes, can be gratified by men and women who do not possess large means, and who work hard; and so can love of good books—not of good bindings and of first editions, excellent enough in their way but sheer luxuries—I mean love of reading books, owning them if possible of course, but, if that is not possible, getting them from a circulating library. . . .

170

At Sagamore Hill* we love a great many things—birds and trees and books, and all things beautiful, and horses and rifles and children and hard work and the joy of life. We have great fireplaces, and in them the logs roar and crackle during the long winter evenings. The big piazza is for the hot, still afternoons of summer. As in every house, there are things that appeal to the householder because of their associations, but which would not mean much to others. Naturally, any man who has been President, and filled other positions, accumulates such things, with scant regard to his own personal merits. Perhaps our most cherished possessions are a Remington bronze, "The Bronco-Buster," given me by my men when the regiment was mustered out, and a big Tiffany silver vase given to Mrs. Roosevelt by the enlisted men of the battleship *Louisianna* after we returned from a cruise on her to Panama. It was a real surprise gift, presented to her in the White House, on behalf of the whole crew, by four as strapping man-of-war's men as ever swung a turret or pointed a twelve-inch gun. The enlisted men of the Army I already knew well—of course I knew well the officers of both Army and Navy. But the enlisted men of the Navy I only grew to know well when I was President. On the *Louisiana* Mrs. Roosevelt and I once dined at the chief petty officers' mess, and on another battleship, the *Missouri* (when I was in company with Admiral Evans and Captain Cowles), and again on the *Sylph* and on the *Mayflower*, we also dined as guests of the crew.

When we finished our trip on the *Louisiana* I made a short speech to the assembled crew, and at its close one

* Sagamore Hill, TR's house at Oyster Bay, Long Island, dates from 1884. It is now open to the public. [Editor's note]

of the petty officers, the very picture of what a man-of-war's man should look like, proposed three cheers for me in terms that struck me as curiously illustrative of America at her best; he said: "Now then, men, three cheers for Theodore Roosevelt, the typical American citizen!" That was the way in which they thought of the American President—and a very good way, too. It was an expression that would have come naturally only to men in whom the American principles of government and life were ingrained, just as they were ingrained in the men of my regiment. . . .

There are various bronzes in the house: Saint-Gaudens's "Puritan," a token from my staff officers when I was governor; Proctor's cougar, the gift of the Tennis Cabinet —who also gave us a beautiful silver bowl, which is always lovingly pronounced to rhyme with "owl" because that was the pronunciation used at the time of the giving by the valued friend who acted as spokesman for his fellow members, and who was himself the only non-American member of the said Cabinet. There is a horseman by Mac-Monnies, and a big bronze vase by Kemys, an adaptation or development of the pottery vases of the southwestern Indians. Mixed with all of these are gifts from varied sources, ranging from a brazen Buddha sent me by the Dalai Lama and a wonderful psalter from the Emperor Menelik to a priceless ancient Samurai sword, coming from Japan in remembrance of the peace of Portsmouth, and a beautifully inlaid miniature suit of Japanese armor, given me by a favorite hero of mine, Admiral Togo, when he visited Sagamore Hill. There are things from European friends; a mosaic picture of Pope Leo XIII in his garden; a huge, very handsome edition of the "Nibelungenlied"; a striking miniature of John Hampden from Windsor

Castle; editions of Dante, and the campaigns of "Eugenio von Savoy" (another of my heroes, a dead hero this time); a Viking cup; the state sword of a Uganda king; the gold box in which the "freedom of the city of London" was given me; a beautiful head of Abraham Lincoln given me by the French authorities after my speech at the Sorbonne; and many other things from sources as diverse as the Sultan of Turkey and the Dowager Empress of China. Then there are things from home friends: a polar-bear skin from Peary; a Sioux buffalo-robe with, on it, painted by some long-dead Sioux artist, the picture story of Custer's fight; a bronze portrait plaque of Joel Chandler Harris; the candlestick used in sealing the Treaty of Portsmouth, sent me by Captain Cameron Winslow; a shoe worn by Dan Patch when he paced a mile in 1:59, sent me by his owner. There is a picture of a bull moose by Carl Rungius, which seems to me as spirited an animal painting as I have ever seen. In the North Room, with its tables and mantelpiece and desks and chests made of woods sent from the Philippines by army friends, or by other friends for other reasons; with its bison and wapiti heads; there are three paintings by Marcus Symonds—"Where Light and Shadow Meet," "The Porcelain Towers," and "The Seats of the Mighty"; he is dead now, and he had scant recognition while he lived, yet surely he was a great imaginative artist, a wonderful colorist, and a man with a vision more wonderful still. There is one of Lungren's pictures of the Western plains; and a picture of the Grand Canyon; and one by a Scandinavian artist who could see the fierce picturesqueness of workaday Pittsburgh; and sketches of the White House by Sargent and by Hopkinson Smith.

The books are everywhere. . . . I could not name any principle upon which the books have been gathered.

Books are almost as individual as friends. There is no earthly use in laying down general laws about them. Some meet the needs of one person, and some of another; and each person should beware of the book-lover's besetting sin, of what Mr. Edgar Allan Poe calls "the mad pride of intellectuality," taking the shape of arrogant pity for the man who does not like the same kind of books. Of course there are books which a man or woman uses as instruments of a profession—law-books, medical books, cookery books, and the like. I am not speaking of these, for they are not properly "books" at all; they come in the category of timetables, telephone directories, and other useful agencies of civilized life. I am speaking of books that are meant to be read. Personally, granted that these books are decent and healthy, the one test to which I demand that they all submit is that of being interesting. If the book is not interesting to the reader, then in all but an infinitesimal number of cases it gives scant benefit to the reader. Of course any reader ought to cultivate his or her taste so that good books will appeal to it, and that trash won't. But after this point has once been reached, the needs of each reader must be met in a fashion that will appeal to those needs. Personally the books by which I have profited infinitely more than by any others have been those in which profit was a by-product of the pleasure; that is, I read them because I enjoyed them, because I liked reading them, and the profit came in as part of the enjoyment.

Of course each individual is apt to have some special tastes in which he cannot expect that any but a few friends will share. Now, I am very proud of my big-game library. I suppose there must be many big-game libraries in Continental Europe, and possibly in England, more extensive than mine, but I have not happened to come across any

such library in this country. Some of the originals go back
to the sixteenth century, and there are copies or repro-
ductions of the two or three most famous hunting-books of
the Middle Ages, such as the Duke of York's translation
of Gaston Phoebus, and the queer book of the Emperor
Maximilian. It is only very occasionally that I meet any
one who cares for any of these books. On the other hand,
I expect to find many friends who will turn naturally to
some of the old or the new books of poetry or romance or
history to which we of the household habitually turn. Let
me add that ours is in no sense a collector's library. Each
book was procured because some one of the family wished
to read it. We could never afford to take overmuch thought
for the outsides of books; we were too much interested
in their insides.

Now and then I am asked as to "what books a statesman
should read," and my answer is, poetry and novels—including short stories under the head of novels. I don't mean
that he should read only novels and modern poetry. If he
cannot also enjoy the Hebrew prophets and the Greek
dramatists, he should be sorry. He ought to read interesting
books on history and government, and books of science
and philosophy; and really good books on these subjects
are as enthralling as any fiction ever written in prose or
verse. Gibbon and Macaulay, Herodotus, Thucydides and
Tacitus, the Heimskringla, Froissart, Joinville and Ville-
hardouin, Parkman and Mahan, Mommsen and Ranke—
why! there are scores and scores of solid histories, the best
in the world, which are as absorbing as the best of all the
novels, and of as permanent value. The same thing is true of
Darwin and Huxley and Carlyle and Emerson, and parts of
Kant, and of volumes like Sutherland's "Growth of the
Moral Instinct," or Acton's Essays and Lounsbury's studies

—here again I am not trying to class books together, or measure one by another, or enumerate one in a thousand of those worth reading, but just to indicate that any man or woman of some intelligence and some cultivation can in some line or other of serious thought, scientific, or historical or philosophical or economic or governmental, find any number of books which are charming to read, and which in addition give that for which his or her soul hungers. I do not for a minute mean that the statesman ought not to read a great many different books of this character, just as every one else should read them. But, in the final event, the statesman, and the publicist, and the reformer, and the agitator for new things, and the upholder of what is good in old things, all need more than anything else to know human nature, to know the needs of the human soul; and they will find this nature and these needs set forth as nowhere else by the great imaginative writers, whether of prose or of poetry. . . .

A book must be interesting to the particular reader at that particular time. But there are tens of thousands of interesting books, and some of them are sealed to some men and some are sealed to others; and some stir the soul at some given point of a man's life and yet convey no message at other times. The reader, the book-lover, must meet his own needs without paying too much attention to what his neighbors say those needs should be. He must not hypocritically pretend to like what he does not like. Yet at the same time he must avoid that most unpleasant of all the indications of puffed-up vanity which consists in treating mere individual, and perhaps unfortunate, idiosyncrasy as a matter of pride. I happen to be devoted to "Macbeth," whereas I very seldom read "Hamlet" (though I like parts of it). Now I am humbly and sincerely conscious that this is a demerit in me and not in "Hamlet"; and yet it would not do me any good to pretend that I like "Hamlet" as much as "Macbeth" when, as a matter of fact, I don't. I am very fond of simple epics and of ballad poetry, from the "Nibelungenlied" and the "Roland Song" through "Chevy Chase" and "Patrick Spens" and "Twa Corbies" to Scott's poems and Longfellow's "Saga of King Olaf" and "Othere." On the other hand, I don't care to read dramas as a rule; I cannot read them with enjoyment unless they appeal to me very strongly. They must almost be Æschylus or Euripides, Goethe or Molière, in order that I may not feel after finishing them a sense of virtuous pride in having achieved a task. Now I would be the first to deny that even the most delightful old English ballad should be put on a par with any one of scores of dramatic works by authors whom I have not mentioned; I know that each of these dramatists has written what is of more worth than the ballad; only, I enjoy the ballad, and I don't enjoy the drama; and therefore the ballad is better for me, and this fact is not altered by other fact that my own shortcomings are to blame in the matter. I still read a number of Scott's novels over and over again, whereas if I finish anything by Miss Austen I have a feeling that duty performed is a rainbow to the soul. But other book-lovers who are very close kin to me, and whose taste I know to be better than mine, read Miss Austen all the time—and, moreover, they are very kind, and never pity me in too offensive a manner for not reading her myself.

Aside from the masters of literature, there are all kinds of books which one person will find delightful, and which he certainly ought not to surrender just because nobody else is able to find as much in the beloved volume. There is on our book-shelves a little pre-Victorian novel or tale called "The Semi-Attached Couple."* It is told with much humor; it is a story of gentlefolk who are really gentlefolk; and to me it is altogether delightful. But outside the members of my own family I have never met a human being who had even heard of it, and I don't suppose I ever shall meet one. I often enjoy a story by some living author so much that I write to tell him so—or to tell her so; and at least half the time I regret my action, because it encourages the writer to believe that the public shares my views, and he then finds that the public doesn't.

Books are all very well in their way, and we love them at Sagamore Hill; but children are better than books. Sagamore Hill is one of three neighboring houses in which small cousins spent very happy years of childhood. In the three houses there were at one time sixteen of these small cousins, all told, and once we ranged them in order of size and took their photograph. There are many kinds of success in life worth having. It is exceedingly interesting and attractive to be a successful business man, or railroad man, or farmer, or a successful lawyer or doctor; or a writer, or a President, or a ranchman, or the colonel of a fighting regiment, or to kill grizzly bears and lions. But for unflagging interest and enjoyment, a household of children, if things go reasonably well, certainly makes all other forms of success and achievement lose their importance by comparison. It may be true that he travels farthest who travels alone; but the goal thus reached is not worth reaching. And as for a life deliberately devoted to pleasure as an end—why, the greatest happiness is the happiness that comes as a by-product of striving to do what must be done, even though sorrow is met in the doing. . . .

* Emily Eden's novel was actaully published in the twenty-second year of Victoria's reign. [Editor's note]

The country is the place for children, and if not the country, a city small enough so that one can get out into the country. When our own children were little, we were for several winters in Washington, and each Sunday afternoon the whole family spent in Rock Creek Park, which was then very real country indeed. I would drag one of the children's wagons; and when the very smallest pairs of feet grew tired of trudging bravely after us, or of racing on rapturous side trips after flowers and other treasures, the owners would clamber into the wagon. One of these wagons, by the way, a gorgeous red one, had "Express" painted on it in gilt letters, and was known to the younger children as the " 'spress" wagon. They evidently associated the color with the term. Once while we were at Sagamore something happened to the cherished " 'spress" wagon to the distress of the children, and especially of the child who owned it. Their mother and I were just starting for a drive in the buggy, and we promised the bereaved owner that we would visit a store we knew in East Norwich, a village a few miles away, and bring back another " 'spress" wagon. When we reached the store, we found to our dismay that the wagon which we had seen had been sold. We could not bear to return without the promised gift, for we knew that the brains of small persons are much puzzled when their elders seem to break promises. Fortunately, we saw in the store a delightful little bright-red chair and bright-red table, and these we brought home and handed solemnly over to the expectant recipient, explaining that as there unfortunately was not a " 'spress" wagon we had brought him back a " 'spress" chair and " 'spress" table. It worked beautifully! The " 'spress" chair and table were received with such rapture that we had to get duplicates for the other small member of the family who was the particular crony of the proprietor of the new treasures.

When their mother and I returned from a row, we would often see the children waiting for us, running like sand-spiders along the beach. They always liked to swim in company with a grown-up of buoyant temperament and inventive mind, and the float offered limitless opportunities for enjoyment while bathing. All dutiful parents know the game of "stage-coach"; each child is given a name, such as the whip, the nigh leader, the off wheeler, the old lady passenger, and, under penalty of paying a forfeit, must get up and turn round when the grown-up, who is improvising a thrilling story, mentions that particular object; and when the word "stage-coach" is mentioned, everybody has to get up and turn round. Well, we used to play stage-coach on the float while in swimming, and instead of tamely getting up and turning round, the child whose turn it was had to plunge overboard. When I mentioned "stage-coach," the water fairly foamed with vigorously kicking little legs; and then there was always a moment of interest while I counted, so as to be sure that the number of heads that came up corresponded with the number of children who had gone down.

No man or woman will ever forget the time when some child lies sick of a disease that threatens its life. Moreover, much less serious sickness is unpleasant enough at the time. Looking back, however, there are elements of comedy in certain of the less serious cases. I well remember one such instance which occurred when we were living in Washington, in a small house, with barely enough room for everybody when all the chinks were filled. Measles descended on the household. In the effort to keep the children that were well and those that were sick apart, their mother and I had to camp out in improvised fashion. When the eldest small boy was getting well, and had re- covered his spirits, I slept on a sofa beside his bed—the sofa being so short that my feet projected over anyhow. One afternoon the small boy was given a toy organ by a sympathetic friend. Next morning early I was waked to find the small boy very vivacious and requesting a story. Having drowsily told the story, I said, "Now, father's told you a story, so you amuse yourself and let father go to sleep"; to which the small boy responded most virtuously, "Yes, father will go to sleep and I'll play the organ," which he did, at a distance of two feet from my head. Later his sister, who had just come down with the measles, was put into the same room. The small boy was convalescing, and was engaged in playing on the floor with some tin ships, together with two or three pasteboard monitors and rams of my own manufacture. He was giving a vivid rendering of Farragut at Mobile Bay, from memories of how I had told the story. My pasteboard rams and monitors were fascinating—if a naval architect may be allowed to praise his own work—and as property they were equally divided between the little girl and the small boy. The little girl looked on with alert suspicion from the bed, for she was not yet convalescent enough to be allowed down on the floor. The small boy was busily reciting the phases of the fight, which now approached its climax, and the little girl evidently suspected that her monitor was destined to play the part of victim.

Little boy. "And then they steamed bang into the monitor."

Little girl. "Brother, don't you sink my monitor!"

Little boy (without heeding, and hurrying toward the climax). "And the torpedo went at the monitor!"

Little girl. "My monitor is not to sink!"

Little boy, dramatically: "And bang the monitor sank!"

Little girl. "It didn't do any such thing. My monitor always goes to bed at seven, and it's now quarter past. My monitor was in bed and *couldn't* sink!"

When I was assistant secretary of the navy, Leonard Wood and I used often to combine forces and take both families of children out to walk, and occasionally some of their playmates. Leonard Wood's son, I found, attributed the paternity of all of those not of his own family to me. Once we were taking the children across Rock Creek on a fallen tree. I was standing on the middle of the log trying to prevent any of the children from falling off, and while making a clutch at one peculiarly active and heedless child I fell off myself. As I emerged from the water I heard the little Wood boy calling frantically to the general, "Oh! oh! The father of all the children fell into the creek!"— which made me feel like an uncommonly moist patriarch. Of course the chlidren took much interest in the trophies I occasionally brought back from my hunts. When I started for my regiment, in '98, the stress of leaving home, which was naturally not pleasant, was somewhat lightened by the next to the youngest boy, whose ideas of what was about to happen were hazy, clasping me round the legs with a beaming smile and saying: "And is my father going to the war? And will he bring me back a bear?" When, some five months later, I returned, of course in my uniform, this little boy was much puzzled as to my identity, although he greeted me affably with "Good afternoon, Colonel." Half an hour later somebody asked him, "Where's father?" to which he responded: "I don't know; but the Colonel is taking a bath."

Of course the children anthropomorphized—if that is

the proper term—their friends of the animal world. Among these friends at one period was the baker's horse, and on a very rainy day I heard the little girl, who was looking out of the window, say, with a melancholy shake of her head: "Oh! there's poor Kraft's horse, all soppin' wet!"

While I was in the White House the youngest boy became an *habitué* of a small and rather noisome animal shop, and the good-natured owner would occasionally let him take pets home to play with. On one occasion I was holding a conversation with one of the leaders in Congress, Uncle Pete Hepburn, about the railroad-rate bill. The children were strictly trained not to interrupt business, but on this particular occasion the little boy's feelings overcame him. He had been loaned a king-snake, which, as all nature-lovers know, is not only a useful but a beautiful snake, very friendly to human beings; and he came rushing home to show the treasure. He was holding it inside his coat, and it contrived to wiggle partly down the sleeve. Uncle Pete Hepburn naturally did not understand the full import of what the little boy was saying to me as he endeavored to wriggle out of his jacket, and kindly started to help him—and then jumped back with alacrity as the small boy and the snake both popped out of the jacket.

There could be no healthier and pleasanter place in which to bring up children than in that nook of old-time America around Sagamore Hill. Certainly I never knew small people to have a better time or a better training for their work in after-life than the three families of cousins at Sagamore Hill. It was real country, and—speaking from the somewhat detached point of view of the masculine parent—I should say there was just the proper mixture of freedom and control in the management of the children. They were never allowed to be disobedient or to shirk lessons or work; and they were encouraged to have all the fun possible. They often went barefoot, especially during the many hours passed in various enthralling pursuits along and in the waters of the bay. They swam, they tramped, they boated, they coasted and skated in winter, they were intimate friends with the cows, chickens, pigs, and other live stock. They had in succession two ponies, General Grant and, when the general's legs became such that he lay down too often and too unexpectedly in the road, a calico pony named Algonquin, who is still living a life of honorable leisure in the stable and in the pasture—where he has to be picketed, because otherwise he chases the cows. Sedate Pony Grant used to draw the cart in which the children went driving when they were very small, the driver being their old nurse Mame, who had held their mother in her arms when she was born, and who was knit to them by a tie as close as any tie of blood. I doubt whether I ever saw Mame really offended with them except once when, out of pure but misunderstood affection, they named a pig after her. They loved Pony Grant. Once I saw the then little boy of three hugging Pony Grant's fore legs. As he leaned over, his broad straw hat tilted on end, and Pony Grant meditatively munched the brim; whereupon the small boy looked up with a wail of anguish, evidently thinking the pony had decided to treat him like a radish.

The children had pets of their own, too, of course. Among them guinea-pigs were the stand-bys—their highly unemotional nature fits them for companionship with adoring but overenthusiastic young masters and mistresses. Then there were flying squirrels, and kangaroo-rats, gentle and trustful, and a badger whose temper was short but whose nature was fundamentally friendly. The badger's name was Josiah; the particular little boy whose property he was used to carry him about, clasped firmly around what would have been his waist if he had had any. Inasmuch as when on the ground the badger would play energetic games of tag with the little boy and nip his bare legs, I suggested that it would be uncommonly disagreeable if he took advantage of being held in the little boy's arms to bite his face; but this suggestion was repelled with scorn as an unworthy assault on the character of Josiah. "He bites legs sometimes, but he never bites faces," said the little boy. We also had a young black bear whom the children christened Jonathan Edwards, partly out of compliment to their mother, who was descended from that great Puritan divine, and partly because the bear possessed a temper in which gloom and strength were combined in what the children regarded as Calvinistic proportions. As for the dogs, of course there were many, and during their lives they were intimate and valued family friends, and their deaths were household tragedies. One of them, a large yellow animal of several good breeds and valuable rather because of psychical than physical traits, was named "Susan" by his small owners, in commemoration of another retainer, a white cow; the fact that the cow and the dog were not of the same sex being treated with indifference. Much the most individual of the dogs and the one with the strongest character was Sailor Boy, a Chesapeake Bay dog. He had a masterful temper and a strong sense of both dignity and duty. He would never let the other dogs fight, and he himself never fought unless circumstances imperatively demanded it; but he was a murderous animal when he did fight. He was not only exceedingly fond of the water, as was to be expected, but passionately devoted to gunpowder in every form, for he loved firearms and fairly revelled in the Fourth of July celebrations —the latter being rather hazardous occasions, as the children strongly objected to any "safe and sane" element being injected into them, and had the normal number of close shaves with rockets, Roman candles, and firecrackers.

One of the stand-bys for enjoyment, especially in rainy weather, was the old barn. This had been built nearly a century previously, and was as delightful as only the pleasantest kind of old barn can be. It stood at the meeting-spot of three fences. A favorite amusement used to be an obstacle race when the barn was full of hay. The contestants were timed and were started successively from outside the door. They rushed inside, clambered over or burrowed through the hay, as suited them best, dropped out of a place where a loose board had come off, got over, through, or under the three fences, and raced back to the starting-point. When they were little, their respective fathers were expected also to take part in the obstacle race, and when with the advance of years the fathers finally refused to be contestants, there was a general feeling of pained regret among the children at such a decline in the sporting spirit.

Another famous place for handicap races was Cooper's Bluff, a gigantic sand-bank rising from the edge of the bay, a mile from the house. If the tide was high there was an added thrill, for some of the contestants were sure to run into the water.

As soon as the little boys learned to swim they were allowed to go off by themselves in rowboats and camp out for the night along the Sound. Sometimes I would go along so as to take the smaller children. Once a schooner was wrecked on a point half a dozen miles away. She held together well for a season or two after having been cleared of everything down to the timbers, and this gave us the chance to make camping-out trips in which the girls could also be included, for we put them to sleep in the wreck, while the boys slept on the shore; squaw picnics, the children called them.

My children, when young, went to the public school near us, the little Cove School, as it is called. For nearly thirty years we have given the Christmas-tree to the school. Before the gifts are distributed I am expected to make an address, which is always mercifully short, my own children having impressed upon me with frank sincerity the attitude of other children to addresses of this kind on such occasions. There are of course performances by the children themselves, while all of us parents look admiringly on, each sympathizing with his or her particular offspring in the somewhat wooden recital of "Darius Green and his Flying Machine" or "The Mountain and the Squirrel had a Quarrel." But the tree and the gifts make up for all short-comings.

We had a sleigh for winter; but if, when there was much snow, the whole family desired to go somewhere, we would put the body of the farm wagon on runners and all bundle in together. We always liked snow at Christmas-time, and the sleigh-ride down to the church on Christmas eve. One of the hymns always sung at this Christmas-eve festival begins: "It's Christmas eve on the river; it's Christmas eve on the bay." All good natives of the village firmly believe that this hymn was written here, and with direct reference to Oyster Bay; although if such were the case the word "river" would have to be taken in a hyperbolic sense, as the nearest approach to a river is the village pond. I used to share this belief myself, until my faith was shaken by a Denver lady who wrote that she had sung that hymn when a child in Michigan, and that at the present time her little Denver babies also loved it, although in their case the river was not represented by even a village pond.

When we were in Washington, the children usually went with their mother to the Episcopal church, while I went to the Dutch Reformed. But if any child misbehaved itself, it was sometimes sent next Sunday to church with me, on the theory that my companionship would have a sedative effect—which it did, as I and the child walked along with rather constrained politeness, each eyeing the other with watchful readiness for the unexpected. On one occasion, when the child's conduct fell just short of warranting such extreme measures, his mother, as they were on the point of entering church, concluded a homily by a quotation which showed a certain haziness of memory concerning the marriage and baptismal services: "No, little boy, if this conduct continues, I shall think that you neither love, honor, nor obey me!" However, the culprit was much impressed with a sense of shortcoming as to the obligations he had undertaken; so the result was as satisfactory as if the quotation had been from the right service.

As for the education of the children, there was of course much of it that represented downright hard work and drudgery. There was also much training that came as a by-product and was perhaps almost as valuable—not as a substitute but as an addition. After their supper, the children, when little, would come trotting up to their mother's room to be read to, and it was always a surprise to me to notice the extremely varied reading which interested them from Howard Pyle's "Robin Hood," Mary Alicia Owen's "Voodo Tales," and Joel Chandler Harris's "Aaron in the Wild Woods" to "Lycides" and "King John." If their mother was absent I would try to act as vice-mother—a poor substitute, I fear—superintending the supper and reading aloud afterward. The children did not wish me to read the books they desired their mother to read, and I usually took some such book as "Hereward the Wake," or "Guy Mannering," or "The Last of the Mohicans" or else some story about a man-eating tiger, or a man-eating lion, from one of the hunting-books in my library. These latter stories were always favorites, and as the authors told them in the first person, my interested auditors grew to know them by the name of the "I" stories, and regarded them as adventures all of which happened to the same individual. When Selous, the African hunter, visited us, I had to get him to tell to the younger children two or three of the stories with which they were already familiar from my reading; and as Selous is a most graphic narrator, and always enters thoroughly into the feeling not only of himself but of the opposing lion or buffalo, my own rendering of the incidents was cast entirely into the shade. . . .

Occasionally bits of self-education proved of unexpected help to the children in later years. Like other children, they were apt to take to bed with them treasures which they particularly esteemed. One of the boys, just before his sixteenth birthday, went moose-hunting with the family doctor, and close personal friend of the entire family, Alexander Lambert. Once night overtook them before they camped, and they had to lie down just where they were. Next morning Doctor Lambert rather enviously congratulated the boy on the fact that stones and roots evidently did not interfere with the soundness of his sleep; to which the boy responded: "Well, Doctor, you see it isn't very long since I used to take fourteen china animals to bed with me every night!"

As the children grew up, Sagamore Hill remained delightful for them. There were picnics and riding-parties, there were dances in the north room—sometimes fancy-dress dances—and open-air plays on the green tennis-court of one of the cousin's houses. The children are no longer children now. Most of them are men and women, working out their own fates in the big world; some in our own land, others across the great oceans or where the Southern Cross blazes in the tropic nights. Some of them have children of their own; some are working at one thing, some at another; in cable ships, in business offices, in factories, in newspaper offices, building steel bridges, bossing gravel-trains and steam-shovels, or laying tracks and superintending freight traffic. They have had their share of accidents and escapes; as I write, word comes from a far-off land that one of them, whom Seth Bullock used to call "Kim" because he was the friend of all mankind, while bossing a dangerous but necessary steel structural job has had two ribs and two back teeth broken, and is back at work. They have known and they will know joy and sorrow, triumph and temporary defeat. But I believe they are all the better off because of their happy and healthy childhood.

It is impossible to win the great prizes of life without running risks, and the greatest of all prizes are those connected with the home. No father and mother can hope to escape sorrow and anxiety, and there are dreadful moments when death comes very near those we love, even if for the time being it passes by. But life is a great adventure, and the worst of all fears is the fear of living. There are many forms of success, many forms of triumph. But there is no other success that in any shape or way approaches that which is open to most of the many, many men and women who have the right ideals. These are the men and women who see that it is the intimate and homely things that count most. They are the men and women who have the courage to strive for the happiness which comes only with labor and effort and self-sacrifice, and only to those whose joy in life springs in part from power of work and sense of duty.

CHAPTER 10

The Presidency:
Making an Old Party Progressive

On SEPTEMBER 6, 1901, President McKinley was shot by an Anarchist in the city of Buffalo. I went to Buffalo at once. The President's condition seemed to be improving, and after a day or two we were told that he was practically out of danger. I then joined my family, who were in the Adirondacks, near the foot of Mount Tahawus. A day or two afterward we took a long tramp through the forest, and in the afternoon I climbed Mount Tahawus. After reaching the top I had descended a few hundred feet to a shelf of land where there was a little lake, when I saw a guide coming out of the woods on our trail from below. I felt at once that he had bad news and, sure enough, he handed me a telegram saying that the President's condition was much worse and that I must come to Buffalo immediately. It was late in the afternoon, and darkness had fallen by the time I reached the club-house where we were staying. It was some time afterward before I could get a wagon

192

to drive me out to the nearest railway-station, North Creek, some forty or fifty miles distant. The roads were the ordinary wilderness roads and the night was dark. But we changed horses two or three times—when I say "we" I mean the driver and I, as there was no one else with us— and reached the station just at dawn, to learn from Mr. Loeb, who had a special train waiting, that the President was dead. That evening I took the oath of office, in the house of Ansley Wilcox, at Buffalo.

On three previous occasions the Vice-President had succeeded to the presidency on the death of the President. In each case there had been a reversal of party policy, and a nearly immediate and nearly complete change in the personnel of the higher offices, especially the Cabinet. I had never felt that this was wise from any standpoint. If a man is fit to be President, he will speedily so impress himself in the office that the policies pursued will be his anyhow, and he will not have to bother as to whether he is changing them or not; while as regards the offices under him, the important thing for him is that his subordinates shall make a success in handling their several departments. The subordinate is sure to desire to make a success of his department for his own sake, and if he is a fit man, whose views on public policy are sound, and whose abilities entitle him to his position, he will do excellently under almost any chief with the same purposes.

I at once announced that I would continue unchanged McKinley's policies for the honor and prosperity of the country, and I asked all the members of the Cabinet to stay. There were no changes made among them save as changes were made among their successors whom I myself appointed. I continued Mr. McKinley's policies, changing and developing them and adding new policies only as the questions before the public changed and as the needs of the public developed. Some of my friends shook their heads over this, telling me that the men I retained would not be "loyal to me," and that I would seem as if I were "a pale copy of McKinley." I told them that I was not nervous on this score, and that if the men I retained were loyal to their work they would be giving me the loyalty for which I most cared; and that if they were not, I would change them anyhow; and that as for being "a pale copy of McKinley," I was not primarily concerned with either following or not following in his footsteps, but in facing the new problems that arose; and that if I were competent I would find ample opportunity to show my competence by my deeds without worrying myself as to how to convince people of the fact.

For the reasons I have already given in my chapter on the governorship of New York, the Republican party, which in the days of Abraham Lincoln was founded as the radical progressive party of the nation, had been obliged during the last decade of the nineteenth century to uphold the interests of popular government against a foolish and ill-judged mock-radicalism. It remained the Nationalist as against the particularist or States'-rights party, and in so far it remained absolutely sound; for little permanent good can be done by any party which worships the States'-rights fetich or which fails to regard the State, like the county or the municipality, as merely a convenient unit for local self-government, while in all national matters, of importance to the whole people, the nation is to be supreme over State, county, and town alike. But the States'-rights fetich, although still effectively used at certain times by both courts and Congress to block needed national legislation directed against the huge corporations or in the interests of working men, was not a prime issue at the time of which I speak. In 1896, 1898, and 1900 the campaigns were waged on two great moral issues: (1) the imperative need of a sound and honest currency; (2) the need, after 1898, of meeting in manful and straightforward fashion the extraterritorial problems arising from the Spanish War. On these great moral issues the Republican party was right, and the men who were opposed to it, and who claimed to be the radicals, and their allies among the sentimentalists, were utterly and hopelessly wrong. This had, regrettably but perhaps inevitably, tended to throw the party into the hands not merely of the conservatives but of the reactionaries; of men who, sometimes for personal and improper reasons, but more often with entire sincerity and uprightness of purpose, distrusted anything that was progressive and dreaded radicalism. These men still from force of habit applauded what Lincoln had done in the way of radical dealing with the abuses of his day; but they did not apply the spirit in which Lincoln worked to the abuses of their own day. Both houses of Congress were controlled by these men. . . . I made a resolute effort to get on with all three and with their followers, and I have no question that they made an equally resolute effort to get on with me. We succeeded in working together, although with increasing friction, for some years, I pushing forward and they hanging back. Gradually, however, I was forced to abandon the effort to persuade them to come my way, and then I achieved results only by appealing over the heads of the Senate and House leaders to the people, who were the masters of both of us. I continued in this way to get results until almost the close of my term; and the

Republican party became once more the progressive and indeed the fairly radical progressive party of the nation. . . .

There were, of course, many senators and members of the Lower House with whom up to the very last I continued to work in hearty accord, and with a growing understanding. I have not the space to enumerate, as I would like to, these men. For many years Senator Lodge had been my close personal and political friend, with whom I discussed all public questions that arose, usually with agreement; and our intimately close relations were of course unchanged by my entry into the White House. He was of all our public men the man who had made the closest and wisest study of our foreign relations, and more clearly than almost any other man he understood the vital fact that the efficiency of our navy conditioned our national efficiency in foreign affairs. Anything relating to our international relations, from Panama and the navy to the Alaskan boundary question, the Algeciras negotiations, or the peace of Portsmouth, I was certain to discuss with Senator Lodge. . . .

I do not think I overstate the case when I say that most of the men who did the best work under me felt that ours was a partnership, that we all stood on the same level of purpose and service, and that it mattered not what position any one of us held so long as in that position he gave the very best that was in him. We worked very hard; but I made a point of getting a couple of hours off each day for equally vigorous play. The men with whom I then played, whom we laughingly grew to call the "Tennis Cabinet," have been mentioned in a previous chapter of this book in connection with the gift they gave me at the last breakfast which they took at the White House. There were many others in the public service under me with whom I happened not to play, but who did their share of our common work just as effectively as it was done by us who did play. Of course nothing could have been done in my administration if it had not been for the zeal, intelligence, masterful ability, and downright hard labor of these men in countless positions under me. I was helpless to do anything except as my thoughts and orders were translated into action by them; and, moreover, each of them, as he grew specially fit for his job, used to suggest to me the right thought to have, and the right order to give, concerning that job. It is of course hard for me to speak with cold and dispassionate partiality of these men, who were as close to me as were the men of my regiment. But the outside observers best fitted to pass judgment about them felt as I did. At the end of my administration Mr. Bryce, the British ambassador, told me that in a long life, during which he had studied intimately the government of many different countries, he had never in any country seen a more eager, high-minded, and efficient set of public servants, men more useful and more creditable to their country, than the men then doing the work of the American Government in Washington and in the field. . . .

My view was that every executive officer, and above all every executive officer in high position, was a steward of the people bound actively and affirmatively to do all he could for the people, and not to content himself with the negative merit of keeping his talents undamaged in a napkin. I declined to adopt the view that what was imperatively necessary for the nation could not be done by the President unless he could find some specific authorization to do it. My belief was that it was not only his right but his duty to do anything that the needs of the nation demanded unless such action was forbidden by the Constitution or by the laws. Under this interpretation of executive power I did and caused to be done many things not previously done by the President and the heads of the departments. I did not usurp power, but I did greatly broaden the use of executive power. In other words, I acted for the public welfare, I acted for the common well-being of all our people, whenever and in whatever manner was necessary, unless prevented by direct constitutional or legislative prohibition. . . .

The course I followed, of regarding the Executive as subject only to the people, and, under the Constitution, bound to serve the people affirmatively in cases where the Constitution does not explicity forbid him to render the service, was substantially the course followed by both Andrew Jackson and Abraham Lincoln. Other honorable and well-meaning Presidents, such as James Buchanan, took the opposite and, as it seems to me, narrowly legalistic view that the President is the servant of Congress rather than of the people, and can do nothing, no matter how necessary it be to act, unless the Constitution explicitly commands the action. Most able lawyers who are past middle age take this view, and so do large numbers of well-meaning, respectable citizens. My successor in office took this, the Buchanan, view of the President's powers and duties.

For example, under my administration we found that one of the favorite methods adopted by the men desirous of stealing the public domain was to carry the decision of the secretary of the interior into court. By vigorously opposing such action, and only by so doing, we were able to carry out the policy of properly protecting the public domain. My successor not only took the opposite view, but recommended to Congress the passage of a bill which would have given the courts direct appellate power over the secretary of the interior in these land matters. . . . Fortunately, Congress declined to pass the bill. Its passage would have been a veritable calamity.

I acted on the theory that the President could at any time in his discretion withdraw from entry any of the public lands of the United States and reserve the same for forestry, for water-power sites, for irrigation, and other public purposes. Without such action it would have been impossible to stop the activity of the land-thieves. No one ventured to test its legality by lawsuit. My successor, however, himself questioned it, and referred the matter to Congress. Again Congress showed its wisdom by passing a law which gave the President the power which he had long exercised, and of which my successor had shorn himself.

Perhaps the sharp difference between what may be called the Lincoln-Jackson and the Buchanan-Taft schools, in their views of the power and duties of the President, may be best illustrated by comparing the attitude of my successor toward his Secretary of the Interior, Mr. Ballinger, when the latter was accused of gross misconduct in office, with my attitude toward my chiefs of department and other subordinate officers. More than once while I was President my officials were attacked by Congress, generally because these officials did their duty well and fearlessly. In every such cash I stood by the official and refused to recognize the right of Congress to interfere with me excepting by impeachment or in other constitutional manner. On the other hand, wherever I found the officer unfit for his position, I promptly removed him, even although the most influential men in Congress fought for his retention. The Jackson-Lincoln view is that a President who is fit to do good work should be able to form his own judgment as to his own subordinates, and, above all, of the subordinates standing highest and in closest and most intimate touch with him. My secretaries and their subordinates were responsible to me, and I accepted the responsibility for all their deeds. As long as they were satisfactory to me I stood by them against every critic or assailant, within or without Congress; and as for getting Congress to make up my mind for me about them, the thought would have been inconceivable to me. My successor took the opposite, or Buchanan, view when he permitted and requested Congress to pass judgment on the charges made against Mr. Ballinger as an executive officer. These charges were made to the President; the President had the facts before him and could get at them at any time, and he alone had power to act if the charges were true. However, he permitted and requested Congress to investigate Mr. Ballinger. The party minority of the committee that investigated him, and one member of the majority, declared that the charges were well-founded and that Mr. Ballinger should be removed. The other members of the majority declared the charges ill-founded. The President abode by the view of the majority. Of course believers in the Jackson-Lincoln theory of the presidency would not be content with this town-meeting majority and minority method of determining by another branch of the government what it seems the especial duty of the President himself to determine for himself in dealing with his own subordinate in his own department. . . .

There was one cartoon made while I was President, in which I appeared incidentally, that was always a great favorite of mine. It pictured an old fellow with chin-whiskers, a farmer, in his shirt-sleeves, with his boots off, sitting before the fire, reading the President's message. On his feet were stockings of the kind I have seen hung up by the dozen in Joe Ferris's store at Medora, in the days when I used to come in to town and sleep in one of the rooms over the store. The title of the picture was "His Favorite Author." This was the old fellow whom I always used to keep in my mind. He had probably been in the Civil War in his youth; he had worked hard ever since he left the army; he had been a good husband and father; he had brought up his boys and girls to work; he did not wish to do injustice to any one else, but he wanted justice done to himself and to others like him; and I was bound to secure that justice for him if it lay in my power to do so.

TR did justice to his children, too, while in the White House. To Kermit in the winter of 1903 he wrote of dogs and cats:

Tom Quartz is certainly the cunningest kitten I have ever seen. He is always playing pranks on Jack and I get very nervous lest Jack should grow too irritated. The other evening they were both in the library—Jack sleeping before the fire—Tom Quartz scampering about, an exceedingly playful little wild creature,—which is about what he is. He would race across the floor and then jump upon the curtains or play with the tassels. Suddenly he spied Jack and galloped up to him. Jack, looking exceedingly sullen and shamefaced, jumped out of the way and got upon the sofa, where Tom Quartz instantly jumped upon him again. Jack suddenly shifted to the other sofa where Tom Quartz again went after him. Then Jack started for the door, while Tom made a rapid turn under the sofa and around the table and just as Jack reached the door leaped on his hind quarters. Jack bounded forward and away and the two went tandem out of the room—Jack not reappearing at all; and after about five minutes Tom Quartz stalked solemnly back.

Another evening the next Speaker of the House, Mr. Cannon, an exceedingly solemn, elderly gentleman with chin whiskers, who certainly does not look to be of playful nature, came to call upon me. He is a great friend of mine and we sat talking over what our policies for the session should be until about eleven o'clock; and when he went I accompanied him to the head of the stairs. He had gone about halfway down when Tom Quartz strolled by, his tail erect and very fluffy. He spied Mr. Cannon going down the stairs, and jumped to the conclusion that he was a playmate escaping, and raced after him, suddenly grasping him by the leg the way he does Archie and Quentin when they play hide and seek with him; then loosening his hold he tore downstairs ahead of Mr. Cannon, who eyed him with iron calm and not one particle of surprise.

A little later he was telling Kermit of Archie's doings and Quentin's:

The last two or three nights I have had terrific pillow fights with Archie and Quentin, Mr. John McIlhenny, who has come to visit us, occasionally joining in. Quentin's idea is to get as many pillows as possible in a heap and then lie on them apparently on the theory that he is protecting them from me. This enrages Archie, who addresses him with lofty contempt as "kid," and adjures him to stand up manfully and "fight the bear." If mother is tired I usually read to them, but if I cannot then Archie solemnly reads aloud to Quentin. Today, for our sins, Archie has a mask and a tin horn with which he runs about, armed also

with divers wooden swords and spears, to assail the policemen, ushers, and even me in my capacity as dragon.

To Ethel he sent one of his picture letters:

WHITE HOUSE
WASHINGTON June 22d
1904

Darling Ethel,
        Here goes for the
picture letter!

Ethel administers necessary
discipline to Archie and
Quentin.

Ethel gives sick Yagenka
a bottle of medicine

Father plays tennis
with Mr. Cooley. ————
[Father's shape & spectacles are reproduced
  with photographic fidelity; also notice

Leo chases a squirrel
which fortunately he can't catch

A nice policeman feeding
a squirrel with bread;
I fed two with bread
this afternoon.

Mr. Cooley's mile

There! My invention has given out. Mother & Aunt Emily have been on a picnic down the river with General Crozier; we have been sitting on the portico in the moonlight. Sister is very good.

Your loving
father

And to Kermit he admitted that novels were too often concerned with low life:

I sympathize with every word you say in your letter, about Nicholas Nickleby, and about novels generally.

Normally I only care for a novel if the ending is good, and I quite agree with you that if the hero has to die he ought to die worthily and nobly, so that our sorrow at the tragedy shall be tempered with the joy and pride one always feels when a man does his duty well and bravely. There is quite enough sorrow and shame and suffering and baseness in real life, and there is no need for meeting it unnecessarily in fiction. As Police Commissioner it was my duty to deal with all kinds of squalid misery and hideous and unspeakable infamy, and I should have been worse than a coward if I had shrunk from doing what was necessary; but there would have been no use whatever in my reading novels detailing all this misery and squalor and crime, or at least in reading them as a steady thing. Now and then there is a powerful but sad story which really is interesting and which really does good; but normally the books which do good and the books which healthy people find interesting are those which are not in the least of the sugar-candy variety, but which, while portraying foulness and suffering when they must be portrayed, yet have a joyous as well as a noble side.

When not giving advice on novel-reading, the President of the United States found the time to rescue a kitten. To Ethel he wrote in the summer of 1906:

Today as I was marching to church, with Sloan some twenty-five yards behind, I suddenly saw two terriers racing to attack a kitten which was walking down the sidewalk. I bounced forward with my umbrella, and after

some active work put to flight the dogs while Sloan captured the kitten, which was a friendly, helpless little thing,
evidently too well accustomed to being taken care of to
know how to shift for itself. I inquired of all the bystanders
and of people on the neighboring porches to know if they
knew who owned it; but as they all disclaimed, with
many grins, any knowledge of it, I marched ahead with it
in my arms for about a half a block. Then I saw a very
nice colored woman and little colored girl looking out of
the window of a small house with on the door a dress-
maker's advertisement, and I turned and walked up the
steps and asked them if they did not want the kitten. They
said they did, and the little girl welcomed it lovingly; so
I felt I had gotten it a home and continued toward
church. . . .

Has the lordly Ted turned up yet? Is his loving sister
able, unassisted, to reduce the size of his head, or does
she need any assistance from her male parent?

Your affectionate father,

CHAPTER 11

The Natural Resources
of the Nation

. . . WHILE I HAD LIVED in the West I had come to realize the vital need of irrigation to the country, and I had been both amused and irritated by the attitude of Eastern men who obtained from Congress grants of national money to develop harbors and yet fought the use of the nation's power to develop the irrigation work of the West. Major John Wesley Powell, the explorer of the Grand Canyon, and director of the Geological Survey, was the first man who fought for irrigation, and he lived to see the Reclamation Act passed and construction actually begun. Mr. F. H. Newell, . . . director of the Reclamation Service, began his work as an assistant hydraulic engineer under Major Powell; and, unlike Powell, he appreciated the need of saving the forests and the soil as well as the need of irrigation. . . . Senator Francis G. Newlands, of Nevada, fought hard for the cause of reclamation in Congress. . . . But Gifford Pinchot is the man to whom the nation owes most

209

for what has been accomplished as regards the preservation of the natural resources of our country. He led, and indeed during its most vital period embodied, the fight for the preservation through use of our forests. He played one of the leading parts in the effort to make the National Government the chief instrument in developing the irrigation of the arid West. He was the foremost leader in the great struggle to co-ordinate all our social and governmental forces in the effort to secure the adoption of a rational and far-seeing policy for securing the conservation of all our national resources. He was already in the government service as head of the Forestry Bureau when I became President; he continued throughout my term, not only as head of the forest service, but as the moving and directing spirit in most of the conservation work, and as counsellor and assistant on most of the other work connected with the internal affairs of the country. Taking into account the varied nature of the work he did, its vital importance to the nation and the fact that as regards much of it he was practically breaking new ground, and taking into account also his tireless energy and activity, his fearlessness, his complete disinterestedness, his single-minded devotion to the interests of the plain people, and his extraordinary efficiency, I believe it is but just to say that among the many, many public officials who under my administration rendered literally invaluable service to the people of the United States, he, on the whole, stood first. A few months after I left the presidency he was removed from office by President Taft.

The first work I took up when I became President was the work of reclamation. . . . At that time a narrowly legalistic point of view toward natural resources obtained in the departments, and controlled the governmental administrative machinery. Through the General Land Office and other government bureaus, the public resources were being handled and disposed of in accordance with the small considerations of petty legal formalities, instead of for the large purposes of constructive development, and the habit of deciding, whenever possible, in favor of private interests against the public welfare was firmly fixed. . . .

The idea that our natural resources were inexhaustible still obtained, and there was as yet no real knowledge of their extent and condition. The relation of the conservation of natural resources to the problems of national welfare and national efficiency had not yet dawned on the public mind. The reclamation of arid public lands in the West was still a matter for private enterprise alone; and our magnificent river system, with its superb possibilities for public usefulness, was dealt with by the National Government not as a unit, but as a disconnected series of pork-barrel problems, whose only real interest was in their effect on the re-election or defeat of a congressman here and there . . .

The place of the farmer in the national economy was still regarded solely as that of a grower of food to be eaten by others, while the human needs and interests of himself and his wife and children still remained wholly outside the recognition of the government. . . .

Such was the condition of things when Newell and Pinchot called on me. I was a warm believer in reclamation and in forestry, and, after listening to my two guests, I asked them to prepare material on the subject for me to use in my first message to Congress, of December 3, 1901. This message laid the foundation for the development of irrigation and forestry during the next seven and one-half years. . . .

On the day the message was read, a committee of Western senators and congressmen was organized to prepare a reclamation bill in accordance with the recommendations. By far the most effective of the senators in drafting and pushing the bill, which became known by his name, was Newlands. . . .

On June 17, 1902, the Reclamation Act was passed. It set aside the proceeds of the disposal of public lands for the purpose of reclaiming the waste areas of the arid West by irrigating lands otherwise worthless, and thus creating new homes upon the land. The money so appropriated was to be repaid to the government by the settlers, and to be used again as a revolving fund continuously available for the work.

The impatience of the Western people to see immediate results from the Reclamation Act was so great that red tape was disregarded, and the work was pushed forward at a rate previously unknown in government affairs. Later, as in almost all such cases, there followed the criticisms of alleged illegality and haste which are so easy to make after results have been accomplished and the need for the measures without which nothing could have been done has gone by. These criticisms were in character precisely the same as that made about the acquisition of Panama, the settlement of the anthracite-coal strike, the suits against the big trusts, the stopping of the panic of 1907 by the action of the Executive concerning the Tennessee Coal and Iron Company; and, in short, about most of the best work done during my administration.

With the reclamation work, as with much other work under me, the men in charge were given to understand that they must get into the water if they would learn to swim; and, furthermore, they learned to know that if they acted honestly, and boldly and fearlessly accepted responsibility, I would stand by them to the limit. In this, as in every other case, in the end the boldness of the action fully justified itself. . . .

Although the gross expenditure under the Reclamation Act is not yet as large as that for the Panama Canal, the engineering obstacles to be overcome have been almost as great, and the political impediments many times greater. The reclamation work had to be carried on at widely separated points, remote from railroads, under the most difficult pioneer conditions. The twenty-eight projects begun in the years 1902 to 1906 contemplated the irrigation of more than three million acres and the watering of more than thirty thousand farms. Many of the dams required for this huge task are higher than any previously built anywhere in the world. They feed main-line canals over seven thousand miles in total length, and involve minor constructions, such as culverts and bridges, tens of thousands in number. . . .

When I became President, the Bureau of Forestry (since 1905 the United States Forest Service) was a small but growing organization, under Gifford Pinchot, occupied mainly with laying the foundation of American forestry by scientific study of the forests, and with the promotion of forestry on private lands. It contained all the trained foresters in the government service, but had charge of no public timber-land whatsoever. The government forest reserves of that day were in the care of a division in the General Land Office, under the management of clerks wholly without knowledge of forestry, few if any of whom had ever seen a foot of the timber-lands for which they were responsible. Thus the reserves were neither well protected nor well used. . . .

In my first message to Congress I strongily recommended the consolidation of the forest work in the hands of the trained men of the Bureau of Forestry. This recommendation was repeated in other messages, but Congress did not give effect to it until three years later. In the meantime, by thorough study of the Western public timber-lands, the groundwork was laid for the responsibilities which were to fall upon the Bureau of Forestry when the care of the national forests came to be transferred to it. It was evident that trained American foresters would be needed in considerable numbers, and a forest school was established at Yale to supply them.

In 1901, at my suggestion as President, the Secretary of the Interior, Mr. Hitchcock, made a formal request for technical advice from the Bureau of Forestry in handling the national forests, and an extensive examination of their condition and needs was accordingly taken up. The same year a study was begun of the proposed Appalachian national forest, the plan of which, already formulated at that time, has since been carried out. A year later experimental planting on the national forests was also begun, and studies preparatory to the application of practical forestry to the Indian reservations were undertaken. In 1903, so rapidly did the public work of the Bureau of Forestry increase, that the examination of land for new forest reserves was added to the study of those already created, the forest-lands of the various States were studied, and co-operation with several of them in the examination and handling of their forest-lands was undertaken. While these practical tasks were pushed forward, a technical knowledge of American forests was rapidly accumulated. The special knowledge gained was made public in printed bulletins; and at the same time the bureau undertook, through the newspaper and periodical press, to make all the people of the United States acquainted with the needs and the purposes of practical forestry. It is doubtful whether there has ever been elsewhere under the government such effective publicity—publicity purely in the interest of the people—at so low a cost. Before the educational work of the forest service was stopped by the Taft administration, it was securing the publication of facts about forestry in fifty million copies of newspapers a month at a total expense of six thousand dollars a year. Not one cent has ever been paid by the forest service to any publication of any kind for the printing of this material. It was given out freely, and published without cost because it was news. Without this publicity the forest service could not have survived the attacks made upon it by the representatives of the great special interests in Congress; nor could forestry in America have made the rapid progress it has.

The result of all the work outlined above was to bring together in the Bureau of Forestry, by the end of 1904, the only body of forest experts under the government, and practically all of the first-hand information about the public forests which was then in existence. In 1905, the obvious foolishness of continuing to separate the foresters and the forests, reinforced by the action of the First National Forest Congress, held in Washington, brought about the Act of February 1, 1905, which transferred the national forests from the care of the Interior Department to the Department of Agriculture, and resulted in the creation of the present United States Forest Service.

The men upon whom the responsibility of handling some sixty million acres of national forest-lands was thus thrown were ready for the work, both in the office and in the field, because they had been preparing for it for more than five years. Without delay they proceeded, under the leadership of Pinchot, to apply to the new work the principles they had already formulated. One of these was to open all the resources of the national forests to regulated use. Another was that of putting every part of the land to that use in which it would best serve the public. Following this principle, the Act of June 11, 1906, was drawn, and its passage was secured from Congress. This law throws open to settlement all land in the national forests that is found, on examination, to be chiefly valuable for agriculture. Hitherto all such land had been closed to the settler.

The principles thus formulated and applied may be summed up in the statement that the rights of the public to the natural resources outweigh private rights, and must be given its first consideration. Until that time, in dealing with the national forests, and the public lands generally, private rights had almost uniformly been allowed to over-balance public rights. The change we made was right, and was vitally necessary; but, of course, it created bitter opposition from private interests.

One of the principles whose application was the source of much hostility was this: It is better for the government to help a poor man to make a living for his family than to help a rich man make more profit for his company. This principle was too sound to be fought openly. It is the kind of principle to which politicians delight to pay unctuous homage in words. But we translated the words into deeds; and when they found that this was the case, many rich men, especially sheep-owners, were stirred to hostility, and they used the congressmen they controlled to assault us—getting most aid from certain demagogues, who were equally glad improperly to denounce rich men in public and improperly to serve them in private. . . .

Another principle which led to the bitterest antagonism of all was this—whoever (except a bona-fide settler) takes public property for private profit should pay for what he gets. In the effort to apply this principle, the forest service obtained a decision from the attorney-general that it was legal to make the men who grazed sheep and cattle on the national forests pay for what they got. Accordingly, in the summer of 1906, for the first time, such a charge was made; and, in the face of the bitterest opposition, it was collected.

Up to the time the national forests were put under the charge of the forest service, the Interior Department had made no effort to establish public regulation and control of water powers. Upon the transfer, the service immediately began its fight to handle the power resources of the national forests so as to prevent speculation and monopoly and to yield a fair return to the government. . . .

In 1907, the area of the national forests was increased by presidential proclamation more than forty-three million acres; the plant necessary for the full use of the forests, such as roads, trails, and telephone-lines, began to be provided on a large scale; the interchange of field and office men, so as to prevent the antagonism between them, which is so destructive of efficiency in most great businesses, was established as a permanent policy; and the really effective management of the enormous area of the national forests began to be secured. . . .

By March 4, 1909, nearly half a million acres of agricultural land in the national forests had been opened to settlement under the Act of June 11, 1906. . . . The area of the national forests had increased from forty-three to one hundred and ninety-four million acres; the force from about five hundred to more than three thousand. There was saved for public use in the national forests more government timber-land during the seven and a half years prior to March 4, 1909, than during all previous and succeeding years put together. . . .

In its administration of the national forests, the forest service found that valuable coal-lands were in danger of passing into private ownership without adequate money return to the government and without safeguard against monopoly; and that existing legislation was insufficient to prevent this. When this condition was brought to my attention I withdrew from all forms of entry about sixty-eight million acres of coal-land in the United States, including Alaska. The refusal of Congress to act in the public interest was solely responsible for keeping these lands from entry.

The conservation movement was a direct outgrowth of the forest movement. It was nothing more than the application to our other natural resources of the principles which had been worked out in connection with the forests. Without the basis of public sentiment which had been built up for the protection of the forests, and without the example of public foresight in the protection of this, one of the great natural resources, the conservation movement would have been impossible. The first formal step was the creation of the Inland Waterways Commission, appointed on March 14, 1907. . . .

In the November following I wrote to each of the governors of the several States and to the presidents of various important national societies concerned with natural resources, inviting them to attend the conference, which took place May 13 to 15, 1908, in the East Room of the White House. It is doubtful whether, except in time of war, any new idea of like importance has ever been presented to a nation and accepted by it with such effectiveness and rapidity, as was the case with this conservation movement when it was introduced to the American people by the conference of governors. The first result was the unanimous declaration of the governors of all the States and Territories upon the subject of conservation, a document which ought to be hung in every schoolhouse throughout the land. A further result was the appointment of thirty-six State conservation commissions and, on June 8, 1908, of the National Conservation Commission. The task of this commission was to prepare an inventory, the first ever made for any nation, of all the natural resources which underlay its property. The making of this inventory was made possible by an Executive order which placed the resources of the government departments at the command of the commission, and made possible the organization of subsidiary committees by which the actual facts for the inventory were prepared and digested. Gifford Pinchot was made chairman of the commission.

The report of the National Conservation Commission was not only the first inventory of our resources, but was unique in the history of government in the amount and variety of information brought together. It was completed in six months. It laid squarely before the American people the essential facts regarding our natural resources, when facts were greatly needed as the basis for constructive action. . . .

Our land laws have of recent years proved inefficient; yet the land laws themselves have not been so much to blame as the lax, unintelligent, and often corrupt administration of these laws. The appointment on March 4, 1907, of James R. Garfield as Secretary of the Interior led to a new era in the interpretation and enforcement of the laws governing the public lands. His administration of the Interior Department was beyond comparison the best we have ever had. It was based primarily on the conception that it is as much the duty of public-land officials to help the honest settler get title to his claim as it is to prevent the looting of the public lands. The essential fact about public-land frauds is not merely that public property is stolen, but that every claim fraudulently acquired stands in the way of the making of a home or a livelihood by an honest man.

As the study of the public-land laws proceeded and their administration improved, a public-land policy was formulated in which the saving of the resources on the public domain for public use became the leading principle. There followed the withdrawal of coal-lands . . . of oil-lands and phosphate-lands, and finally, just at the end of the Administration, of water-power sites on the public domain. These withdrawals were made by the Executive in order to afford to Congress the necessary opportunity to pass wise laws dealing with their use and disposal; and the great crooked special interests fought them with incredible bitterness. . . .

The things accomplished that have been enumerated above were of immediate consequence to the economic well-being of our people. In addition certain things were done of which the economic bearing was more remote, but which bore directly upon our welfare, because they add to the beauty of living and therefore to the joy of life. Securing a great artist, Saint-Gaudens, to give us the most beautiful coinage since the decay of Hellenistic Greece was one such act. In this case I had power myself to direct the Mint to employ Saint-Gaudens. The first, and most beautiful, of his coins were issued in thousands before Congress assembled or could intervene; and a great and permanent improvement was made in the beauty of the coinage. In the same way, on the advice and suggestion of Frank Millet, we got some really capital medals by sculptors of the first rank. Similarly, the new buildings in Washington were erected and placed in proper relation to one another, on plans provided by the best architects and landscape-architects. I also appointed a Fine Arts Council, an unpaid body of the best architects, painters, and sculptors in the country, to advise the government as to the erection and decoration of all new buildings. The "pork-barrel" senators and congressmen felt for this body an instinctive, and perhaps from their standpoint a natural, hostility; and my successor a couple of months after taking office revoked the appointment and disbanded the council.

Even more important was the taking of steps to preserve from destruction beautiful and wonderful wild creatures whose existence was threatened by greed and wantonness. During the seven and a half years closing on March 4, 1909, more was accomplished for the protection of wild life in the United States than during all the previous years, excepting only the creation of the Yellowstone National Park. The record includes the creation of five national parks—Crater Lake, Oregon; Wind Cave, South Dakota; Platt, Oklahoma; Sully Hill, North Dakota, and Mesa Verde, Colorado; four big-game refuges in Oklahoma, Arizona, Montana, and Washington; fifty-one bird reservations; and the enactment of laws for the protection of wild life in Alaska, the District of Columbia, and on national bird reserves. . . .

CHAPTER 12

The Big Stick
and the Square Deal

ONE OF THE VITAL QUESTIONS with which as President I had to deal was the attitude of the nation toward the great corporations. Men who understand and practise the deep underlying philosophy of the Lincoln school of American political thought are necessarily Hamiltonian in their belief in a strong and efficient National Government and Jeffersonian in their belief in the people as the ultimate authority, and in the welfare of the people as the end of government. The men who first applied the extreme democratic theory in American life were, like Jefferson, ultraindividualists, for at that time what was demanded by our people was the largest liberty for the individual. During the century that had elapsed since Jefferson became President the need had been exactly reversed. There had been in our country a riot of individualistic materialism, under which complete freedom for the individual . . . turned out in practice to mean perfect freedom for the strong to wrong the

222

weak. . . . In no other country in the world had such enormous fortunes been gained. In no other country in the world was such power held by the men who had gained these fortunes; and these men almost always worked through, and by means of, the giant corporations which they controlled. The power of the mighty industrial over-lords of the country had increased with giant strides, while the methods of controlling them, or checking abuses by them on the part of the people, through the government, remained archaic and therefore practically impotent. The courts, not unnaturally but most regrettably, and to the grave detriment of the people and of their own standing, had for a quarter of a century been on the whole the agents of reaction, and by conflicting decisions which, however, in their sum, were hostile to the interests of the people, had left both the nation and the several States well-nigh impotent to deal with the great business combinations. . . .

One of the main troubles was the fact that the men who saw the evils and who tried to remedy them attempted to work in two wholly different ways, and the great majority of them in a way that offered little promise of real betterment. They tried (by the Sherman-law method) to bolster up an individualism already proved to be both futile and mischievous; to remedy by more individualism the concentration that was the inevitable result of the already existing individualism. They saw the evil done by the big combinations, and sought to remedy it by destroying them and restoring the country to the economic conditions of the middle of the nineteenth century. This was a hopeless effort, and those who went into it, although they regarded themselves as radical progressives, really represented a form of sincere rural toryism. They confounded monopolies with big business combinations, and in the effort to prohibit both alike, instead of where possible prohibiting one and drastically controlling the other, they succeeded merely in preventing any effective control of either.

On the other hand, a few men recognized that corporations and combinations had become indispensable in the business world, that it was folly to try to prohibit them, but that it was also folly to leave them without thoroughgoing control. These men realized that the doctrines of the old *laissez-faire* economists, of the believers in unlimited competition, unlimited individualism, were in the actual state of affairs false and mischievous. They realized that the government must now interfere to protect labor, to subordinate the big corporation to the public welfare, and to shackle cunning and fraud exactly as centuries before it had interfered to shackle the physical force which does wrong by violence.

The big reactionaries of the business world and their allies and instruments among politicians and newspaper editors took advantage of this division of opinion, and especially of the fact that most of their opponents were on the wrong path; and fought to keep matters absolutely unchanged. These men demanded for themselves an immunity from governmental control which, if granted, would have been as wicked and as foolish as immunity to the barons of the twelfth century. Many of them were evil men. Many others were just as good men as were some of these same barons; but they were as utterly unable as any mediæval castle-owner to understand what the public interest really was. There have been aristocracies which have played a great and beneficent part at stages in the growth of mankind; but we had come to the stage where for our people what was needed was a real democracy; and of all forms of tyranny the least attractive and the most vulgar is the tyranny of mere wealth, the tyranny of a plutocracy.

When I became President, the question as to the *method* by which the United States Government was to control the corporations was not yet important. The absolutely vital question was whether the government had power to control them at all. This question had not yet been decided in favor of the United States Government. It was useless to discuss methods of controlling big business by the National Government until it was definitely settled that the National Government had the power to control it. A decision of the Supreme Court had, with seeming definiteness, settled that the National Government had not the power.

This decision I caused to be annulled by the court that had rendered it; and the present power of the National Government to deal effectively with the trusts is due solely to the success of the Administration in securing this reversal of its former decision by the Supreme Court. . . .

The Sherman antitrust law was enacted in 1890 because the formation of the Tobacco Trust and the Sugar Trust, the only two great trusts then in the country (aside from the Standard Oil Trust, which was a gradual growth), had awakened a popular demand for legislation to destroy monopoly and curb industrial combinations. This demand the antitrust law was intended to satisfy. The administrations of Mr. Harrison and Mr. Cleveland evidently construed this law as prohibiting such combinations in the future, not as condemning those which had been formed prior to its enactment. In 1895, however, the Sugar Trust, whose output originally was about fifty-five per cent of all sugar produced in the United States, obtained control of three other companies in Philadelphia by exchanging its stock for theirs, and thus increased its business until it controlled ninety-eight per cent of the entire product. Under Cleveland, the government brought proceedings against the Sugar Trust, invoking the antitrust law, to set aside the acquisition of these corporations. The test case was on the absorption of the Knight Company.* The Supreme Court of the United States, with but one dissenting vote, held adversely to the government. They took the ground that the power conferred by the Constitution to regulate and control interstate commerce did not extend to the production or manufacture of commodities within a State, and that nothing in the Sherman antitrust law prohibited a corporation from acquiring all the stock of other corporations through exchange of its stock for theirs, such exchange not being "commerce" in the opinion of the court, even though by such acquisition the corporation was enabled to control the entire production of a commodity that was a necessary of life. The effect of this decision was not merely the absolute nullification of the antitrust law, so fas as industrial corporations were concerned, but was also in effect a declaration that, under the Constitution, the National Government could pass no law really effective for the destruction or control of such combinations.

This decision left the National Government, that is, the people of the nation, practically helpless to deal with the large combinations of modern business. The courts in other cases asserted the power of the Federal Government to enforce the antitrust law so far as transportation rates by railways engaged in interstate commerce were concerned. But so long as the trusts were free to control the production of commodities without interference from the general

* The case is known in the law-books as U. S. *vs.* E. C. Knight, 156 U. S., Sept., p. 1.

government, they were well content to let the transportation of commodities take care of itself—especially as the
law against rebates was at that time a dead letter; and the
court by its decision in the Knight case had interdicted any
interference by the President or by Congress with the
production of commodities. It was on the authority of this
case that practically all the big trusts in the United States,
excepting those already mentioned, were formed. Usually
they were organized as "holding" companies, each one
acquiring control of its constituent corporations by exchanging its stock for theirs, an operation which the Supreme Court had thus decided could not be prohibited,
controlled, regulated, or even questioned by the Federal
Government.

Such was the condition of our laws when I acceded to
the presidency. Just before my accession, a small group of
financiers, desiring to profit by the governmental impotence to which we had been reduced by the Knight decision, had arranged to take control of practically the
entire railway system in the Northwest—possibly as the
first step toward controlling the entire railway system of
the country. This control of the northwestern railway
systems was to be effected by organizing a new "holding"
company, and exchanging its stock against the stock of
the various corporations engaged in railway transportation
throughout that vast territory, exactly as the Sugar Trust
had acquired control of the Knight company and other
concerns. This company was called the Northern Securities Company. Not long after I became President, on the
advice of the attorney-general, Mr. Knox, and through
him, I ordered proceedings to be instituted for the dissolution of the company. As far as could be told by their utterances at the time, among all the great lawyers in the

United States Mr. Knox was the only one who believed that this action could be sustained. The defense was based expressly on the ground that the Supreme Court in the Knight case had explicitly sanctioned the formation of such a company as the Northern Securities Company. . . .

By a vote of five to four the Supreme Court reversed its decision in the Knight case, and in the Northern Securities case sustained the government. The power to deal with industrial monopoly and suppress it and to control and regulate combinations, of which the Knight case had deprived the Federal Government, was thus restored to it by the Northern Securities case. After this later decision was rendered, suits were brought by my direction against the American Tobacco Company and the Standard Oil Company. Both were adjudged criminal conspiracies, and their dissolution ordered. The Knight case was finally overthrown. The vicious doctrine it embodied no longer remains as an obstacle to obstruct the pathway of justice when it assails monopoly. Messrs. Knox, Moody, and Bonaparte, who successively occupied the position of attorney-general under me, were profound lawyers and fearless and able men; and they completely established the newer and more wholesome doctrine under which the Federal Government may now deal with monopolistic combinations and conspiracies.

The decisions rendered in these various cases brought under my direction constitute the entire authority upon which any action must rest that seeks through the exercise of national power to curb monopolistic control. The men who organized and directed the Northern Securities Company were also the controlling forces in the Steel Corporation, which has since been prosecuted under the act. . . .

From the standpoint of giving complete control to the National Government over big corporations engaged in interstate business, it would be impossible to overestimate the importance of the Northern Securities decision and of the decisions afterward rendered in line with it in connection with the other trusts whose dissolution was ordered. The success of the Northern Securities case definitely established the power of the government to deal with all great corporations.* Without this success the National Government must have remained in the impotence to which it had been reduced by the Knight decision as regards the most important of its internal functions. But our success in establishing the power of the National Government to curb monopolies did not establish the right method of exercising that power. We had gained the power. We had not devised the proper method of exercising it.

Monopolies can, although in rather cumbrous fashion, be broken up by lawsuits. Great business combinations, however, cannot possibly be made useful instead of noxious industrial agencies merely by lawsuits, and especially by lawsuits supposed to be carried on for their destruction and not for their control and regulation. I at once began to urge upon Congress the need of laws supplementing the antitrust law—for this law struck at all big business, good and bad, alike, and as the event proved was very inefficient in checking bad big business, and yet was a constant threat against decent business men. I strongly urged the inauguration of a system of thoroughgoing and drastic governmental regulation and control over all big business combinations engaged in interstate industry.

* By this decision in 1904 the Morgan-Hill-Harriman plan of controlling the Great Northern, Northern Pacific, and Burlington lines by means of a holding company was checkmated. [*Editor's note*]

Here I was able to accomplish only a small part of what I desired to accomplish. I was opposed both by the foolish radicals who desired to break up all big business, with the impossible ideal of returning to mid-nineteenth-century industrial conditions; and also by the great privileged interests themselves, who used these ordinarily—but sometimes not entirely—well-meaning "stool-pigeon progressives" to further their own cause. The worst representatives of big business encouraged the outcry for the total abolition of big business, because they knew that they could not be hurt in this way, and that such an outcry distracted the attention of the public from the really efficient method of controlling and supervising them, in just but masterly fashion, which was advocated by the sane representatives of reform. However, we succeeded in making a good beginning by securing the passage of a law creating the Department of Commerce and Labor, and with it the erection of the Bureau of Corporations. . . .

The Standard Oil Company took the lead in opposing all this legislation. This was natural, for it had been the worst offender in the amassing of enormous fortunes by improper methods of all kinds, at the expense of business rivals and of the public, including the corruption of public servants. If any man thinks this condemnation extreme, I refer him to the language officially used by the Supreme Court of the nation in its decision against the Standard Oil Company. Through their counsel, and by direct telegrams and letters to senators and congressmen from various heads of the Standard Oil organization, they did their best to kill the bill providing for the Bureau of Corporations. I got hold of one or two of these telegrams and letters, however, and promptly published them; and, as generally happens in such a case, the men who were all-powerful as long as they could work in secret and behind closed doors became powerless as soon as they were forced into the open. The bill went through without further difficulty.

The true way of dealing with monopoly is to prevent it by administrative action before it grows so powerful that even when courts condemn it they shrink from destroying it. The Supreme Court in the Tobacco and Standard Oil cases, for instance, used very vigorous language in condemning these trusts; but the net result of the decision was of positive advantage to the wrong-doers, and this has tended to bring the whole body of our law into disrepute in quarters where it is of the very highest importance that the law be held in respect and even in reverence. My effort was to secure the creation of a Federal commission which should neither excuse nor tolerate monopoly, but prevent it when possible and uproot it when discovered; and which should in addition effectively control and regulate all big combinations, and should give honest business certainty as to what the law was and security as long as the law was obeyed. Such a commission would furnish a steady expert control, a control adapted to the problem; and dissolution is neither control nor regulation, but is purely negative; and negative remedies are of little permanent avail. Such a commission would have complete power to examine into every big corporation engaged or proposing to engage in business between the States. It would have the power to discriminate sharply between corporations that are doing well and those that are doing ill; and the distinction between those who do well and those who do ill would be defined in terms so clear and unmistakable that no one could misapprehend them. . . . Such a commission, with the power I advocate, would put a stop to abuses of big corporations and small corporations alike; it would draw the line on conduct and not on size; it would destroy monopoly, and make the biggest business man in the country conform squarely to the principles laid down by the American people, while at the same time giving fair play to the little man and certainty of knowledge as to what was wrong and what was right both to big man and little man.

Although under the decision of the courts the National Government had power over the railways, I found, when I became President, that this power was either not exercised at all or exercised with utter inefficiency. The law against rebates was a dead letter. All the unscrupulous railway men had been allowed to violate it with impunity; and because of this, as was inevitable, the scrupulous and decent railway men had been forced to violate it themselves, under penalty of being beaten by their less scrupulous rivals. It was not the fault of these decent railway men. It was the fault of the government. . . .

We not only secured the stopping of rebates, but in the Hepburn rate bill we were able to put through a measure which gave the Interstate Commerce Commission for the first time real control over the railways. . . . Thanks to this law and to the way in which the Interstate Commerce Commission was backed by the Administration, the commission. . . . became a most powerful force for good. Some of the good that we had accomplished was undone after the close of my administration by the unfortunate law creating a Commerce Court; but the major part of the immense advance we had made remained. There was one point on which I insisted, and upon which it is necessary always to insist. The commission cannot do permanent good unless it does justice to the corporations precisely as it exacts justice from them. The public, the shippers, the stock and bond holders, and the employees, all have their rights, and none should be allowed unfair privileges at the expense of the others. Stock-watering and swindling of any kind should of course not only be stopped but punished. When, however, a road is managed fairly and honestly, and when it renders a real and needed service, then the government must see that it is not so burdened as to make it impossible to run it at a profit. There is much wise legislation necessary for the safety of the public, or—like workmen's compensation—necessary to the well-being of the employee, which nevertheless imposes such a burden on the road that the burden must be distributed between the general public and the corporation, or there will be no dividends. In such a case it may be the highest duty of the commission to raise rates; and the commission, when satisfied that the necessity exists, in order to do justice to the owners of the road, should no more hesitate to raise rates than under other circumstances to lower them.

So much for the "big stick" in dealing with the corporations when they went wrong. Now for a sample of the square deal.

In the fall of 1907 there were severe business disturbances and financial stringency, culminating in a panic which arose in New York and spread over the country. The damage actually done was great, and the damage threatened was incalculable. Thanks largely to the action of the government, the panic was stopped before, instead of being merely a serious business check, it became a frightful and nation-wide calamity, a disaster fraught with untold misery and woe to all our people. . . .

During these days both the Secretary of the Treasury and I personally were in hourly communication with New

York, following every change in the situation, and trying to anticipate every development. It was the obvious duty of the Administration to take every step possible to prevent appalling disaster by checking the spread of the panic before it grew so that nothing could check it. And events moved with such speed that it was necessary to decide and to act on the instant, as each successive crisis arose, if the decision and action were to accomplish anything. The Secretary of the Treasury took various actions, some on his own initiative, some by my direction. Late one evening I was informed that two representatives of the Steel Corporation wished to see me early the following morning, the precise object not being named. Next morning, while at breakfast, I was informed that Messrs. Frick and Gary were waiting at the office. I at once went over, and, as the Attorney-General, Mr. Bonaparte, had not yet arrived from Baltimore, where he had been passing the night, I sent a message asking the Secretary of State, Mr. Root, who was also a lawyer, to join us, which he did. . . .

I was intimately acquainted with the situation in New York. The word "panic" means fear, unreasoning fear; to stop a panic it is necessary to restore confidence; and at the moment the so-called Morgan interests were the only interests which retained a full hold on the confidence of the people of New York—not only the business people, but the immense mass of men and women who owned small investments or had small savings in the banks and trust companies. Mr. Morgan and his associates were of course fighting hard to prevent the loss of confidence and the panic distrust from increasing to such a degree as to bring any other big financial institutions down; for this would probably have been followed by a general, and very likely a world-wide, crash. The Knickerbocker Trust

Company had already failed, and runs had begun on, or were threatened as regards, two other big trust companies. These companies were now on the fighting-line, and it was to the interest of everybody to strengthen them, in order that the situation might be saved. It was a matter of general knowledge and belief that they, or the individual prominent in them, held the securities of the Tennessee Coal and Iron Company, which securities had no market value, and were useless as a source of strength in the emergency. The Steel Corporation securities, on the contrary, were immediately marketable, their great value being known and admitted all over the world—as the event showed. The proposal of Messrs. Frick and Gary was that the Steel Corporation should at once acquire the Tennessee Coal and Iron Company, and thereby substitute, among the assets of the threatened institutions (which, by the way, they did not name to me), securities of great and immediate value for securities which at the moment were of no value. It was necessary for me to decide on the intant, before the Stock Exchange opened, for the situation in New York was such that any hour might be vital, and failure to act for even an hour might make all subsequent efforts to act utterly useless. From the best information at my disposal, I believe (what was actually the fact) that the addition of the Tennessee Coal and Iron property would only increase the proportion of the Steel Company's holdings by about four per cent, making them about sixty-two per cent instead of about fifty-eight per cent of the total value in the country; an addition which, by itself, in my judgment (concurred in, not only by the Attorney-General but by every competent lawyer), worked no change in the legal status of the Steel Corporation. The diminution in the percentage of holdings, and production, has gone on steadily, and the percentage is now about ten per cent less than it was ten years ago.

The action was emphatically for the general good. It offered the only chance for arresting the panic, and it did arrest the panic. I answered Messrs. Frick and Gary, . . . to the effect that I did not deem it my duty to interfere, that is, to forbid the action which more than anything else in actual fact saved the situation. The result justified my judgment. The panic was stopped, public confidence in the solvency of the threatened institution being at once restored.

Business was vitally helped by what I did. The benefit was not only for the moment. It was permanent. Particularly was this the case in the South. Three or four years afterward I visited Birmingham. Every man I met, without exception, who was competent to testify, informed me voluntarily that the results of the action taken had been of the utmost benefit to Birmingham, and therefore to Alabama, the industry having profited to an extraordinary degree, not only from the standpoint of the business, but from the standpoint of the community at large and of the wage-workers, by the change in ownership. The results of the action I took were beneficial from every standpoint, and the action itself, at the time when it was taken, was vitally necessary to the welfare of the people of the United States.

I would have been derelict in my duty, I would have shown myself a timid and unworthy public servant, if in that extraordinary crisis I had not acted precisely as I did act. . . . Every step I took in this matter was open as the day, and was known in detail at the moment to all people. The press contained full accounts of the visit to me of Messrs. Frick and Gary, and heralded widely and with acclamation the results of that visit. At the time the relief and rejoicing over what had been done were well-nigh universal. The danger was too imminent and too appalling for men to be willing to condemn those who were successful in saving them from it. But I fully understood and expected that when there was no longer danger, when the fear had been forgotten, attack would be made upon me; and as a matter of fact after a year had elapsed the attack was begun, and has continued at intervals ever since; my ordinary assailant being some politician of rather cheap type. . . .

There were many other things that we did in connection with corporations. One of the most important was the passage of the meat-inspection law because of scandalous abuses shown to exist in the great packing-houses in Chicago and elsewhere. There was a curious result of this law, similar to what occurred in connection with the law providing for effective railway regulation. The big beef men bitterly opposed the law; just as the big railway men opposed the Hepburn Act. Yet three or four years after these laws had been put on the statute-books every honest man both in the beef business and the railway business came to the conclusion that they worked good and not harm to the decent business concerns. They hurt only those who were not acting as they should have acted. The law providing for the inspection of packing-houses, and the Pure Food and Drugs Act, were also extremely important; and the way in which they were administered was even more important. . . .

It would be useless to enumerate all the suits we brought. Some of them I have already touched upon. Others, such as the suits against the Harriman railway corporations, which were successful, and which had been rendered absolutely necessary by the grossly improper action of the corporations concerned, offered no special points of interest. The Sugar Trust proceedings, however, may be mentioned as showing just the kind of thing that was done and the kind of obstacle encountered and overcome in prosecutions of this character.

It was on the advice of my secretary, William Loeb, Jr., afterward head of the New York Custom-House, that the action was taken which started the uncovering of the frauds perpetrated by the Sugar Trust and other companies in connection with the importing of sugar. Loeb had from time to time told me that he was sure that there was fraud in connection with the importations by the Sugar Trust through the New York Custom-House. Finally, some time toward the end of 1904, he informed me that Richard Parr, a sampler at the New York Appraisers' Stores (whose duties took him almost continually on the docks in connection with the sampling of merchandise), had called on him, and had stated that in his belief the sugar companies were defrauding the government in the matter of weights, and had stated that if he could be made an investigating officer of the Treasury Department, he was confident that he could show there was wrongdoing. . . . Parr was assigned to New York early in March, 1907, and at once began an active investigation of the conditions existing on the sugar docks. This terminated in the discovery of a steel spring in one of the scales of the Havemeyer & Elder docks in Brooklyn, November 20, 1907, which enabled us to uncover what were probably the most colossal frauds ever perpetrated in the customs service. . . .

District Attorney Stimson, of New York, assisted by Denison, Frankfurter, Wise, and other employees of the

Department of Justice, took charge of the case, and carried on both civil and criminal proceedings. The trial in the action against the Sugar Trust, for the recovery of duties on the cargo of sugar which was being sent over the scales at the time of the discovery of the steel spring by Parr, was begun in 1908; judgment was rendered against the defendants on March 5, 1909, the day after I left office. Over four million dollars were recovered and paid back into the United States Treasury by the sugar companies which had perpetrated the various forms of fraud. These frauds were unearthed by Parr, Loeb, Stimson, Frankfurter, and the other men mentioned and their associates, and it was to them that the people owed the refunding of the huge sum of money mentioned. We had already secured heavy fines from the Sugar Trust, and from various big railways, and private individuals, such as Edwin Earle, for unlawful rebates. In the case of the chief offender, the American Sugar Refining Company (the Sugar Trust), criminal prosecutions were carried on against every living man whose position was such that he would naturally know about the fraud. All of them were indicted, and the biggest and most responsible ones were convicted. The evidence showed that the president of the company, Henry O. Havemeyer, virtually ran the entire company, and was responsible for all the details of the management. . . .

Among the big corporations themselves, even where they did wrong, there was a wide difference in the moral obliquity indicated by the wrong-doer. There was a wide distinction between the offenses committed in the case of the Northern Securities Company and the offenses because of which the Sugar Trust, the Tobacco Trust, and the Standard Oil Trust were successfully prosecuted under my administration. It was vital to destroy the Northern Securities Company; but the men creating it had done so in open and aboveboard fashion, acting under what they, and most of the members of the bar, thought to be the law established by the Supreme Court in the Knight sugar case. But the Supreme Court in its decree dissolving the Standard Oil and Tobacco Trusts, condemned them in the severest language for moral turpitude; and an even severer meed of condemnation should be visited on the Sugar Trust. . . .

Understandably, in the midst of his campaign to educate businessmen to be better citizens, TR was giving careful thought to the choice of new members of the Supreme Court. Here, in a letter to Henry Cabot Lodge, is his estimate of Oliver Wendell Holmes, Jr., whom he appointed to the Court on December 4, 1902:

Now as to Holmes: . . . I wish to go over the reasons why I am in his favor. He possesses the high character and the high reputation both of which should if possible attach to any man who is to go upon the highest court of the entire civilized world. His father's name entitles the son to honor; and if the father had been an utterly unknown man the son would nevertheless now have won the highest honor. The position of Chief Justice of Massachusetts is in itself a guarantee of the highest professional standing. Moreover, Judge Holmes has behind him the kind of career and possesses the kind of personality which make a good American proud of him as a representative of our country. He has been a most gallant soldier, a most able and upright public servant, and in public and private life alike a citizen whom we like to think of as typical of the American character at its best. The labor decisions which have been criticized by some of the big railroad men and other members of large corporations constitute to my mind a strong point in Judge Holmes' favor. The ablest lawyers and greatest judges are men whose past has naturally brought them into close relationship with the wealthiest and most powerful clients, and I am glad when I can find a judge who has been able to preserve his aloofness of mind so as to keep his broad humanity of feeling and his sympathy for the class from which he has not drawn his clients. I think it eminently desirable that our Supreme Court should show in unmistakable fashion their entire sympathy with all proper effort to secure the most favorable possible consideration for the men who most need that consideration.

Finally, Judge Holmes' whole mental attitude, as shown for instance by his great Phi Beta Kappa speech at Harvard is such that I should naturally expect him to be in favor of those principles in which I so earnestly believe.

Now a word as to the other side. It may seem to be, but it is not really, a small matter that his speech on Marshall should be unworthy of the subject, and above all should show a total incapacity to grasp what Marshall did. In the ordinary and low sense which we attach to the words "partisan" and "politician," a judge of the Supreme Court should be neither. But in the higher sense, in the proper sense, he is not in my judgment fitted for the position unless he is a party man, a constructive statesman, constantly keeping in mind his adherence to the principles and policies under which this nation has been built up and in accordance with which it must go on; and keeping in mind also his relations with his fellow statesmen who in other branches of the government are striving in cooperation with him to advance the ends of government. Marshall rendered such invaluable service because he was a statesman of the national type, like Adams who appointed him, like Washington whose mantle fell upon him. Taney was a curse to our national life because he belonged to the wrong party and faithfully carried out the criminal and foolish views of the party which stood for such a construction of the Constitution as would have rendered it impossible even to preserve the national life. The Supreme Court of the sixties was good exactly in so far as its members fitly represented the spirit of Lincoln.

This is true at the present day. The majority of the present Court who have, although without satisfactory unanimity, upheld the policies of President McKinley and the Republican party in Congress, have rendered a great service to mankind and to this nation. The minority—a minority so large as to lack but one vote of being a majority —have stood for such reactionary folly as would have hampered well-nigh hopelessly this people in doing efficient and honorable work for the national welfare, and for the welfare of the islands themselves, in Porto Rico and the Philippines. No doubt they have possessed excellent motives and without doubt they are men of excellent personal character; but this no more excuses them than the same conditions excused the various upright and honorable men who took part in the wicked folly of secession in 1860 and 1861.

Now I should like to know that Judge Holmes was in entire sympathy with our views, . . . before I would feel justified in appointing him. . . . I should hold myself as guilty of an irreparable wrong to the nation if I should appoint any man who was not absolutely sane and sound on the great national policies for which we stand in public life.

Ultimately, Holmes proved a disappointment to Roosevelt. In the Northern Securities case, he issued a dissenting opinion.

While bearing down on corporations that misbehaved, TR grew more and more convinced that the men with the biggest bank balances were not always the most desirable citizens. As he wrote his English friend Spring-Rice in the spring of 1908:

I am simply unable to understand the value placed by so many people upon great wealth. I very thoroly understand the need of sufficient means to enable the man or woman to be comfortable; I also entirely understand the pleasure of having enough more than this so as to add certain luxuries, and above all, that greatest of all luxuries, the escape from the need of considering at every turn whether it is possible to spend a dollar or two extra; but when the last limit has been reached, then increase in wealth means but little, certainly as compared with all kinds of other things. In consequence, I am simply unable to make myself take the attitude of respect toward the very wealthy men which such an enormous multitude of people evidently really feel. I am delighted to show any courtesy to Pierpont Morgan or Andrew Carnegie or James J. Hill; but as for regarding any one of them as, for instance, I regard Professor Bury, or Peary, the Arctic explorer, or Admiral Evans, or Rhodes, the historian, or Selous, the big game hunter (to mention at random guests who have been at the White House not long ago)—why, I could not force myself to do it even if I wanted to, which I do not. The very luxurious, grossly material life of the average multi-millionaire whom I know, does not appeal to me in the least, and nothing would hire me to lead it. It is an exceedingly nice thing to have enough money to be able to take a hunting trip in Africa after big game (if you are not able to make it pay for itself in some other way). It is an exceedingly nice thing, if you are young, to have one or two good jumping horses and to be able to occasionally hunt—altho Heaven forfend that anyone for whom I care should treat riding to hounds as the serious business of life! It is an exceedingly nice thing to have a good house and to be able to purchase good books and good pictures, and especially to have that house isolated from others. But I wholly fail to see where any real enjoyment comes from a dozen automobiles, a couple of hundred horses, and a good many different homes luxuriously upholstered. From the standpoint of real pleasure I should selfishly prefer my old-time ranch on the Little Missouri to anything in Newport.

TR could scarcely sympathize with the men responsible for the conditions in the Chicago Stockyards. To James Walcott Wadsworth, Chairman of the House Committee on Agriculture, he wrote in the spring of 1906:

I have recently had an investigation made by Commissioner Neill of the Labor Bureau and Mr. J. B. Reynolds, of the situation in Chicago packing houses. It is hideous, and it must be remedied at once. I was at first so indignant that I resolved to send in the full report to Congress. As far as the beef packers themselves are concerned I should do this now with a clear conscience, for the great damage that would befall them in consequence would be purely due to their own actions. But the damage would also come to all the stock growers of the country and the effect of such a report would undoubtedly be well-nigh ruinous to our export trade in meat for the time being, and doubtless the damaging effect would be apparent long after we had remedied the wrongs. I am therefore going to withhold the report for the time being, and until I can also report that the wrongs have been remedied, provided that without making it public I can get the needed legislation; that is, provided we can have the meat inspection amendment that has been put on in the Senate in substance enacted into law. Of course what I am after is not to do damage even to the packers, still less to the stockmen and farmers. What I want is the immediate betterment of the dreadful conditions that prevail, and moreover the providing against a possible recurrence of these conditions. The beef packers have told me through Mr. Louis Swift that if I will not make this report public they will guarantee to remedy all the wrongs which we have found or may find to exist. This is good as far as it goes, but it does not go far enough, and it is absolutely necessary that we shall have legislation which will prevent the recurrence of these wrongs. I should not make the report public with the idea of damaging the packers. I should do it only if it were necessary in order to secure the remedy.

There was wisdom, TR felt, in a threat well-timed. "Speak softly and carry a big stick; you will go far" was a West African proverb that the President made famous. He quoted it in a letter to the lawyer Henry L. Sprague on January 26, 1900.

At the same time TR feared the muck-rakers then denouncing big businessmen in the popular magazines were carrying their campaign beyond the bounds of decency. In an address on April 14, 1906 at the laying of the cornerstone of the new office building for the House of Representatives he said:

In Bunyan's "Pilgrim's Progress" you may recall the description of the Man with the Muck-rake, the man who could look no way but downward, with the muck-rake in his hand; who was offered a celestial crown for his muck-rake, but who would neither look up nor regard the crown he was offered, but continued to rake to himself the filth of the floor.

In "Pilgrim's Progress" the Man with the Muck-rake is set forth as the example of him whose vision is fixed on carnal instead of on spiritual things. Yet he also typifies the man who in this life consistently refuses to see aught that is lofty, and fixes his eyes with solemn intentness only on that which is vile and debasing. Now, it is very necessary that we should not flinch from seeing what is vile and debasing. There is filth on the floor, and it must be scraped up with the muck-rake; and there are times and places where this service is the most needed of all the services that can be performed. But the man who never does anything else, who never thinks or speaks or writes, save of his feats with the muck-rake, speedily becomes, not a help to so-

ciety, not an incitement to good, but one of the most
potent forces for evil.

There are, in the body politic, economic and social,
many and grave evils, and there is urgent necessity for the
sternest war upon them. There should be relentless ex-
posure of and attack upon every evil man whether politician or business man, every evil practice, whether in
politics, in business, or in social life. I hail as a benefactor
every writer or speaker, every man who, on the platform,
or in book, magazine, or newspaper, with merciless se-
verity makes such attack, provided always that he in his
turn remembers that the attack is of use only if it is absolutely truthful. The liar is no whit better than the thief,
and if his mendacity takes the form of slander, he may be
worse than most thieves. It puts a premium upon knavery
untruthfully to attack an honest man, or even with hys-
terical exaggeration to assail a bad man with untruth. An
epidemic of indiscriminate assault upon character does not
good, but very great harm. The soul of every scoundrel
is gladdened whenever an honest man is assailed, or even
when a scoundrel is untruthfully assailed.

He was even more explicit on this subject when he wrote in the
fall of 1905 to S. S. McClure, the publisher of McClure's Maga-
zine.

It is an unfortunate thing to encourage people to believe
that all crimes are connected with business, and that the
crime of graft is the only crime. I wish very much that

you could have articles showing up the hideous iniquity of which mobs are guilty, the wrongs of violence by the poor as well as the wrongs of corruption by the rich. I feel that very great good is done by a crusade against corruption such as you have carried on, provided only it is clearly shown that we must *not* confine our hostility to the wealthy, nor feel indignant only at corruption. There are other classes just as guilty, and other crimes as bad.

CHAPTER 13

Social and Industrial Justice

By the time I became President I had grown to feel with deep intensity of conviction that governmental agencies must find their justification largely in the way in which they are used for the practical betterment of living and working conditions among the mass of the people. I felt that the fight was really for the abolition of privilege; and one of the first stages in the battle was necessarily to fight for the rights of the working man. For this reason I felt most strongly that all that the government could do in the interest of labor should be done. The Federal Government can rarely act with the directness that the State governments act. It can, however, do a good deal. My purpose was to make the National Government itself a model employer of labor, the effort being to make the per diem employee just as much as the Cabinet officer regard himself as one of the partners employed in the service of the public, proud of his work, eager to do it in the best possible manner, and confident of just treatment. Our aim was also to secure good laws wherever the National Government had power, notably in the Territories, in the District of Columbia, and in connection with interstate commerce. I found the eight-hour law a mere farce, the departments rarely enforcing it with any degree of efficiency. This I remedied by executive action. Unfortunately, thoroughly efficient government servants often proved to be the prime offenders so far as the enforcement of the eight-hour law was concerned, because in their zeal to get good work done for the government they became harsh taskmasters, and declined to consider the needs of their fellow employees who served under them. The more I had studied the subject the more strongly I had become convinced that an eight-hour day under the conditions of labor in the United States was all that could, with wisdom and propriety, be required either by the government or by private employers; that more than this meant, on the average, a decrease in the qualities that tell for good citizenship. . . .

We passed a good law protecting the lives and health of miners in the Territories, and other laws providing for the supervision of employment agencies in the District of Columbia, and protecting the health of motormen and conductors on street-railways in the District. We practically started the Bureau of Mines. We provided for safeguarding factory employees in the District against accidents, and for the restriction of child labor therein. We passed a workmen's compensation law for the protection of government employees; a law which did not go as far as I wished, but which was the best I could get, and which committed the government to the right policy. We provided for an investigation of woman and child labor in the United States. We incorporated the National Child-Labor Committee. Where we had most difficulty was with the railway companies engaged in interstate business. We passed an act improving safety appliances on railway-trains without much opposition, but we had more trouble with acts regulating the hours of labor of railway employees and making those railways which were engaged in interstate commerce liable for injuries to or the death of their employees while on duty. . . .

Our desire was to make the Federal Government efficient as an instrument for protecting the rights of labor within its province, and therefore to secure and enforce judicial decisions which would permit us to make this desire effective. Not only some of the Federal judges, but some of the State courts invoked the Constitution in a spirit of the narrowest legalistic obstruction to prevent the government from acting in defense of labor on interstate railways. In effect, these judges took the view that while Congress had complete power as regards the goods transported by the railways, and could protect wealthy or well-to-do owners of these goods, yet that it had no power to protect the lives of the men engaged in transporting the goods. Such judges freely issued injunctions to prevent the obstruction of traffic in the interest of the property-owners, but declared unconstitutional the action of the government in seeking to safeguard the men, and the families of the men, without whose labor the traffic could not take place. It was an instance of the largely unconscious way in which the courts had been twisted into the exaltation of property rights over human rights, and the subordination of the welfare of the laborer when compared with the profit of the man for whom he labored. By what I fear my conservative friends regarded as frightfully aggressive missionary work, which included some uncommonly plain speaking as to certain unjust and antisocial judicial decisions, we succeeded in largely, but by no means altogether, correcting this view, at least so far as the best and most enlightened judges were concerned.

Very much the most important action I took as regards labor had nothing to do with legislation, and represented executive action which was not required by the Constitution. It illustrated as well as anything that I did the theory which I have called the Jackson-Lincoln theory of the presidency; that is, that occasionally great national crises arise which call for immediate and vigorous executive action, and that in such cases it is the duty of the President to act upon the theory that he is the steward of the people, and that the proper attitude for him to take is that he is bound to assume that he has the legal right to do whatever the needs of the people demand, unless the Constitution or the laws explicitly forbid him to do it.

Early in the spring of 1902 a universal strike began in the anthracite regions. The miners and the operators became deeply embittered, and the strike went on throughout the summer and the early fall without any sign of reaching an end, and with almost complete stoppage of mining. . . . In consequence, the coal famine became a national menace as the winter approached. In most big cities and many farming districts east of the Mississippi the shortage of anthracite threatened calamity. In the populous industrial States, from Ohio eastward, it was not merely calamity, but the direst disaster, that was threatened. Ordinarily conservative men, men very sensitive as to the rights of property under normal conditions, when faced by this crisis felt, quite rightly, that there must be some radical action. . . .

The big coal operators had banded together, and positively refused to take any steps looking toward an accommodation. They knew that the suffering among the miners was great; they were confident that if order were kept, and nothing further done by the government, they would win; and they refused to consider that the public had any rights in the matter. They were, for the most part, men of unquestionably good private life, and they were merely taking the extreme individualistic view of the rights of property and the freedom of individual action upheld in the *laissez-faire* political economics. The mines were in the State of Pennsylvania. There was no duty whatever laid upon me by the Constitution in the matter, and I had in theory no power to act directly unless the Governor of Pennsylvania or the legislature, if it were in session, should notify me that Pennsylvania could not keep order, and request me as Commander-in-Chief of the Army of the United States to intervene and keep order.

. . . As September passed without any sign of weakening either among the employers or the striking workmen, the situation became so grave that I felt I would have to try to do something. The thing most feasible was to get both sides to agree to a commission of arbitration, with a promise to accept its findings; the miners to go to work as soon as the commission was appointed, at the old rate of wages. To this proposition the miners, headed by John Mitchell, agreed, stipulating only that I should have power to name the commission. The operators, however, positively refused. They insisted that all that was necessary to do was for the State to keep order, using the militia as a police force; although both they and the miners asked me to intervene under the Interstate Commerce law, each side requesting that I proceed against the other, and both requests being impossible.

Finally, on October 3, the representatives of both the

operators and the miners met before me, in pursuance of my request. The representatives of the miners included as their head and spokesman John Mitchell, who kept his temper admirably and showed to much advantage. The representatives of the operators, on the contrary, came down in a most insolent frame of mind, refused to talk of arbitration or other accommodation of any kind, and used language that was insulting to the miners and offensive to me. They were curiously ignorant of the popular temper; and when they went away from the interview they, with much pride, gave their own account of it to the papers, exulting in the fact that they had "turned down" both the miners and the President.

I refused to accept the rebuff, however, and continued the effort to get an agreement between the operators and the miners. I was anxious to get this agreement, because it would prevent the necessity of taking the extremely drastic action I meditated. . . .

Fortunately, this time we were successful. Yet we were on the verge of failure, because of self-willed obstinacy on the part of the operators. This obstinacy was utterly silly from their own standpoint, and well-nigh criminal from the standpoint of the people at large. The miners proposed that I should name the commission, and that if I put on a representative of the employing class I should also put on a labor-union man. The operators positively declined to accept the suggestion. They insisted upon my naming a commission of only five men, and specified the qualifications these men should have, carefully choosing these qualifications so as to exclude those whom it had leaked out I was thinking of appointing, including Ex-President Cleveland. They made the condition that I was to appoint one officer of the engineer corps of the Army or Navy, one man with experience of mining, one "man of prominence," "eminent as a sociologist," one Federal judge of the Eastern District of Pennsylvania, and one mining engineer.

They positively refused to have me appoint any representative of labor, or to put on an extra man. I was desirous of putting on the extra man, because Mitchell and the other leaders of the miners had urged me to appoint some high Catholic ecclesiastic. Most of the miners were Catholics, and Mitchell and the leaders were very anxious to secure peaceful acquiescence by the miners in any decision rendered, and they felt that their hands would be strengthened if such an appointment were made. They also, quite properly, insisted that there should be one representative of labor on the commission, as all of the others represented the propertied classes. The operators, however, absolutely refused to acquiesce in the appointment of any representative of labor, and also announced that they would refuse to accept a sixth man on the commission; although they spoke much less decidedly on this point. The labor men left everything in my hands.

The final conferences with the representatives of the operators took place in my rooms on the evening of October 15. Hour after hour went by while I endeavored to make the operators through their representatives see that the country would not tolerate their insisting upon such conditions; but in vain. The two representatives of the operators were Robert Bacon and George W. Perkins. They were entirely reasonable. But the operators themselves were entirely unreasonable. They had worked themselves into a frame of mind where they were prepared to sacrifice everything and see civil war in the country rather than back down and acquiesce in the appointment of a representative of labor. It looked as if a deadlock were inevitable.

Then, suddenly, after about two hours' argument, it dawned on me that they were not objecting to the thing, but to the name. I found that they did not mind my appointing any man, whether he was a labor man or not, so long as he was not appointed *as* a labor man, or *as* a representative of labor; they did not object to my exercising any latitude I chose in the appointments so long as they were made under the headings they had given. I shall never forget the mixture of relief and amusement I felt when I thoroughly grasped the fact that while they would heroically submit to anarchy rather than have Tweedledum, yet if I would call it Tweedledee they would accept it with rapture; it gave me an illuminating glimpse into one corner of the mighty brains of these "captains of industry." In order to carry the great and vital point and secure agreement by both parties, all that was necessary for me to do was to commit a technical and nominal absurdity with a solemn face. This I gladly did. I announced at once that I accepted the terms laid down. With this understanding, I appointed the labor man I had all along had in view, Mr. E. E. Clark, the head of the Brotherhood of Railway Conductors, calling him an "eminent sociologist"—a term which I doubt whether he had ever previously heard. He was a first-class man, whom I afterward put on the Interstate Commerce Commission. I added to the Arbitration Commission, on my own authority, a sixth member, in the person of Bishop Spalding, a Catholic bishop, of Peoria, Ill., one of the very best men to be found in the entire country. The man whom the operators had expected me to appoint as the sociologist was Carroll Wright—who really was an eminent sociologist. I put him on as recorder of the commission, and added him as a seventh member as soon as the commission got fairly started. In publishing the list of the commissioners, when I came to Clark's appointment, I added: "As a sociologist—the President assuming that for the purposes of such a commission, the term sociologist means a man who has thought and studied deeply on social questions and has practically applied his knowledge."

The relief of the whole country was so great that the sudden appearance of the head of the Brotherhood of Railway Conductors as an "eminent sociologist" merely furnished material for puzzled comment on the part of the press. It was a most admirable commission. It did a noteworthy work, and its report is a monument in the history of the relations of labor and capital in this country. . . .

A democracy can be such in fact only if there is some rough approximation to similarity in stature among the men composing it. One of us can deal in our private lives with the grocer or the butcher or the carpenter or the chicken-raiser, or if we are the grocer or carpenter or butcher or farmer, we can deal with our customers, because *we are all of about the same size*. Therefore a simple and poor society can exist as a democracy on a basis of sheer individualism. But a rich and complex industrial society cannot so exist; for some individuals, and especially those artificial individuals called corporations, become so very big that the ordinary individual is utterly dwarfed beside them, and cannot deal with them on terms of equality. It therefore becomes necessary for these ordinary individuals to combine in their turn, first in order to act in their collective capacity through that biggest of all combinations called the government, and second, to act, also in their own self-defense, through private combinations, such as farmers' associations and trade-unions.

This the great coal operators did not see. They did not see that their property rights, which they so stoutly defended, were of the same texture as were the human rights, which they so blindly and hotly denied. They did not see that the power which they exercised by representing their stockholders was of the same texture as the power which the union leaders demanded of representing the workmen, who had democratically elected them. They did not see that the right to use one's property as one will can be maintained only so long as it is consistent with the maintenance of certain fundamental human rights, of the rights to life, liberty, and the pursuit of happiness, or, as we may restate them in these later days, of the rights of the worker to a living wage, to reasonable hours of labor, to decent working and living conditions, to freedom of thought and speech and industrial representation—in short, to a measure of industrial democracy and, in return for his arduous toil, to a worthy and decent life according to American standards. Still another thing these great business leaders did not see. They did not see that both their interests and the interests of the workers must be accommodated, and if need be, subordinated, to the fundamental permanent interests of the whole community. No man and no group of men may so exercise their rights as to deprive the nation of the things which are necessary and vital to the common life. A strike which ties up the coal-supplies of a whole section is a strike invested with a public interest. . . .

Of course, in labor controversies it was not always possible to champion the cause of the workers, because in many cases strikes were called which were utterly unwarranted and were fought by methods which cannot be too harshly condemned. No straightforward man can believe, and no fearless man will assert, that a trade-union is always right. That man is an unworthy public servant who by speech or silence, by direct statement or cowardly evasion, invariably throws the weight of his influence on the side of the trade-union, whether it is right or wrong. It has occasionally been my duty to give utterance to the feelings of all right-thinking men by expressing the most emphatic disapproval of unwise or even immoral actions by representatives of labor. The man is no true democrat, and if an American is unworthy of the traditions of his country who, in problems calling for the exercise of a moral judgment, fails to take his stand on conduct and not on class. There are good and bad wage-workers just as there are good and bad employers, and good and bad men of small means and of large means alike.

But a willingness to do equal and exact justice to all citizens, irrespective of race, creed, section, or economic interest and position, does not imply a failure to recognize the enormous economic, political, and moral possibilities of the trade-union. Just as democratic government cannot be condemned because of errors and even crimes committed by men democratically elected, so trade-unionism must not be condemned because of errors or crimes of occasional trade-union leaders. The problem lies deeper. While we must repress all illegalities and discourage all immoralities, whether of labor organizations or of corporations, we must recognize the fact that to-day the organization of labor into trade-unions and federations is necessary, is beneficent, and is one of the greatest possible agencies in the attainment of a true industrial, as well as a true political, democracy in the United States. . . .

Because of things I have done on behalf of justice to the working man, I have often been called a Socialist. Usually I have not taken the trouble even to notice the epithet. I am not afraid of names, and I am not one of those who fear to do what is right because some one else will confound me with partisans with whose principles I am not in accord. Moreover, I know that many American Socialists are high-minded and honorable citizens, who in reality are merely radical social reformers. They are oppressed by the brutalities and industrial injustices which we see everywhere about us. When I recall how often I have seen Socialists and ardent non-Socialists working side by side for some specific measure of social or industrial reform, and how I have found opposed to them on the side of privilege many shrill reactionaries who insist on calling all reformers Socialists, I refuse to be panic-stricken by having this title mistakenly applied to me.

None the less, without impugning their motives, I do disagree most emphatically with both the fundamental philosophy and the proposed remedies of the Marxian Socialists. These Socialists are unalterably opposed to our whole industrial system. They believe that the payment of wages means everywhere and inevitably an exploitation of the laborer by the employer, and that this leads inevitably to a class war between those two groups, or as they would say, between the capitalists and the proletariat. They assert that this class war is already upon us and can only be ended when capitalism is entirely destroyed and all the machines, mills, mines, railroads, and other private property used in production are confiscated, expropriated, or taken over by the workers. They do not as a rule claim— although some of the sinister extremists among them do —that this class war is a war of blood and bullets, but they do claim that there is and must be a continual struggle between two great classes, whose interests are opposed and cannot be reconciled. In this war they insist that the whole government—national, state, and local—is on the side of the employers and is used by them against the workmen, and that our law and even our common morality are class weapons, like a policeman's club or a Gatling gun.

I have never believed, and do not to-day believe, that such a class war is upon us, or need ever be upon us; nor do I believe that the interests of wage-earners and employers cannot be harmonized, compromised, and adjusted. It would be idle to deny that wage-earners have certain different economic interests from, let us say, manufacturers or importers, just as farmers have different interests from sailors, and fishermen from bankers. There is no reason why any of these economic groups should not consult their group interests by any legitimate means and with due regard to the common, over-lying interests of all. I do not even deny that the majority of wage-earners, because they have less property and less industrial security than others and because they do not own the machinery with which they work (as does the farmer), are perhaps in greater need of acting together than are other groups in the community. But I do insist (and I believe that the great majority of wage-earners take the same view) that employers and employees have overwhelming interests in common, both as partners in industry and as citizens of the Republic, and that where these interests are apart they can be adjusted by so altering our laws and their interpretation as to secure to all members of the community social and industrial justice.

I have always maintained that our worst revolutionaries to-day are those reactionaries who do not see and will not admit that there is any need for change. Such men seem to believe that the four and a half million Progressive voters, who in 1912 registered their solemn protest against our social and industrial injustices, are "anarchists," who are not willing to let ill enough alone. If these reactionaries had lived at an earlier time in our history, they would have advocated sedition laws, opposed free speech and free assembly, and voted against free schools, free access by settlers to the public lands, mechanics' lien laws, the prohibition of truck stores and the abolition of imprisonment for debt; and they are the men who to-day oppose minimum-wage laws, insurance of workmen against the ills of industrial life, and the reform of our legislators and our courts, which can alone render such measures possible. Some of these reactionaries are not bad men, but merely short-sighted and belated. It is these reactionaries, however, who, by "standing pat" on industrial injustices, incite inevitably to industrial revolt, and it is only we who advocate political and industrial democracy who render possible the progress of our American industry on large constructive lines with a minimum of friction because with a maximum of justice. . . .

It was not always easy to avoid feeling very deep anger with the selfishness and short-sightedness shown both by the representatives of certain employers' organizations and by certain great labor federations or unions. One such employers' association was called the National Association of Manufacturers. Extreme though the attacks sometimes made upon me by the extreme labor organizations were, they were not quite as extreme as the attacks made upon me by the head of the National Association of Manufacturers, and as regards their attitude toward legislation I came to the conclusion toward the end of my term that the latter had actually gone further the wrong way than did the former—and the former went a good distance also. The opposition of the National Association of Manufacturers to every rational and moderate measure for benefiting working men, such as measures abolishing child labor, or securing workmen's compensation, caused me real and grave concern; for I felt that it was ominous of evil for the whole country to have men who ought to stand high in wisdom and in guiding force take a course and use language of such reactionary type as directly to incite revolution—for this is what the extreme reactionary always does. . . .

Celebrating his victory in 1904 over the Democratic candidate Alton B. Parker, TR told his old friend the novelist Owen Wister that he could take coal operator George F. Baer in his stride. Though Baer believed that "the rights and interests of the laboring man will be protected and cared for—not by the labor agitators, but by the Christian men to whom God in his infinite wisdom has given the control of the property interests of this country," he was not half so irritating, the President thought, as the respectable intellectuals who presumed to criticize White House policies. To Wister TR wrote:

It is a peculiar gratification to me to have owed my election not to the politicians primarily, although of course I have done my best to get on with them; not to the financiers, although I have staunchly upheld the rights of property; but above all to Abraham Lincoln's "plain people"; to the folk who work hard on farm, in shop, or on the railroads, or who own little stores, little businesses which they manage themselves. I would literally not figuratively, rather cut off my right hand than forfeit by any improper act of mine the trust and regard of these people. I may have to do something of which they will diapprove, because I deem it absolutely right and necessary; but most assuredly I shall endeavor not to merit their disapproval by any act inconsistent with the ideal they have formed of me.

But the gentle folk, the people whom you and I meet at the houses of our friends and at our clubs; the people who went to Harvard as we did, or to other colleges more or less like Harvard: these people have contained many of those who have been most bitter in their opposition to me, and their support on the whole has been much more lukewarm than the support of those whom I have called the plain people. As you say, I do not at all mind what Mr. Baer or Mr. J. J. Hill or Mr. Thomas F. Ryan does in the way of opposing me. Mr. Baer was doing what I thought wrong in the coal strike. Mr. Hill was doing what I thought wrong in the Northern Securities Company. Mr. Ryan was doing what I thought wrong about the franchise tax law in New York. And I upset them all. They are all three big men and very wealthy. They are accustomed to being treated with great consideration, and they have doubtless quite sincerely come to feel that their own wisdom and rightmindedness are such that it is improper to oppose them. I do not wonder that they are bitter towards me.

But the *Evening Post* crowd, the Carl Schurz and Charles Francis Adams crowd, are hypocritical and insincere when they oppose me. They have loudly professed to demand just exactly the kind of government I have given, and yet they have done their futile best to defeat me. They have not been able to do me personally any harm; but they continually do the cause of good government a certain amount of harm by diverting into foolish channels of snarling and critical impotence the energies of fine young fellows who ought to be a power for good.

No one, not even Carl Schurz, could keep TR from promoting reforms he deemed essential to the welfare of his fellow citizens. In the summer of 1906, the President, who had always had a weakness for spelling as he pleased, plunged with all of his usual vigor into the cause of simplified spelling. He gave orders to the Public Printer to alter about 300 commonly-used words in all government publications, and retreated only when Congress threatened to debate his prerogative. To James Brander Matthews he wrote, wistfully:

I could not by fighting have kept the new spelling in, and it was evidently worse than useless to go into an undignified contest when I was beaten. Do you know I think that the one word as to which I thought the new spelling was wrong—thru—was more responsible than anything else for our discomfiture? But I am mighty glad I did the thing anyhow. In my own correspondence I shall continue using the new spelling.

Another cause for which TR fought the good fight was that of truth in nature writing. In the September, 1907 issue of Everybody's Magazine *he denounced all "nature-fakers" and took William J. Long to task for a number of errors concerning the habits of our animal friends.*

The modern "nature-faker" is . . . an object of derision to every scientist worthy of the name, to every real lover of the wilderness, to every faunal naturalist, to every true hunter or nature-lover. But it is evident that he completely deceives many good people who are wholly ignorant of wild life. Sometimes he draws on his own imagination for his fictions; sometimes he gets them second-hand from irresponsible guides or trappers or Indians. . . .

Of all these "nature-fakers," the most reckless and least responsible is Mr. Long; but there are others who run him close in the "yellow journalism of the woods," as John Burroughs has aptly called it. It would take a volume merely to catalogue the comic absurdities with which the books of these writers are filled. There is no need of discussing their theories; the point is that their alleged "facts" are not facts at all, but fancies. Their most striking stories are not merely distortions of facts, but pure inventions; and not only are they inventions, but they are inventions by men who know so little of the subject concerning which they write, and who to ignorance add such utter recklessness, that they are not even able to distinguish between what is possible, however wildly improbable, and mechanical impossibilities. Be it remembered that I am not speaking of ordinary mistakes, of ordinary errors of observation, of differences of interpretation and opinion; I am dealing only with deliberate invention, deliberate perversion of fact. . . .

In one story a wolf is portrayed as guiding home some lost children, in a spirit of thoughtful kindness; let the overtrustful individual who has girded up his loins to believe this think of the way he would receive the statement of some small farmer's boy that when lost he was guided home by a coon, a possum, or a woodchuck. Again, one of these story-book wolves, when starving, catches a red squirrel, which he takes round as a present to propitiate a bigger wolf. If any man seriously thinks a starving wolf would act in this manner, let him study hounds when feeding, even when they are not starving. . . .

. . . No man who has really studied nature in a spirit of seeking the truth, whether he be big or little, can have any controversy with these writers; it would be as absurd as to expect some genuine student of anthropology or archæology to enter into a controversy with the clumsy fabricators of the Cardiff Giant. Their books carry their own refutation; and affidavits in support of the statements they contain are as worthless as the similar affidavits once solemnly issued to show that the Cardiff "giant" was a petrified pre-Adamite man. There is now no more excuse for being deceived by their stories than for being still in doubt about the silly Cardiff hoax. . . .

Long, who refused to let the President have the last word, reported that he was impressed by an episode in Roosevelt's The Wilderness Hunter, *in which one deer was shot, and another, untouched, stayed close to watch the sportsman in action. "A nature writer would say that the deer was looking for its lost mate, but that, of course, would be a lie," Long commented. "He was merely ashamed at not letting himself be killed by so great a hunter."*

CHAPTER 14

The Monroe Doctrine
and the Panama Canal

No NATION can claim rights without acknowledging the duties that go with the rights. It is a contemptible thing for a great nation to render itself impotent in international action, whether because of cowardice or sloth, or sheer inability or unwillingness to look into the future. It is a very wicked thing for a nation to do wrong to others. But the most contemptible and most wicked course of conduct is for a nation to use offensive language or be guilty of offensive actions toward other people and yet fail to hold its own if the other nation retaliates; and it is almost as bad to undertake responsibilities and then not fulfil them. During the seven and a half years that I was President, this nation behaved in international matters toward all other nations precisely as an honorable man behaves to his fellow men. We made no promise which we could not and did not keep. We made no threat which we did not carry out. We never failed to assert our rights in the face of the

268

strong, and we never failed to treat both strong and weak
with courtesy and justice; and against the weak when they
misbehaved we were slower to assert our rights than we
were against the strong.

As a legacy of the Spanish War we were left with peculiar relations to the Philippines, Cuba, and Porto Rico,
and with an immensely added interest in Central America
and the Caribbean Sea. As regards the Philippines my
belief was that we should train them for self-government as rapidly as possible, and then leave them free to
decide their own fate. I did not believe in setting the time-
limit within which we would give them independence,
because I did not believe it wise to try to forecast how soon
they would be fit for self-government; and once having
made the promise I would have felt that it was imperative
to keep it. . . .

I do not believe that America has any special beneficial
interest in retaining the Philippines. Our work there has
benefited us only as any efficiently done work performed
for the benefit of others does incidentally help the character of those who do it. The people of the islands have
never developed so rapidly, from every standpoint, as during the years of the American occupation. The time will
come when it will be wise to take their own judgment as
to whether they wish to continue their association with
America or not. There is, however, one consideration upon
which we should insist. Either we should retain complete
control of the islands, or absolve ourselves from all responsibility for them. Any half-and-half course would be both
foolish and disastrous. . . .

We made the promise to give Cuba independence; and
we kept the promise. Leonard Wood was left in as governor for two or three years, and evolved order out of chaos,

raising the administration of the island to a level, moral and material, which it had never before achieved. We also by treaty gave the Cubans substantial advantages in our markets. Then we left the island, turning the government over to its own people. After four or five years a revolution broke out, during my administration, and we again had to intervene to restore order. We promptly sent thither a small army of pacification. Under General Barry, order was restored and kept, and absolute justice done. The American troops were then withdrawn and the Cubans re-established in complete possession of their own beautiful island, and they are in possession of it now. There are plenty of occasions in our history when we have shown weakness or inefficiency, and some occasions when we have not been as scrupulous as we should have been as regards the rights of others. But I know of no action by any other government in relation to a weaker power which showed such disinterested efficiency in rendering service as was true in connection with our intervention in Cuba.

In Cuba, as in the Philippines and as in Porto Rico, Santo Domingo, and later in Panama, no small part of our success was due to the fact that we put in the highest grade of men as public officials. This practice was inaugurated under President McKinley. I found admirable men in office, and I continued them and appointed men like them as their successors. . . .

The Philippines, Cuba, and Porto Rico came within our own sphere of governmental action. In addition to this we asserted certain rights in the western hemisphere under the Monroe Doctrine. My endeavor was not only to assert these rights, but frankly and fully to acknowledge the duties that went with the rights.

The Monroe Doctrine lays down the rule that the western hemisphere is not hereafter to be treated as subject to settlement and occupation by Old World powers. It is not international law; but it is a cardinal principle of our foreign policy. There is no difficulty at the present day in maintaining this doctrine, save where the American power whose interest is threatened has shown itself in international matters both weak and delinquent. The great and prosperous civilized commonwealths, such as the Argentine, Brazil, and Chile, in the southern half of South America, have advanced so far that they no longer stand in any position of tutelage toward the United States. They occupy toward us precisely the position that Canada occupies. Their friendship is the friendship of equals for equals. My view was that as regards these nations there was no more necessity for asserting the Monroe Doctrine than there was to assert it in regard to Canada. They were competent to assert it for themselves. Of course if one of these nations, or if Canada, should be overcome by some Old World power, which then proceeded to occupy its territory, we would undoubtedly, if the American nation needed our help, give it in order to prevent such occupation from taking place. But the initiative would come from the nation itself, and the United States would merely act as a friend whose help was invoked.

The case was (and is) widely different as regards certain—not all—of the tropical states in the neighborhood of the Caribbean Sea. Where these states are stable and prosperous, they stand on a footing of absolute equality with all other communities. But some of them have been a prey to such continuous revolutionary misrule as to have grown impotent either to do their duties to outsiders or to enforce their rights against outsiders. The United States has not the slightest desire to make aggressions on any one of these states. On the contrary, it will submit to much from them without showing resentment. . . . In the case of two states, however, affairs reached such a crisis that we had to act. These two states were Santo Domingo and the then owner of the Isthmus of Panama, Colombia.

Santo Domingo had fallen into such chaos that once for some weeks there were two rival governments in it, and a revolution was being carried on against each. At one period one government was at sea in a small gunboat, but still stoutly maintained that it was in possesion of the island and entitled to make loans and declare peace or war. The situation had become intolerable by the time that I interfered. . . .

It was the custom-houses that caused the trouble, for they offered the only means of raising money, and the revolutions were carried on to get possession of them. Accordingly I secured an agreement with the governmental authorities, who for the moment seemed best able to speak for the country, by which these custom-houses were placed under American control. The arrangement was that we should keep order and prevent any interference with the custom-houses or the places where they stood, and should collect the revenues. Forty-five per cent of the revenue was then turned over to the Santo Domingan Government, and fifty-five per cent put in a sinking fund in New York for the benefit of the creditors. The arrangement worked in capital style. On the forty-five per cent basis the Santo Domingan Government received from us a larger sum than it had ever received before when nominally all the revenue went to it. The creditors were entirely satisfied with the arrangement, and no excuse for interference by European powers remained. Occasional disturbances occurred in the island, of course, but on the whole there ensued a degree of peace and prosperity which the island had not known before for at least a century. . . .

Under these circumstances those who do not know the nature of the professional international philanthropists would suppose that these apostles of international peace would have been overjoyed with what we had done. As a matter of fact, when they took any notice of it at all it was to denounce it; and those American newspapers which are fondest of proclaiming themselves the foes of war and the friends of peace violently attacked me for averting war from, and bringing peace to, the island. They insisted I had no power to make the agreement, and demanded the rejection of the treaty which was to perpetuate the agreement. They were, of course, wholly unable to advance a single sound reason of any kind for their attitude. I suppose the real explanation was partly their dislike of me personally, and unwillingness to see peace come through or national honor upheld by me; and in the next place their sheer, simple devotion to prattle and dislike of efficiency. . . .

It cannot in the long run prove possible for the United States to protect delinquent American nations from punishment for the non-performance of their duties unless she undertakes to make them perform their duties. People may theorize about this as much as they wish, but whenever a sufficiently strong outside nation becomes sufficiently aggrieved, then either that nation will act or the United States Government itself will have to act. We were face to face at one period of my administration with this condition of affairs in Venezuela, when Germany, rather feebly backed by England, undertook a blockade against Venezuela to make Venezuela adopt the German and English view about certain agreements. There was real danger that the blockade would finally result in Germany's taking possession of certain cities or custom-houses. I succeeded, however, in getting all the parties in interest to submit their cases to the Hague Tribunal.

By far the most important action I took in foreign affairs during the time I was President related to the Panama Canal. Here again there was much accusation about my having acted in an "unconstitutional" manner—a position which can be upheld only if Jefferson's action in acquiring Louisiana be also treated as unconstitutional; and at different stages of the affair believers in a do-nothing policy denounced me as having "usurped authority"—which meant, that when nobody else could or would exercise efficient authority, I exercised it.

During the nearly four hundred years that had elapsed since Balboa crossed the Isthmus, there had been a good deal of talk about building an Isthmus Canal, and there had been various discussions of the subject and negotiations about it in Washington for the previous half-century. So far it had all resulted merely in conversation; and the time had come when unless somebody was prepared to act with decision we would have to resign ourselves to at least half a century of further conversation. Under the Hay-Pauncefote Treaty signed shortly after I became President; and thanks to our negotiations with the French Panama Company, the United States at last acquired a possession, so far as Europe was concerned, which warranted her in immediately undertaking the task. It remained to decide where the canal should be, whether along the line already pioneered by the French company in Panama, or in Nicaragua. Panama belonged to the Republic of Colombia. Nicaragua bid eagerly for the privilege of having the United States build the canal through her territory. As long as it was doubtful which route we would decide upon, Colombia extended every promise of friendly co-operation: at the Pan-American Congress in Mexico her delegate joined in the unanimous vote which requested the United States forthwith to build the canal; and at her eager request we negotiated the Hay-Herran Treaty with her, which gave us the right to build the canal across Panama. A board of experts sent to the Isthmus had reported that this route was better than the Nicaragua route, and that it would be well to build the canal over it provided we could purchase the rights of the French Company for forty million dollars; but that otherwise they would advise taking the Nicaragua route. Ever since 1846 we had had a treaty with the power then in control of the Isthmus, the Republic of New Granada, the predecessor of the Republic of Colombia and of the present Republic of Panama, by which treaty the United States was guaranteed free and open right of way across the Isthmus of Panama by any mode of communication that might be constructed, while in return our government guaranteed the perfect neutrality of the Isthmus with a view to the preservation of free transit. . . .

I took final action in 1903. During the preceding fifty-three years the governments of New Granada and of its successor, Colombia, had been in a constant state of flux; and the state of Panama had sometimes been treated as almost independent, in a loose Federal league, and sometimes as the mere property of the government at Bogota; and there had been innumerable appeals to arms, sometimes for adequate, sometimes for inadequate, reasons. . . .

Consideration of the above facts ought to be enough to show any human being that we were not dealing with normal conditions on the Isthmus and in Colombia. We were dealing with the government of an irresponsible alien dictator, and with a condition of affairs on the Isthmus itself which was marked by one uninterrupted series of outbreaks and revolutions. As for the "consent-of-the-governed" theory, that absolutely justified our action; the people on the Isthmus were the "governed"; they were governed by Colombia, without their consent, and they unanimously repudiated the Colombian Government, and demanded that the United States build the canal.

I had done everything possible, personally and through Secretary Hay, to persuade the Colombian Government to keep faith. Under the Hay-Pauncefote Treaty, it was explicitly provided that the United States should build the canal, should control, police, and protect it, and keep it open to the vessels of all nations on equal terms. We had assumed the position of guarantor of the canal, including, of course, the building of the canal, and of its peaceful use by all the world. The enterprise was recognized everywhere as responding to an international need. It was a mere travesty on justice to treat the government in possession of the Isthmus as having the right . . . to close the gates of intercourse on one of the great highways of the world. When we submitted to Colombia the Hay-Herran Treaty, it had been settled that the time for delay, the time for permitting any government of antisocial character, or of imperfect development, to bar the work, had passed. The United States had assumed in connection with the canal certain responsibilities not only to its own people, but to the civilized world which imperatively demanded that there should be no further delay in beginning the work. The Hay-Herran Treaty, if it erred at all, erred in being overgenerous toward Colombia. The people of Panama were delighted with the treaty, and the president of Co-

lombia, who embodied in his own person the entire government of Colombia, had authorized the treaty to be made.
But after the treaty had been made the Colombia Government thought it had the matter in its own hands; and the
further thought, equally wicked and foolish, came into
the heads of the people in control at Bogotá that they
would seize the French Company at the end of another
year and take for themselves the forty million dollars which
the United States had agreed to pay the Panama Canal
Company.

President Maroquin, through his minister, had agreed
to the Hay-Herran Treaty in January, 1903. He had the
absolute power of an unconstitutional dictator to keep his
promise or break it. He determined to break it. To furnish
himself an excuse for breaking it he devised the plan of
summoning a congress especially called to reject the canal
treaty. This the congress—a congress of mere puppets—
did, without a dissenting vote; and the puppets adjourned
forthwith without legislating on any other subject. . . .

When, in August, 1903, I became convinced that Colombia intended to repudiate the treaty made the preceding
January, under cover of securing its rejection by the Colombian legislature, I began carefully to consider what
should be done. By my direction, Secretary Hay, personally and through the minister at Bogotá, repeatedly
warned Colombia that grave consequences might follow
her rejection of the treaty. The possibility of ratification
did not wholly pass away until the close of the session of
the Colombian congress on the last day of October. There
would then be two possibilities. One was that Panama
would remain quiet. In that case I was prepared to recom-
mend to Congress that we should at once occupy the Isthmus anyhow, and proceed to dig the canal; and I had

drawn out a draft of my message to this effect. But from the information I received, I deemed it likely that there would be a revolution in Panama as soon as the Colombian congress adjourned without ratifying the treaty, for the entire population of Panama felt that the immediate building of the canal was of vital concern to their well-being. Correspondents of the different newspapers on the Isthmus had sent to their respective papers widely published forecasts indicating that there would be a revolution in such event.

Moreover, on October 16, . . . two army officers who had returned from the Isthmus, saw me and told me that there would unquestionably be a revolution on the Isthmus, that the people were unanimous in their criticism of the Bogotá Government and their disgust over the failure of that government to ratify the treaty; and that the revolution would probably take place immediately after the adjournment of the Colombian congress. They did not believe that it would be before October 20, but they were confident that it would certainly come at the end of October or immediately afterward, when the Colombian congress had adjourned. Accordingly I directed the Navy Department to station various ships within easy reach of the Isthmus, to be ready to act in the event of need arising.

These ships were barely in time. On November 3 the revolution occurred. Practically everybody on the Isthmus, including all the Colombian troops that were already stationed there, joined in the revolution, and there was no bloodshed. But on that same day four hundred new Colombian troops were landed at Colón. Fortunately, the gunboat *Nashville*, under Commander Hubbard, reached Colón almost immediately afterward, and when the commander of the Colombian forces threatened the lives and property of the American citizens, including women and children, in Colón, Commander Hubbard landed a few score sailors and marines to protect them. By a mixture of firmness and tact he not only prevented any assault on our citizens, but persuaded the Colombian commander to reembark his troops for Cartagena. On the Pacific side a Colombian gunboat shelled the city of Panama, with the result of killing one Chinaman—the only life lost in the whole affair.

No one connected with the American Government had any part in preparing, inciting, or encouraging the revolution, and except for the reports of our military and naval officers, which I forwarded to Congress, no one connected with the government had any previous knowledge concerning the proposed revolution, except such as was accessible to any person who read the newspapers and kept abreast of current questions and current affairs. By the unanimous action of its people, and without the firing of a shot, the state of Panama declared themselves an independent republic. The time for hesitation on our part had passed.

My belief then was, and the events that have occurred since have more than justified it, that from the standpoint of the United States it was imperative, not only for civil but for military reasons, that there should be the immediate establishment of easy and speedy communication by sea between the Atlantic and the Pacific. These reasons were not of convenience only, but of vital necessity, and did not admit of indefinite delay. The action of Colombia had shown not only that the delay would be indefinite, but that she intended to confiscate the property and rights of the French Panama Canal Company. The report of the Panama Canal Committee of the Colombian senate on

October 14, 1903, on the proposed treaty with the United States, proposed that all consideration of the matter should be postponed until October 31, 1904, when the next Colombian congress would have convened, because by that time the new Congress would be in condition to determine whether through lapse of time the French Company had not forfeited its property and rights. . . . The naked meaning of this was that Colombia proposed to wait a year, and then enforce a forfeiture of the rights and property of the French Panama Company, so as to secure the forty million dollars our government had authorized as payment to this company. If we had sat supine, this would doubtles have meant that France would have interfered to protect the company, and we should then have had on the Isthmus, not the company but France; and the gravest international complications might have ensued. Every consideration of international morality and expediency, of duty to the Panama people, and of satisfaction of our own national interests and honor, bade us take immediate action. I recognized Panama forthwith on behalf of the United States, and practically all the countries of the world immediately followed suit. The State Department immediately negotiated a canal treaty with the new republic. One of the foremost men in securing the independence of Panama, and the treaty which authorized the United States forthwith to build the canal, was M. Philippe Bunau-Varilla, an eminent French engineer formerly associated with De Lesseps and then living on the Isthmus; his services to civilization were notable, and deserve the fullest recognition.

From the beginning to the end our course was straightforward and in absolute accord with the highest of standards of international morality. Criticism of it can come only from misinformation, or else from a sentimentality which represents both mental weakness and a moral twist. To have acted otherwise than I did would have been on my part betrayal of the interests of the United States, indifference to the interests of Panama, and recreancy to the interests of the world at large. . . .

After a sufficient period of wrangling, the Senate ratified the treaty with Panama, and work on the canal was begun. The first thing that was necessary was to decide the type of canal. I summoned a board of engineering experts, foreign and native. They divided on their report. The majority of the members, including all the foreign members, approved a sea-level canal. The minority, including most of the American members, approved a lock canal. Studying these conclusions, I came to the belief that the minority was right. The two great traffic canals of the world were the Suez and the Soo. The Suez Canal is a sea-level canal, and it was the one best known to European engineers. The Soo Canal, through which an even greater volume of traffic passes every year, is a lock canal, and the American engineers were thoroughly familiar with it; whereas, in my judgment, the European engineers had failed to pay proper heed to the lessons taught by its operation and management. Moreover, the engineers who were to do the work at Panama all favored a lock canal. I came to the conclusion that a sea-level canal would be slightly less exposed to damage in the event of war; that the running expenses, apart from the heavy cost of interest on the amount necessary to build it, would be less; and that for small ships the time of transit would be less. But I also came to the conclusion that the lock canal at the proposed level would cost only about half as much to build and would be built in half the time, with much less risk; that for large ships the transit would be quicker, and that, taking into account the interest saved, the cost of maintenance would be less. Accordingly I recommended to Congress, on February 19, 1906, that a lock canal should be built, and my recommendation was adopted. Congress insisted upon having it built by a commission of several men. I tried faithfully to get good work out of the commission, and found it quite impossible; for a many-headed commission is an extremely poor executive instrument. At last I put Colonel Goethals in as head of the commission. Then, when Congress still refused to make the commission single-headed, I solved the difficulty by an executive order of January 6, 1908, which practically accomplished the object by enlarging the powers of the chairman, making all the other members of the commission dependent upon him, and thereby placing the work under one-man control. Doctor Gorgas had already performed an inestimable service by caring for the sanitary conditions so thoroughly as to make the Isthmus as safe as a health resort. Colonel Goethals proved to be the man of all others to do the job. It would be impossible to overstate what he has done. It is the greatest task of any kind that any man in the world has accomplished during the years that Colonel Goethals has been at work. It is the greatest task of its own kind that has ever been performed in the world at all. . . .

When he looked back on the building of the Panama Canal, TR found that he could not always praise Secretary of State John Hay. To Henry Cabot Lodge TR wrote early in 1909:

Hay was a man of remarkable ability. I think he was the most delightful man to talk to I ever met, for in his conversation he continually made out of hand those delightful epigrammatic remarks which we would all like to make, and which in books many people appear as making, but which in actual life hardly anyone ever does more than think about when it is too late to say them. He was moreover, I think without exception, the best letter-writer of his age; altho the present volume does not give this impression, as it is atrociously edited. His dignity, his remarkable literary ability, his personal charm, and the respect his high character and long service commanded thruout the country, together with his wide acquaintance with foreign statesmen and foreign capitals, made him one of the public servants of real value to the United States. But he was not a great Secretary of State. For instance, he was not to be mentioned in the same breath with Root. He was no administrator. He had a very ease-loving nature and a moral timidity which made him shrink from all that was rough in life, and therefore from practical affairs. He was at his best at a dinner table or in a drawing room, and in neither place have I ever seen anyone's best that was better than his; but his temptation was to associate as far as possible only with men of refined and cultivated tastes, who lived apart from the world of affairs, and who, if Americans, were wholly lacking in robustness of fiber. His close intimacy with Henry James and Henry Adams—charming men, but exceedingly undesirable companions for any man not of strong nature—and the tone of satirical cynicism which they admired, and which he always affected in writing them, marked that phase of his character which so impaired his usefulness as a public man. In public life during the time he was Secretary of State under me he accomplished little. I was personally extremely fond of him. I had a great admiration for his fastidious literary skill, and liked to listen to him; I saw much of him, and found his company a relaxation; but in the Department of State his usefulness to me was almost exclusively the usefulness of a fine figurehead. He never initiated a policy or was of real assistance in carrying thru a policy; but he sometimes phrased what I desired said in a way that was of real service; and the general respect for him was such that his presence in the Cabinet was a strength to the administration. He was always afraid of Senators and Congressmen who possess any power or robustness, this fear being due in part to timidity and nervousness, and in part to a sheer fastidiousness which made him unwilling to face the rather intimate association which is implied in a fight. Accordingly, in actual practice he hardly ever opposed a Senator or Congressman, especially in the matter of patronage, and almost always did, especially in the matter of appointment or promotion, whatever any one of them, even the worst, asked, no matter how bad it might be. The result was thoroly bad for the Department and the service, and it had the further and rather unexpected effect of making Hay himself talk against Senators and Congressmen with extraordinary violence, the Senators being the especial object of his wrath. The very fact that in action in the presence of a Senator he was always feeble, made him try to atone to his own self-respect by being very forcible about him afterwards in speech. . . .

It is distressing to read the letters in which Hay harps on how tired he is of the "sordid wrangles" he lives among; they are not the letters of a strong or brave man. He was dealing with great affairs, he was backed by me in every way. In the Panama business, after the revolution, he did good work, but not as good as Knox and Root. The vital work, getting Panama as an independent Republic, on which all else hinged, was done by me without the aid or advice of anyone, save in so far as they carried out my instructions; and without the knowledge of anyone.

CHAPTER 15

The Peace of Righteousness

THERE CAN BE no nobler cause for which to work than the peace of righteousness; and high honor is due those serene and lofty souls who with wisdom and courage, with high idealism tempered by sane facing of the actual facts of life, have striven to bring nearer the day when armed strife between nation and nation, between class and class, between man and man shall end throughout the world. Because all this is true, it is also true that there are no men more ignoble or more foolish, no men whose actions are fraught with greater possibility of mischief to their country and to mankind, than those who exalt unrighteous peace as better than righteous war. The men who have stood highest in our history, as in the history of all countries, are those who scorned injustice, who were incapable of oppressing the weak, or of permitting their country, with their consent, to oppress the weak, but who did not hesitate to draw the sword when to leave it undrawn meant inability to arrest triumphant wrong. . . .

Yet amiable but fatuous persons, with all these facts

before their eyes, pass resolutions demanding universal arbitration for everything, and the disarmament of the free civilized powers and their abandonment of their armed forces; or else they write well-meaning, solemn little books, or pamphlets or editorials, and articles in magazines or newspapers, to show that it is "an illusion" to believe that war ever pays, because it is expensive. This is precisely like arguing that we should disband the police and devote our sole attention to persuading criminals that it is "an illusion" to suppose that burglary, highway robbery, and white slavery are profitable. . . .

Throughout the seven and a half years that I was President, I pursued without faltering one consistent foreign policy, a policy of genuine international good-will and of consideration for the rights of others, and at the same time of steady preparedness. The weakest nations knew that they, no less than the strongest, were safe from insult and injury at our hands; and the strong and the weak alike also knew that we possessed both the will and the ability to guard ourselves from wrong or insult at the hands of any one.

It was under my administration that the Hague Court was saved from becoming an empty farce. It had been established by joint international agreement, but no power had been willing to resort to it. Those establishing it had grown to realize that it was in danger of becoming a mere paper court, so that it would never really come into being at all. M. d'Estournelles de Constant had been especially alive to this danger. By correspondence and in personal interviews he impressed upon me the need not only of making advances by actually applying arbitration—not merely promising by treaty to apply it—no questions that were up for settlement, but of using the Hague Tribunal for this purpose. I cordially sympathized with these views. On the recommendation of John Hay, I succeeded in getting an agreement with Mexico to lay a matter in dispute between the two republics before the Hague Court. This was the first case ever brought before the Hague Court. It was followed by numerous others; and it definitely established that court as the great international peace tribunal. By mutual agreement with Great Britain, through the decision of a joint commission, of which the American members were Senators Lodge and Turner, and Secretary Root, we were able peacefully to settle the Alaska boundary question, the only question remaining between ourselves and the British Empire which it was not possible to settle by friendly arbitration; this therefore represented the removal of the last obstacle to absolute agreement between the two peoples. We were of substantial service in bringing to a satisfactory conclusion the negotiations at Algeciras concerning Morocco. We concluded with Great Britain, and with most of the other great nations, arbitration treaties specifically agreeing to arbitrate all matters, and especially the interpretation of treaties, save only as regards questions affecting territorial integrity, national honor, and vital national interest. We made with Great Britain a treaty guaranteeing the free use of the Panama Canal on equal terms to the ships of all nations, while reserving to ourselves the right to police and fortify the Canal, and therefore to control it in time of war. Under this treaty we are in honor bound to arbitrate the question of Canal tolls for coastwise traffic between the western and eastern coasts of the United States. I believe that the American position as regards this matter is right; but I also believe that under the arbitration treaty we are in honor bound to submit the matter to arbitration in view of Great

Britain's contention—although I hold it to be an unwise contention—that our position is unsound. I emphatically disbelieve in making universal arbitration treaties which neither the makers nor any one else would for a moment dream of keeping. I no less emphatically insist that it is our duty to keep the limited and sensible arbitration treaties which we have already made. The importance of a promise lies not in making it, but in keeping it; and the poorest of all positions for a nation to occupy in such a matter is readiness to make impossible promises at the same time that there is failure to keep promises which have been made, which can be kept, and which it is discreditable to break.

During the early part of the year 1905, the strain on the civilized world caused by the Russo-Japanese War became serious. The losses of life and of treasure were frightful. From all the sources of information at hand, I grew most strongly to believe that a further continuation of the struggle would be a very bad thing for Japan, and an even worse thing for Russia. Japan was already suffering terribly from the drain upon her men, and especially upon her resources, and had nothing further to gain from continuance of the struggle; its continuance meant to her more loss than gain, even if she were victorious. Russia, in spite of her gigantic strength, was, in my judgment, apt to lose even more than she had already lost if the struggle continued. I deemed it probable that she would no more be able successfully to defend eastern Siberia and northern Manchuria than she had been able to defend southern Manchuria and Korea. If the war went on, I thought it, on the whole, likely that Russia would be driven west of Lake Baikal. But it was very far from certain. There is no certainty in such a war. Japan might have met defeat, and defeat to her would have spelled overwhelming disaster; and even if she had continued to win, what she thus won would have been of no value to her, and the cost in blood and money would have left her drained white. I believed, therefore, that the time had come when it was greatly to the interest of both combatants to have peace, and when therefore it was possible to get both to agree to peace.

I first satisfied myself that each side wished me to act, but that, naturally and properly, each side was exceedingly anxious that the other should not believe that the action was taken on its initiative. I then sent an identical note to the two powers, proposing that they should meet, through their representatives, to see if peace could not be made directly between them, and offered to act as an intermediary in bringing about such a meeting, but not for any other purpose. Each assented to my proposal in principle. There was difficulty in getting them to agree on a common meeting-place; but each finally abandoned its original contentions in the matter, and the representatives of the two nations finally met at Portsmouth, in New Hampshire. I previously received the two delegations at Oyster Bay on the U. S. S. *Mayflower*, which, together with another naval vessel, I put at their disposal, on behalf of the United States Government, to take them from Oyster Bay to Portsmouth.

As in customary—but both unwise and undesirable in such cases, each side advanced claims which the other could not grant. The chief difficulty came because of Japan's demand for a money indemnity. I felt that it would be better for Russia to pay some indemnity than to go on with the war, for there was little chance, in my judgment, of the war turning out favorably for Russia, and the revolutionary movement already under way bade fair to overthrow the negotiations entirely. I advised the Russian Government to this effect, at the same time urging them to abandon their pretensions on certain other points, notably concerning the southern half of Saghalien, which the Japanese had taken. I also, however, and equally strongly, advised the Japanese that in my judgment it would be the gravest mistake on their part to insist on continuing the war for the sake of a money indemnity; for Russia was absolutely firm in refusing to give them an indemnity, and the longer the war continued the less able she would be to pay. I pointed out that there was no possible analogy between their case and that of Germany in the war with France, which they were fond of quoting. The Germans held Paris and half of France, and gave up much territory in lieu of the indemnity, whereas the Japanese were still many thousand miles from Moscow, and had no territory whatever which they wished to give up. I also pointed out that in my judgment whereas the Japanese had enjoyed the sympathy of most of the civilized powers at the outset of and during the continuance of the war, they would forfeit it if they turned the war into one merely for getting money —and, moreover, they would almost certainly fail to get the money, and would simply find themselves at the end of a year, even if things prospered with them, in possession of territory they did not want, having spent enormous additional sums of money, and lost enormous additional numbers of men, and yet without a penny of remuneration. The treaty of peace was finally signed.

As is inevitable under such circumstances, each side felt that it ought to have got better terms; and when the danger was well past each side felt that it had been overreached by the other, and that if the war had gone on it would have gotten more than it actually did get. The Japanese

Government had been wise throughout, except in the matter of announcing that it would insist on a money indemnity. Neither in national nor in private affairs is it ordinarily advisable to make a bluff which cannot be put through—personally, I never believe in doing it under any circumstances. The Japanese people had been misled by this bluff of their government; and the unwisdom of the government's action in the matter was shown by the great resentment the treaty aroused in Japan, although it was so beneficial to Japan. There were various mob outbreaks, especially in the Japanese cities; the police were roughly handled, and several Christian churches were burned, as reported to me by the American minister. In both Russia and Japan I believe that the net result as regards myself was a feeling of injury, and of dislike of me, among the people at large. I had expected this; I regarded it as entirely natural; and I did not resent it in the least. The governments of both nations behaved toward me not only with correct and entire propriety, but with much courtesy and the fullest acknowledgment of the good effect of what I had done; and in Japan, at least, I believe that the leading men sincerely felt that I had been their friend. I had certainly tried my best to be the friend not only of the Japanese people but of the Russian people, and I believe that what I did was for the best interests of both and of the world at large.

During the course of the negotiations I tried to enlist the aid of the governments of one nation which was friendly to Russia, and of another nation which was friendly to Japan, in helping bring about peace. I got no aid from either. I did, however, receive aid from the Emperor of Germany. His ambassador at St. Petersburg was the one ambassador who helped the American ambassador,

Mr. Meyer, at delicate and doubtful points of the negotiations. Mr. Meyer, who was, with the exception of Mr. White, the most useful diplomat in the American service, rendered literally invaluable aid by insisting upon himself seeing the Czar at critical periods of the transaction, when it was no longer possible for me to act successfully through the representatives of the Czar, who were often at cross-purposes with one another.

As a result of the Portsmouth peace, I was given the Nobel Peace Prize. This consisted of a medal, which I kept, and a sum of forty thousand dollars, which I turned over as a foundation of industrial peace to a board of trustees which included Oscar Straus, Seth Low, and John Mitchell. In the present state of the world's development industrial peace is even more essential than international peace; and it was fitting and appropriate to devote the peace prize to such a purpose. . . .

In my own judgment the most important service that I rendered to peace was the voyage of the battle fleet round the world. I had become convinced that for many reasons it was essential that we should have it clearly understood, by our own people especially, but also by other peoples, that the Pacific was as much our home waters as the Atlantic, and that our fleet could and would at will pass from one to the other of the two great oceans. It seemed to me evident that such a voyage would greatly benefit the navy itself; would arouse popular interest in and enthusiasm for the navy; and would make foreign nations accept as a matter of course that our fleet should from time to time be gathered in the Pacific, just as from time to time it was gathered in the Atlantic, and that its presence in one ocean was no more to be accepted as a mark of hostility to any Asiatic power than its presence in the Atlantic was to be accepted as a mark of hostility to any European power. I determined on the move without consulting the Cabinet, precisely as I took Panama without consulting the Cabinet. . . .

When I left the Presidency I finished seven and a half years of administration, during which not one shot had been fired against a foreign foe. We were at absolute peace, and there was no nation in the world with whom a war cloud threatened, no nation in the world whom we had wronged, or from whom we had anything to fear. The cruise of the battle fleet was not the least of the causes which insured so peaceful an outlook. . . .

When TR came to estimate the results of the Algeciras Conference of 1906, in which the United States sided with France over the question of German influence in Morocco, he found he owed a special debt to the tact and vision of Jean-Jules Jusserand, the French Ambassador to Washington. To Jusserand he wrote:

It is the simple and literal truth to say that in my judgment we owe it to you more than to any other one man that the year which has closed has not seen a war between France and Germany, which, had it begun, would probably have extended to take in a considerable portion of the world. In last May and June the relations between the two countries were so strained that such a war was imminent. Probably the only way it could have been avoided was by an international conference, and such a conference could only have been held on terms compatible with France's honor and dignity. You were the man most instrumental in having just this kind of conference arranged for. I came into the matter at all most unwillingly, and I could not have come into it at all if I had not possessed entire confidence alike in your unfailing soundness of judgment and in your high integrity of personal conduct. Thanks to the fact that these are the two dominant notes in your personality my relationship with you has been such as I think has very, very rarely obtained between any ambassador at any time and the head of the government to which that ambassador was accredited; and certainly no ambassador and no head of a government could ever stand to one another on a footing at once more pleasant and more advantageous to their respective countries than has been the case with you and me. If, in these delicate Morocco negotiations, I had not been able to treat you with the absolute frankness and confidence that I did, no good result could possibly have been obtained; and this frankness and confidence were rendered possible only because of the certainty that you would do and advise what was wisest to be done and advised, and that you would treat all that was said and done between us two as a gentleman of the highest honor treats what is said and done in the intimate personal relations of life. If you had been capable of adopting one line of conduct as a private individual and another as a public man I should have been wholly unable to assume any such relations with you; nor, on the other hand, however high your standard of honor, could I have assumed them had I not felt complete confidence in the soundness and quickness of your judgment. The service you rendered was primarily one to France, but it was also a service to the world at large; and in rendering it you bore yourself as the ideal public servant should bear himself; for such a public servant should with trained intelligence know how

296 THE AUTOBIOGRAPHY OF THEODORE ROOSEVELT

to render the most effective service to his own country while yet never deviating by so much as a hand's breadth from the code of mutual good faith and scrupulous regard for the rights of others, which should obtain between nations no less than between gentlemen. I do not suppose that you will ever gain any personal advantage, and perhaps not even any personal recognition, because of what you have done in the past year; but I desire that you should at least know my appreciation of it.

The fact that he had won the Nobel Prize for peace did not mean that he had turned into a professional pacifist, TR reminded Carl Schurz:

I thank you for your congratulations. As to what you say about disarmament—which I suppose is the rough equivalent of "the gradual diminution of the oppressive burdens imposed upon the world by armed peace"—I am not clear either what can be done or what ought to be done. If I had been known as one of the conventional type of peace advocates I could have done nothing whatever in bringing about peace now, I would be powerless in the future to accomplish anything, and I would not have been able to help confer the boons upon Cuba, the Philippines, Porto Rico and Panama, brought about by our action therein. If the Japanese had not armed during the last twenty years, this would indeed be a sorrowful century for Japan. If this country had not fought the Spanish War; if we had failed to take the action we did about Panama; all mankind would have been the loser. While the Turks were butchering the Armenians the European powers kept the peace and thereby added a burden of infamy to the Nineteenth Century, for in keeping that peace a greater number of lives were lost than in any European war since the days of Napoleon, and these lives were those of women and children as well as of men; while the moral degradation, the brutality inflicted and endured, the aggregate of hideous wrong done, surpassed that of any war of which we have record in modern times. Until people get it firmly fixed in their minds that peace is valuable chiefly as a means to righteousness, and that it can only be considered as an end when it also coincides with righteousness, we can do only a limited amount to advance its coming on this earth. . . .

This does not in the least mean that it is hopeless to make the effort. It may be that some scheme will be developed. America, fortunately, can cordially assist in such an effort, for no one in his senses would suggest our disarmament; and though we should continue to perfect our small navy and our minute army, I do not think it necessary to increase the number of our ships—at any rate as things look now—nor the number of our soldiers. Of course our navy must be kept up to the highest point of efficiency, and the replacing of old and worthless vessels by first-class new ones may involve an increase in the personnel; but not enough to interfere with our action along the lines you have suggested. But before I would know how to advocate such action, save in some such way as commending it to the attention of The Hague Tribunal, I would have to have a feasible and rational plan of action presented.

CHAPTER 16

Hunter and Historian

When TR turned over the White House in the spring of 1909 to his then good friend William Howard Taft, nothing was further from his thoughts than a life of sloth and ease. On March 23 TR and his son Kermit set sail from New York on the Hamburg *for the first lap of their journey to Africa. In* African Game Trails *the former President told the story of his hunt for rhinoceroses, hippopotamuses, elephants and lions. Here is his account of the killing of a lion on the Kapiti Plains:*

ONE DAY we started from the ranch-house in good season for an all-day lion-hunt. Besides Kermit and myself, there was a fellow guest, Medlicott, and not only our host, but our hostess and her daughter; and we were joined by Percival at lunch, which we took under a great fig-tree, at the foot of a high, rocky hill. Percival had with him a little mongrel bulldog, and a Masai "boy," a fine, bold-looking savage, with a handsome head-dress and the usual formida-

298

ble spear; master, man, and dog evidently all looked upon any form of encounter with lions simply in the light of a spree.

After lunch we began to beat down a long donga, or dry watercourse—a creek, as we should call it in the Western plains country. The watercourse with low, steep banks wound in curves, and here and there were patches of brush, which might contain anything in the shape of lion, cheetah, hyena, or wild dog. Soon we came upon lion spoor in the sandy bed; first the footprints of a big male, then those of a lioness. We walked cautiously along each side of the donga, the horses following close behind so that if the lion were missed we could gallop after him and round him up on the plain. The dogs—for besides the little bull, we had a large brindled mongrel named Ben, whose courage belied his looks—began to show signs of scenting the lion; and we beat out each patch of brush, the natives shouting and throwing in stones, while we stood with the rifles where we could best command any probable exit. After a couple of false alarms the dogs drew toward one patch, their hair bristling, and showing such eager excitement that it was evident something big was inside; and in a moment one of the boys called, "simba" (lion), and pointed with his finger. It was just across the little ravine, there about four yards wide and as many feet deep; and I shifted my position, peering eagerly into the bushes for some moments before I caught a glimpse of tawny hide; as it moved, there was a call to me to "shoot," for at that distance, if the lion charged, there would be scant time to stop it; and I fired into what I saw. There was a commotion in the bushes, and Kermit fired; and immediately afterward there broke out on the other side, not the hoped-for big lion, but two cubs the size of mastiffs. Each was badly wounded and we finished them off; even if unwounded they were too big to take alive.

This was a great disappointment, and as it was well on in the afternoon, and we had beaten the country most apt to harbor our game, it seemed unlikely that we would have another chance. Percival was on foot and a long way from his house, so he started for it; and the rest of us also began to jog homeward. But Sir Alfred, although he said nothing, intended to have another try. After going a mile or two he started off to the left at a brisk canter; and we, the other riders, followed, leaving behind our gun-bearers, saises, and porters. A couple of miles away was another donga, another shallow watercourse with occasional big brush patches along the winding bed; and toward this we cantered. Almost as soon as we reached it our leader found the spoor of two big lions; and with every sense acock, we dismounted and approached the first patch of tall bushes. We shouted and threw in stones, but nothing came out; and another small patch showed the same result. Then we mounted our horses again, and rode toward another patch a quarter of a mile off. I was mounted on Tranquillity, the stout and quiet sorrel.

This patch of tall, thick brush stood on the hither bank —that is, on our side of the watercourse. We rode up to it and shouted loudly. The response was immediate, in the shape of loud gruntings, and crashings through the thick brush. We were off our horses in an instant, I throwing the reins over the head of mine; and without delay the good old fellow began placidly grazing, quite unmoved by the ominous sounds immediately in front.

I sprang to one side; and for a second or two we waited, uncertain whether we should see the lions charging out

ten yards distant or running away. Fortunately, they
adopted the latter course. Right in front of me, thirty
yards off, there appeared, from behind the bushes which
had first screened him from my eyes, the tawny, galloping
form of a big maneless lion. Crack! the Winchester spoke;
and as the soft-nosed bullet ploughed forward through his
flank the lion swerved so that I missed him with the second
shot; but my third bullet went through the spine and forward into his chest. Down he came, sixty yards off, his hind
quarters dragging, his head up, his ears back, his jaws open
and lips drawn up in a prodigious snarl, as he endeavored
to turn to face us. His back was broken; but of this we
could not at the moment be sure, and if it had merely been
grazed, he might have recovered, and then, even though
dying, his charge might have done mischief. So Kermit, Sir
Alfred, and I fired, almost together, into his chest. His
head sank, and he died.

This lion had come out on the left of the bushes; the
other, to the right of them, had not been hit, and we saw
him galloping off across the plain, six or eight hundred
yards away. A couple more shots missed, and we mounted
our horses to try to ride him down. The plain sloped gently
upward for three-quarters of a mile to a low crest or divide,
and long before we got near him he disappeared over this.
Sir Alfred and Kermit were tearing along in front and to
the right, with Miss Pease close behind; while Tranquillity
carried me, as fast as he could, on the left, with Medlicott
near me. On topping the divide Sir Alfred and Kermit
missed the lion, which had swung to the left, and they
raced ahead too far to the right. Medlicott and I, however,
saw the lion, loping along close behind some kongoni; and
this enabled me to get up to him as quickly as the lighter
men on the faster horses. The going was now slightly

downhill, and the sorrel took me along very well, while Medlicott, whose horse was slow, bore to the right and joined the other two men. We gained rapidly, and, finding out this, the lion suddenly halted and came to bay in a slight hollow, where the grass was rather long. The plain seemed flat, and we could see the lion well from horseback; but, especially when he lay down, it was most difficult to make him out on foot, and impossible to do so when kneeling.

We were about a hundred and fifty yards from the lion, Sir Alfred, Kermit, Medlicott, and Miss Pease off to one side, and slightly above him on the slope, while I was on the level, about equidistant from him and them. Kermit and I tried shooting from the horses; but at such a distance this was not effective. Then Kermit got off, but his horse would not let him shoot; and when I got off I could not make out the animal through the grass with sufficient distinctness to enable me to take aim. Old Ben the dog had arrived, and, barking loudly, was strolling about near the lion, which paid him not the slightest attention. At this moment my black sais, Simba, came running up to me and took hold of the bridle; he had seen the chase from the line of march and had cut across to join me. There was no other sais or gun-bearer anywhere near, and his action was plucky, for he was the only man afoot, with the lion at bay. Lady Pease had also ridden up and was an interested spectator only some fifty yards behind me.

Now, an elderly man with a varied past which includes rheumatism does not vault lightly into the saddle; as his sons, for instance, can; and I had already made up my mind that in the event of the lion's charging it would be wise for me to trust to straight powder rather than to try to scramble into the saddle and get under way in time. The arrival of my two companions settled matters. I was not sure of the speed of Lady Pease's horse; and Simba was on foot and it was of course out of the question for me to leave him. So I said, "Good, Simba, now we'll see this thing through," and gentle-mannered Simba smiled a shy appreciation of my tone, though he could not understand the words. I was still unable to see the lion when I knelt, but he was now standing up, looking first at one group of horses and then at the other, his tail lashing to and fro, his head held low, and his lips dropped over his mouth in peculiar fashion, while his harsh and savage growling rolled thunderously over the plain. Seeing Simba and me on foot, he turned toward us, his tail lashing quicker and quicker. Resting my elbow on Simba's bent shoulder, I took steady aim and pressed the trigger; the bullet went in between the neck and shoulder, and the lion fell over on his side, one fore leg in the air. He recovered in a moment and stood up, evidently very sick, and once more faced me, growling hoarsely. I think he was on the eve of charging. I fired again at once, and this bullet broke his back just behind the shoulders; and with the next I killed him outright, after we had gathered round him.

TR might not always bring down a lion with the first shot, but he could always take comfort with a good book. He brought with him a formidable number of volumes. Here is his listing of the famous "Pigskin Library":

BIBLE
APOCRYPHA
BORROW: *Bible in Spain. Zingali. Lavengro. Wild Wales. The Romany Rye*

SHAKESPEARE
SPENCER: *Faerie Queene*
MARLOWE
MAHAN: *Sea Power*
MACAULAY: *History. Essays. Poems*
HOMER: *Iliad. Odyssey*
CHANSON DE ROLAND
NIBELUNGENLIED
CARLYLE: *Frederick the Great*
SHELLEY: *Poems*
BACON: *Essays*
LOWELL: *Literary Essays. Biglow Papers*
EMERSON: *Poems*
LONGFELLOW
TENNYSON
POE: *Tales. Poems*
KEATS
MILTON: *Paradise Lost (Books I and II)*
DANTE: *Inferno (Carlyle's translation)*
HOLMES: *Autocrat. Over the Teacups*
BRET HARTE: *Poems. Tales of the Argonauts. Luck of Roaring Camp*
BROWNING: *Selections*
CROTHERS: *Gentle Reader. Pardoner's Wallet*
MARK TWAIN: *Huckleberry Finn. Tom Sawyer*
BUNYAN: *Pilgrim's Progress*
EURIPIDES (*Murray's translation*): *Hippolytus. Bacchæ*
THE FEDERALIST
GREGOROVIUS: *Rome*
SCOTT: *Legend of Montrose. Guy Mannering. Waverley. Rob Roy. Antiquary*
COOPER: *Pilot. Two Admirals*
FROISSART

PERCY'S RELIQUES
THACKERAY: *Vanity Fair. Pendennis*
DICKENS: *Mutual Friend. Pickwick*

. . . In addition to the books originally belonging to the "library," various others were from time to time added; among them, "Alice in Wonderland" and "Through the Looking-Glass" Dumas's "Louves de Machekoule," "Tartarin de Tarascon" (not until after I had shot my lions!), Maurice Egan's "The Wiles of Sexton Maginnis," James Lane Allen's "Summer in Arcady," William Allen White's "A Certain Rich Man," George Meredith's "Farina," and d'Aurevilly's "Chevalier des Touches." I also had sent out to me Darwin's "Origin of Species" and "Voyage of the Beagle," Huxley's Essays, Frazer's "Passages from the Bible," Braithwaite's "Book of Elizabethan Verse," FitzGerald's "Omar Khayyám," Gobineau's "Inégalité des Races Humaines" (a well-written book, containing some good guesses; but for a student to approach it for serious information would be much as if an albatross should apply to a dodo for an essay on flight), "Don Quixote," Montaigne, Molière, Goethe's "Faust," Green's "Short History of the English People," Pascal, Voltaire's "Siècle de Louis XIV," the "Mémoires de St. Simon" (to read on the way home), and "The Soul's Inheritance," by George Cabot Lodge. Where possible I had them bound in pigskin. They were for use, not ornament. I almost always had some volume with me, either in my saddle-pocket or in the cartridge-bag which one of my gun-bearers carried to hold odds and ends. Often my reading would be done while resting under a tree at noon, perhaps beside the carcass of a beast I had killed, or else while waiting for camp to be pitched; and in either case it might be impossible to get water for washing. In consequence the books were stained with blood, sweat, gun-oil, dust, and ashes; ordinary bindings either vanished or became loathsome, whereas pigskin merely grew to look as a well-used saddle looks.

Now, it ought to be evident, on a mere glance at the complete list, both that the books themselves are of unequal value and also that they were chosen for various reasons, and for this particular trip. Some few of them I would take with me on any trip of like length; but the majority I should of course change for others—as good and no better—were I to start on another such trip. On trips of various length in recent years I have taken, among many other books, the "Memoirs of Marbot," Æschylus, Sophocles, Aristotle, Joinville's "History of St. Louis," the Odyssey (Palmer's translation), volumes of Gibbon and Parkman, Lounsbury's Chaucer, Theocritus, Lea's "History of the Inquisition," Lord Acton's Essays, and Ridgeway's "Prehistoric Greece." Once I took Ferrero's "History of Rome," and liked it so much that I got the author to come to America and stay at the White House; once De La Gorce's "History of the Second Republic and Second Empire"—an invaluable book. I did not regard these books as better or worse than those I left behind; I took them because at the moment I wished to read them. The choice would largely depend upon what I had just been reading. This time I took Euripides, because I had just been reading Murray's "History of the Greek Epic."* Having become interested in Mahaffy's essays on Helenistic Greece, I took Polybius on my next trip; having just read Benjamin Ide

* I am writing on the White Nile from memory; the titles I give may sometimes be inaccurate, and I cannot, of course, begin to remember all the books I have at different times taken out with me.—T. R.

Wheeler's "History of Alexander," I took Arrian on my next hunt; something having started me reading German poetry, I once took Schiller, Koerner, and Heine to my ranch; another time I started with a collection of essays on and translations from early Irish poetry; yet another time I took Morris's translations of various Norse Sagas, including the Heimskringla, and liked them so much that I then incautiously took his translation of Beowulf, only to find that while it had undoubtedly been translated out of Anglo-Saxon, it had not been translated into English, but merely into a language bearing a specious resemblance thereto. Once I took Sutherland's "History of the Growth of the Moral Instinct"; but I did not often take sicentific books, simply because as yet scientific books rarely have literary value. Of course a really good scientific book should be as interesting to read as any other good book; and the volume in question was taken because it fulfilled this requirement, its eminent Australian author being not only a learned but a brilliant man.

I as emphatically object to nothing but heavy reading as I do to nothing but light reading—all that is indispensable being that the heavy and the light reading alike shall be both interesting and wholesome. So I have always carried novels with me, including, as a rule, some by living authors, but (unless I had every confidence in the author) only if I had already read the book. Among many, I remember offhand a few such as "The Virginian," "Lin McLean," "Puck of Pook's Hill," "Uncle Remus," "Aaron of the Wild Woods," "Letters of a Self-made Merchant to His Son," "Many Cargoes," "The Gentleman from Indiana," "David Harum," "The Crisis," "The Silent Places," "Marse Chan," "Soapy Sponge's Sporting Tour," "All on the Irish Shore," "The Blazed Trail," "Stratagems and Spoils,"

"Knights in Fustian," "Selma," "The Taskmasters," Edith Wyatt's "Every Man to His Humor," the novels and stories of Octave Thanet—I wish I could remember more of them, for personally I have certainly profited as much by reading really good and interesting novels and stories as by reading anything else, and from the contemporary ones I have often reached, as in no other way I could have reached, an understanding of how real people feel in certain country districts, and in certain regions of great cities like Chicago and New York.

Of course I also generally take out some of the novels of those great writers of the past whom one can read over and over again; and occasionally one by some writer who was not great—like "The Semi-attached Couple,"* a charming little early-Victorian . . . tale which I suppose other people cannot like as I do, or else it would be reprinted.

Above all, let me insist that the books which I have taken were and could only be a tiny fraction of those for which I cared and which I continually read, and that I care for them neither more nor less than for those I left at home. I took "The Deluge" and "Pan Michael" and "Flight of a Tartar Tribe," because I had just finished "Fire and Sword"; "Moby Dick," because I had been rereading "Omoo" and "Typee"; Gogol's "Taras Bulba," because I wished to get the Cossack view of what was described by Sienkiewicz from the Polish side; some of Maurice Jokai, and "St. Peter's Umbrella" (I am not at all sure about the titles), because my attention at the moment was on Hungary; and the novels of Topelius when I happened to be thinking of Finland. I took Dumas's cycle of romances

* "The Semi-attached Couple," by the author of "The Semi-detached House" (the Hon. Emily Eden).

dealing with the French Revolution, because I had just finished Carlyle's work thereon—and I felt that of the two the novelist was decidedly the better historian. I took "Salammbo" and "The Nabob" rather than scores of other French novels simply because at the moment I happened to see them and think that I would like to read them. I doubt if I ever took anything of Hawthorne's, but this was certainly not because I failed to recognize his genius.

Now, all this means that I take with me on any trip, or on all trips put together, but a very small proportion of the books that I like; and that I like very many and very different kinds of books, and do not for a moment attempt anything so preposterous as a continual comparison between books which may appeal to totally different sets of emotions. For instance, one correspondent pointed out to me that Tennyson was "trivial" compared to Browning, and another complained that I had omitted Walt Whitman; another asked why I put Longfellow "on a level" with Tennyson. I believe I did take Walt Whitman on one hunt, and I like Browning, Tennyson, and Longfellow, all of them, without thinking it necessary to compare them. It is largely a matter of personal taste. In a recent English review I glanced at an article on English verse to-day in which, after enumerating various writers of the first and second classes, the writer stated that Kipling was at the head of the third class of "ballad-mongers"; it happened that I had never even heard of most of the men he mentioned in the first two classes, whereas I should be surprised to find that there was any one of Kipling's poems which I did not already know. I do not quarrel with the taste of the critic in question, but I see no reason why any one should be guided by it. So with Longfellow. A man who dislikes or looks down upon simple poetry, ballad poetry, will not care for Longfellow; but if he really cares for "Chevy Chase," "Sir Patrick Spens," "Twa Corbies," Michael Drayton's "Agincourt," Scott's "Harlaw," "Eve of St. John," and the Flodden fight in "Marmion," he will be apt to like such poems as the "Saga of King Olaf," "Othere," "The Driving Cloud," "Belisarius," "Helen of Tyre," "Enceladus," "The Warden of the Cinque Ports," "Paul Revere," and "Simon Danz." I am exceedingly fond of these, and of many, many other poems of Longfellow. This does not interfere in the least with my admiration for "Ulysses," "The Revenge," "The Palace of Art," the little poems in "The Princess," and in fact most of Tennyson. Nor does my liking for Tennyson prevent my caring greatly for "Childe Roland," "Love Among the Ruins," "Proteus," and nearly all the poems that I can understand, and some that I can merely guess at, in Browning. I do not feel the slightest need of trying to apply a common measuring-rule to these three poets, any more than I find it necessary to compare Keats with Shelley, or Shelley with Poe. I enjoy them all. . . .

On his return from Africa TR toured Europe and attended the State Funeral of King Edward VII. On his way he paid a call in Berlin on Kaiser Wilhelm II, of whom he once remarked: "I do admire him, very much as I do a grizzly bear."

In this letter to the British historian Sir George Otto Trevelyan, TR gives his impressions of Imperial Germany, and of His Imperial Majesty Wilhelm II.

At Berlin and in Germany I was well received, that is, the Emperor and all the people high up were more than cordial. So were the professors and the people of the university and the scientific men generally; and the crowds were civil. But it was curious and interesting to notice the contrast between my reception in Germany and my reception in the other countries of Europe which I had already visited or visited afterwards. Everywhere else I was received, as I have said, with practically as much enthusiasm as in my own country when I was President. In Germany I was treated with proper civility, all the civility which I had a right to demand and expect; and no more. In Paris the streets were decorated with French and American flags in my honor, and when I went to the theatre at the Français everyone rose and applauded so that I had to get up in the box and bow repeatedly, first to the actors, who had stopped the piece, and then to the audience. In Berlin the authorities showed me every courtesy, and the people all proper civility. But excepting the university folk, they really did not want to see me. When I left Sweden I left a country where tens of thousands of people gathered on every occasion to see me; every station was jammed with them. When I came into Germany a few hundred might be at each station, or might not be. They were courteous, decorously enthusiastic, and that was all. It was just the same on our trip from Berlin to London. We were given the royal carriage, and every attention shown us by the officials; at each station there were a few score or a few hundred people, polite and mildly curious. Late in the evening we crossed into Holland; and at the first place we stopped there was a wildly enthusiastic mob of ten thousand people cheering and calling. The Swedes and Hollanders, and indeed as I have said the people of all the other countries I visited, felt a quite unwarranted feeling of interest in and liking for me, because to them I symbolized my country, and my country symbolized something that stirred them. The Germans did not like me, and did not like my country; and under the circumstances they behaved entirely correctly, showing me every civility and making no pretense of an enthusiasm which was not present. I do not know quite what the reason of the contrast was; but it was evident that, next to England, America was very unpopular in Germany. The upper classes, stiff, domineering, formal, with the organized army, the organized bureaucracy, the organized industry of their great, highly civilized and admirably administered country behind them, regarded America with a dislike which was all the greater because they could not make it merely contempt. They felt that we were entirely unorganized, that we had no business to be formidable rivals at all in view of our loose democratic governmental methods, and that it was exasperating to feel that our great territory, great natural resources, and strength of individual initiative enabled us in spite of our manifold shortcomings to be formidable industrial rivals of Germany; and, more incredible still, that thanks to our Navy and our ocean-protected position, we were in a military sense wholly independent and slightly defiant; and they felt that I typified the nation they disliked, and, more especially, that as a volunteer soldier and an adventurer who had fought for his own hand and had risen in irregular ways, I typified the very qualities to which they objected. Moreover, the German upper classes, alone among the European upper classes—so far as I knew—really did not like the social type I represented. . . .

Of course my chief interest at Berlin was in the Emperor himself. He is an able and powerful man. The first day we went out to take lunch with him. Afterwards he drove us to Potsdam, and showed us over Sans Souci. He also held army maneuvers at which I was present. On this occasion I rode with him for about five hours, and he talked steadily; and on another afternoon we spent three hours together. He was much interested to find how he was looked at by outsiders, and finally put a practically direct question to me as to how he was regarded in America; and I answered, "Well! your Majesty, I don't know whether you will understand our political terminology; but in America we think that if you lived on our side of the water you would carry your ward and turn up at the convention with your delegation behind you—and I cannot say as much for most of your fellow soverigns!" Of course this needed a little explanation, but he was immensely pleased and amused with it when he understood it. He has a real sense of humor, as is shown by the comments he wrote on the backs of the photographs he sent me, which had been taken of us while we were at the maneuvers by his court photographer. Moreover, he is entirely modest about the many things which he thoroughly knows, such as the industrial and military conditions and needs of Germany. But he lacks all sense of humor when he comes to discuss the things that he does not know, and which he prides himself upon knowing such as matters artistic and scientific. In the fundamentals of domestic morality, and as regards all that side of religion which is moral, we agreed heartily; but there is a good deal of dogmatic theology which to him means much and to me is entirely meaningless; and on the other hand, as is inevitable with a man brought up in the school of Frederick the Great and Bismarck—in contrast to anyone whose heroes are men like Timoleon, John Hampden, Washington, and Lincoln—there were many points in international morality where he and I were completely asunder. But at least we agreed in a cordial dislike of shams and of pretense, and therefore in a cordial dislike of the kind of washy movement for international peace with which Carnegie's name has become so closely associated. The Emperor, as was natural and proper, took a certain sardonic amusement in the fact that the Czar had started the two international peace congresses at The Hague, and between times had fought a needless and unsuccessful war, had seen his country indulge in most revolting massacres of the Jews, had kept Poland under his heel, and had shamefully broken faith with, and prepared for the infamous subjection of, poor little Finland. I do not wonder that cynics take unalloyed enjoyment out of the antics of those professional peace people who have discovered in Russia their champion and ideal.

The Emperor, as everyone knows, talks with the utmost freedom with almost everyone. I especially desired to talk with him about the relations of Germany with England, and these he discussed eagerly and at great length. Moreover, I believe he spoke exactly his mind. He is not down at bottom anything like as hostile to England as his brother Prince Henry, of whom he is rather jealous, by the way. Prince Henry is, I believe, a more really powerful man than the Kaiser, and a more cold-blooded man; and talking with him afterwards I was by no means sure that he did not have clearly in mind the chance of some day using the German fleet against England if exactly the right opportunity arose, simply on the theory that might rules, and that the one capital crime in international matters is weakness. The Kaiser, however, I am confident, never postulates to himself such an idea as the conquest of England. This does not mean that I regard his attitude toward England as free from menace. I do not believe that Germany consciously and of set purpose proposes to herself the idea of a conquest of England, but Germany has the arrogance of a very strong power, as yet almost untouched by that feeble aspiration towards international equity which one or two other strong powers, notably England and America, do at least begin to feel. Germany would like to have a navy (so) strong that whenever England does something she does not like she could at once assume towards England the tone she has assumed toward France. The Morocco incident shows how far Germany is willing to go in doing what she believes her interest and her destiny demand, in disregard of her own engagements and of the equities of other peoples. If she had a Navy as strong as that of England, I do not believe that she would *intend* to use it for the destruction of England; but I do believe that incidents would be very likely to occur which might make her so use it.

I said to the Emperor that it seemed to me that a war between England and Germany would be an unspeakable calamity. He answered eagerly that he quite agreed with me, that such a war he regarded as unthinkable; and he continued "I was brought up in England, very largely; I feel myself partly an Englishman. Next to Germany I care more for England than for any other country." Then with intense emphasis, "I ADORE ENGLAND!" I said that this was a stronger statement than I myself would be willing quite to make, but that I was very glad he felt so, because I believed that the English, Germans and Americans ought to be fundamentally in accord; and that nothing would so make for the peace and progress of the world. He answered that he entirely agreed with me; and then continued to speak of England with a curious mixture of admiration and resentment.

In Paris TR reminded an audience at the Sorbonne that the future belonged to the doers of deeds:

Let the man of learning, the man of lettered leisure, beware of that queer and cheap temptation to pose to himself and to others as the cynic, as the man who has outgrown emotions and beliefs, the man to whom good and evil are as one. The poorest way to face life is to face it with a sneer. There are many men who feel a kind of twisted pride in cynicism; there are many who confine themselves to criticism of the way others do what they themselves dare not even attempt. There is no more unhealthy being, no man less worthy of respect, than he who either really holds, or feigns to hold, an attitude of sneering disbelief toward all that is great and lofty, whether in achievement or in that noble effort which, even if it fails, comes second to achievement. A cynical habit of thought and speech, a readiness to criticise work which the critic himself never tries to perform, an intellectual aloofness which will not accept contact with life's realities—all these are marks, not, as the possessor would fain think, of superiority, but of weakness. They mark the men unfit to bear their part manfully in the stern strife of living, who seek, in the affectation of contempt for the achievements of others, to hide from others and from themselves their own weakness. The rôle is easy; there is none easier, save only the rôle of the man who sneers alike at both criticism and performance.

It is not the critic who counts; not the man who points out how the strong man stumbles, or where the doer of deeds could have done them better. The credit belongs to the man who is actually in the arena, whose face is marred by dust and sweat and blood; who strives valiantly; who errs, and comes short again and again, because there is no effort without error and shortcoming; but who does actually strive to do the deeds; who knows the great enthusiasms, the great devotions; who spends himself in a worthy cause; who at the best knows in the end the triumph of high achievement, and who at the worst, if he fails, at least fails while daring greatly, so that his place shall never be with those cold and timid souls who know neither victory nor defeat. Shame on the man of cultivated taste who permits refinement to develop into a fastidiousness that unfits him for doing the rough work of a workaday world. Among the free peoples who govern themselves there is but a small field of usefulness open for the men of cloistered life who shrink from contact with their fellows. Still less room is there for those who deride or slight what is done by those who actually bear the brunt of the day; nor yet for those others who always profess that they would like to take action, if only the conditions of life were not what they actually are. The man who does nothing cuts the same sordid figure in the pages of history, whether he be cynic, or fop, or voluptuary. There is little use for the being whose tepid soul knows nothing of the great and generous emotion, of the high pride, the stern belief, the lofty enthusiasm, of the men who quell the storm and ride the thunder. . . .

It was, of course, as a man of action that TR studied the history of the West and the exploits of our Navy in the War of 1812. Here is the advice he offered the American Historical Association at its meeting in Boston on December 27, 1912:

History can never be truthfully presented if the presentation is purely emotional. It can never be truthfully or usefully presented unless profound research, patient, laborious, painstaking, has preceded the presentation. No amount of self-communion and of pondering on the soul of mankind, no gorgeousness of literary imagery, can take the place of cool, serious, widely extended study. The vision of the great historian must be both wide and lofty. But it must be sane, clear, and based on full knowledge of the facts and of their interrelations. Otherwise we get merely a splendid bit of serious romance-writing, like Carlyle's "French Revolution." Many hard-working students, alive to the deficiencies of this kind of romance-writing, have grown to distrust not only all historical writing that is romantic, but all historical writing that is vivid. They feel that complete truthfulness must never be sacrificed to color. In this they are right. They also feel that complete truthfulness is incompatible with color. In this they are wrong. The immense importance of full knowledge of a mass of dry facts and gray details has so impressed them as to make them feel that the dryness and the grayness are in themselves meritorious. . . .

Many learned people seem to feel that the quality of readableness in a book is one which warrants suspicion. Indeed, not a few learned people seem to feel that the fact that a book is interesting is proof that it is shallow. This is particularly apt to be the attitude of scientific men.

Very few great scientists have written interestingly, and these few have usually felt apologetic about it. Yet sooner or later the time will come when the mighty sweep of modern scientific discovery will be placed, by scientific men with the gift of expression, at the service of intelligent and cultivated laymen. Such service will be inestimable. Another writer of "Canterbury Tales," another singer of "Paradise Lost," could not add more to the sum of literary achievement than the man who may picture to us the phases of the age-long history of life on this globe, or make vivid before our eyes the tremendous march of the worlds through space.

Indeed, I believe that already science has owed more than it suspects to the unconscious literary power of some of its representatives. Scientific writers of note had grasped the fact of evolution long before Darwin and Huxley; and the theories advanced by these men to explain evolution were not much more unsatisfactory, as full explanations, than the theory of natural selection itself. Yet, where their predecessors had created hardly a ripple, Darwin and Huxley succeeded in effecting a complete revolution in the thought of the age, a revolution as great as that caused by the discovery of the truth about the solar system. I believe that the chief explanation of the difference was the very simple one that what Darwin and Huxley wrote was interesting to read. Every cultivated man soon had their volumes in his library, and they still keep their places on our book-shelves. But Lamarck and Cope are only to be found in the libraries of a few special students. If they had possessed a gift of expression akin to Darwin's, the doctrine of evolution would not in the popular mind have been confounded with the doctrine of natural selection and a juster estimate than at present would obtain as to the relative merits of the explanations of evolution championed by the different scientific schools.

Do not misunderstand me. In the field of historical research an immense amount can be done by men who have no literary power whatever. Moreover, the most painstaking and laborious research, covering long periods of years, is necessary in order to accumulate the material for any history worth writing at all. There are important bypaths of history, moreover, which hardly admit of treatment that would make them of interest to any but specialists. All this I fully admit. In particular I pay high honor to the patient and truthful investigator. He does an indispensable work. My claim is merely that such work should not exclude the work of the great master who can use the materials gathered, who has the gift of vision, the quality of the seer, the power himself to see what has happened and to make what he has seen clear to the vision of others. My only protest is against those who believe that the extension of the activities of the most competent mason and most energetic contractor will supply the lack of great architects. If, as in the Middle Ages, the journeymen builders are themselves artists, why this is the best possible solution of the problem. But if they are not artists, then their work, however much it represents of praiseworthy industry, and of positive usefulness, does not take the place of the work of a great artist. . . .

The greatest historian should also be a great moralist. It is no proof of impartiality to treat wickedness and goodness as on the same level. But of course the obsession of purposeful moral teaching may utterly defeat its own aim. Moreover, unfortunately, the avowed teacher of morality, when he writes history, sometimes goes very far wrong indeed. It often happens that the man who can be of real help in inspiring others by his utterances on abstract principles is wholly unable to apply his own principles to concrete cases. Carlyle offers an instance in point. Very few men have ever been a greater source of insipration to other ardent souls than was Carlyle when he confined himself to preaching morality in the abstract. Moreover, his theory bade him treat history as offering material to support that theory. But not only was he utterly unable to distinguish either great virtues or great vices when he looked abroad on contemporary life—as witness his attitude toward our own Civil War—but he was utterly unable to apply his own principles concretely in history. His "Frederick the Great" is literature of a high order. It may, with reservations, even be accepted as history. But the "morality" therein jubilantly upheld is shocking to any man who takes seriously Carlyle's other writings in which he lays down principles of conduct. In his "Frederick the Great" he was not content to tell the facts. He was not content to announce his admiration. He wished to square himself with his theories, and to reconcile what he admired, both with the actual fact and with his previously expressed convictions on morality. He could only do so by refusing to face the facts and by using words with meanings that shifted to meet his own mental emergencies. He pretended to discern morality where no vestige of it existed. He tortured the facts to support his views. The "morality" he praised had no connection with morality as understood in the New Testament. . . .

History must welcome the entrance upon its domain of every science. . . .

The work of the archæologist, the work of the anthropologist, the work of the palæo—ethnologist—out of all these a great literary historian may gather material indispensable for his use. He, and we, ought fully to acknowledge our debt to the collectors of these indispensable facts. The investigator in any line may do work which puts us all under lasting obligations to him, even though he be totally deficient in the art of literary expression, that is, totally deficient in the ability to convey vivid and lifelike pictures to others of the past whose secrets he has laid bare. I would give no scanty or grudging acknowledgment to the deeds of such a man. He does a lasting service; whereas the man who tries to make literary expression cover his ignorance or misreading of facts renders less than no service. But the service done is immeasurably increased in value when the man arises who from his study of a myriad dead fragments is able to paint some living picture of the past. . . .

The true historian will bring the past before our eyes as if it were the present. He will make us see as living men the hard-faced archers of Agincourt, and the war-worn spearmen who followed Alexander down beyond the rim of the known world. We shall hear grate on the coast of Britain the keels of the Low-Dutch sea-thieves whose children's children were to inherit unknown continents. We shall thrill to the triumphs of Hannibal. Gorgeous in our sight will rise the splendor of dead cities, and the might of the elder empires of which the very ruins crumbled to dust ages ago. . . .

Some day the historians will tell us of these things. Some day, too, they will tell our children of the age and the land in which we now live. They will portray the conquest of the continent. They will show the slow beginnings of settlement, the growth of the fishing and trading towns on the seacoast, the hesitating early ventures into the Indian-haunted forest. Then they will show the backwoodsmen, with their long rifles and their light axes, making their way with labor and peril through the wooded wilderness to the Mississippi; and then the endless march of the white-topped wagon-trains across plain and mountain to the coast of the greatest of the five great oceans. They will show how the land which the pioneers won slowly and with incredible hardship was filled in two generations by the overflow from the countries of western and central Europe. The portentous growth of the cities will be shown, and the change from a nation of farmers to a nation of business men and artisans, and all the far-reaching consequences of the rise of the new industrialism. The formation of a new ethnic type in this melting-pot of the nations will be told. The hard materialism of our age will appear, and also the strange capacity for lofty idealism which must be reckoned with by all who would understand the American character. A people whose heroes are Washington and Lincoln, a peaceful people who fought to a finish one of the bloodiest of wars, waged solely for the sake of a great principle and a noble idea, surely possess an emergency-standard far above mere money-getting.

Those who tell the Americans of the future what the Americans of to-day and of yesterday have done will perforce tell much that is unpleasant. This is but saying that they will describe the arch-typical civilization of this age. Nevertheless, when the tale is finally told, I believe that it will show that the forces working for good in our national life outweigh the forces working for evil, and that, with many blunders and shortcomings, with much halting and turning aside from the path, we shall yet in the end prove our faith by our works, and show in our lives our belief that righteousness exalteth a nation.

The members of the American Historical Association may not have been aware of this, but TR had long had his misgivings about the aims of this academic organization. As early as 1904 he had written Sir George Otto Trevelyan that:

We have a preposterous little organization called I think the American Historical Association, which, when I was just out of Harvard and very ignorant, I joined. Fortunately I had enough good sense, or obstinacy, or something, to retain a subconscious belief that, inasmuch as books were meant to be read, good books ought to be interesting, and the best books capable in addition of giving one a lift upward in some direction. After a while it dawned on me that all of the conscientious industrious, painstaking little pedants, who would have been useful people in a rather small way if they had understood their own limitations, had become because of their conceit distinctly noxious. They solemnly believed that if there were only enough of them, and that if they only collected enough facts of all kinds and sorts, there would cease to be any need hereafter for great writers, great thinkers. They looked for instance at Justin Winsor's conglomerate narrative history of America—a book which is either literature or science in the sense in which a second-rate cyclopedia is literature and science—as showing an "advance" upon Francis Parkman—Heaven save the mark! Each of them was a good-enough day laborer, trundling his barrowful of bricks and worthy of his hire; as long as they saw themselves as they were they were worthy of all respect; but when they imagined that by their activity they rendered the work of an architect unnecessary they became both absurd and mischievous. Unfortunately with us it is these small men who do most of the historic teaching in the colleges. They have done much real harm in preventing the development of students who might have a large grasp of what history should really be. They represent what is in itself the excellent revolt against superficiality and lack of research, but they have grown into the opposite and equally noxious belief that research is all in all, that accumulation of facts is everything, and that the ideal history of the future will consist not even of the work of one huge pedant but of a multitude of articles by a multitude of small pedants. They are honestly unconscious that all they are doing is to gather bricks and stones, and that whether their work will or will not amount to anything really worthy depends entirely upon whether or not some great master builder hereafter arrives who will be able to go over their material, to reject the immense majority of it, and out of what is left to fashion some edifice of majesty and beauty instinct with the truth that both charms and teaches. A thousand Burys, and two thousand of the corresponding Germans whom he reverentially admires, would not in the aggregate begin to add to the wisdom of mankind what another Macaulay, should one arise, would add. The great historian must of course have the scientific spirit which gives the power of research, which enables one to marshal and weigh the facts; but unless his finished work is literature of a very high type small will be his claim to greatness.

CHAPTER 17

Armageddon and Afterward

"*You blessed old trump,*" TR *wrote William Howard Taft in the summer of 1908,* "*I have always said you would be the greatest President, bar only Washington and Lincoln, and I feel mighty inclined to strike out the exceptions.*" *In the fall of 1908 Taft was still* "*just a dear,*" *but no sooner was he in the White House than TR began to revise his opinion.*

The Ex-President wrote Henry Cabot Lodge in the spring of 1910:

FOR A YEAR after Taft took office, for a year and a quarter after he had been elected, I would not let myself think ill of anything he did. I finally had to admit that he had gone wrong on certain points; and I then also had to admit to myself that deep down underneath I had all along known he was wrong, on points as to which I had tried to deceive myself, by loudly proclaiming to myself, that he was right. I went out of the country and gave him the fullest possible chance to work out his own salvation.

But Taft failed to work out his salvation—at least in TR's eyes. Though he started forty-five proceedings leading to indictments under the Sherman Act, twenty more than his predecessor, he made the mistake of hailing the Payne-Aldrich tariff, under which many items in the schedule reached new highs, as "the best ever passed by the Republican Party." Taft also irritated Roosevelt and Roosevelt's friends by refusing to back Chief Forester Gifford Pinchot in his quarrel with R. A. Ballinger over an alleged "give-away" of coal lands in Alaska.

In many ways Taft made an admirable President, but to the millions who had thrilled to Roosevelt's denunciation of iniquity, he was a colorless figure.

To his English friend Arthur Hamilton Lee TR wrote in the fall of 1910:

The situation here politically is anything but pleasant. Taft is a kindly well-meaning man, who was a fine judge and an excellent lieutenant in executive office, but he has no instinct of leadership and he takes his color so completely from his immediate surroundings that he is continually finding himself in situations where he really has broken his word, or betrayed some former associate, and where in consequence, and very naturally, he himself feels irritated against the man to whom he has not behaved very nicely. I do not believe he has been a bad President, and I am sure he has been a thoroughly well-meaning and upright President. I think he is a better President than Mc-Kinley and probably than Harrison, but the times are totally different, and he has not the qualities that are needed at the moment. I am not sure whether he can or cannot redeem himself.

Already TR had come to the conclusion that it was time to preach the gospel of "The New Nationalism." At Osawatomie, Kansas on August 31, 1910 he made an address in which he revealed he had traveled far in the direction of government control of our giant corporations:

I stand for the square deal. But when I say that I am for the square deal, I mean not merely that I stand for fair play under the present rules of the game, but that I stand for having those rules changed so as to work for a more substantial equality of opportunity and of reward for equally good service. One word of warning, which, I think, is hardly necessary in Kansas. When I say I want a square deal for the poor man, I do not mean that I want a square deal for the man who remains poor because he has not got the energy to work for himself. If a man who has had a chance will not make good, then he has got to quit. And you men of the Grand Army, you want justice for the brave man who fought, and punishment for the coward who shirked his work. Is not that so?

Now, this means that our government, national and State, must be freed from the sinister influence or control of special interests. Exactly as the special interests of cotton and slavery threatened our political integrity before the Civil War, so now the great special business interests too often control and corrupt the men and methods of government for their own profit. We must drive the special interests out of politics. That is one of our tasks to-day. Every special interest is entitled to justice—full, fair, and complete—and, now, mind you, if there were any attempt by mob-violence to plunder and work harm to the special interest, whatever it may be, that I most dislike, and the wealthy man, whomsoever he may be, for whom I have the greatest contempt, I would fight for him, and you would if you were worth your salt. He should have justice. For every special interest is entitled to justice, but not one is entitled to a vote in Congress, to a voice on the bench, or to representation in any public office. The Constitution guarantees protection to property, and we must make that promise good. But it does not give the right of suffrage to any corporation.

The true friend of property, the true conservative, is he who insists that property shall be the servant and not the master of the commonwealth; who insists that the creature of man's making shall be the servant and not the master of the man who made it. The citizens of the United States must effectively control the mighty commercial forces which they have themselves called into being.

There can be no effective control of corporations while their political activity remains. To put an end to it will be neither a short nor an easy task, but it can be done.

We must have complete and effective publicity of corporate affairs, so that the people may know beyond peradventure whether the corporations obey the law and whether their management entitles them to the confidence of the public. It is necessary that laws should be passed to prohibit the use of corporate funds directly or indirectly for political purposes; it is still more necessary that such laws should be thoroughly enforced. Corporate expenditures for political purposes, and especially such expenditures by public-service corporations, have supplied one of the principal sources of corruption in our political affairs.

It has become entirely clear that we must have government supervision of the capitalization, not only of public-service corporations, including, particularly, railways, but of all corporations doing an interstate business. I do not wish to see the nation forced into the ownership of the railways if it can possibly be avoided, and the only alternative is thoroughgoing and effective regulation, which shall be based on a full knowledge of all the facts, including a physical valuation of property. This physical valuation is not needed, or, at least, is very rarely needed, for fixing rates; but it is needed as the basis of honest capitalization.

We have come to recognize that franchises should never be granted except for a limited time, and never without proper provision for compensation to the public. It is my personal belief that the same kind and degree of control and supervision which should be exercised over public-service corporations should be extended also to combinations which control necessaries of life, such as meat, oil, and coal, or which deal in them on an important scale. I have no doubt that the ordinary man who has control of them in much like ourselves. I have no doubt he would like to do well, but I want to have enough supervision to help him realize that desire to do well.

I believe that the officers, and, especially, the directors, of corporations should be held personally responsible when any corporation breaks the law.

Combinations in industry are the result of an imperative economic law which cannot be repealed by political legislation. The effort at prohibiting all combination has substantially failed. The way out lies, not in attempting to prevent such combinations, but in completely controlling them in the interest of the public welfare. For that purpose the Federal Bureau of Corporations is an agency of first importance. Its powers, and, therefore, its efficiency, as well as that of the Interstate Commerce Commission, should be largely increased. We have a right to expect from the Bureau of Corporations and from the Interstate Commerce Commission a very high grade of public service. We should be as sure of the proper conduct of the interstate railways and the proper management of interstate business as we are now sure of the conduct and management of the national banks, and we should have as effective supervision in one case as in the other. The Hepburn Act, and the amendment to the act in the shape in which it finally passed Congress at the last session, represent a long step in advance, and we must go yet further.

There is a wide-spread belief among our people that, under the methods of making tariffs which have hitherto obtained, the special interests are too influential. Probably this is true of both the big special interests and the little special interests. These methods have put a premium on selfishness, and, naturally, the selfish big interests have gotten more than their smaller, though equally selfish, brothers. The duty of Congress is to provide a method by which the interest of the whole people shall be all that receives consideration. To this end there must be an expert tariff commission, wholly removed from the possibility of political pressure or of improper business influence. Such a commission can find the real difference between cost of production, which is mainly the difference of labor cost here and abroad. As fast as its recommendations are made, I believe in revising one schedule at a time. A general revision of the tariff almost inevitably leads to log-rolling and the subordination of the general public interest to local and special interests.

The absence of effective State, and, especially, national, restraint upon unfair money-getting has tended to create a small class of enormously wealthy and economically powerful men, whose chief object is to hold and increase their power. The prime need is to change the conditions which enable these men to accumulate power which it is not for the general welfare that they should hold or exercise. We grudge no man a fortune which represents his own power and sagacity, when exercised with entire regard to the welfare of his fellows. Again, comrades over there, take the lesson from your own experience. Not only did you not grudge, but you gloried in the promotion of the great generals who gained their promotion by leading the army to victory. So it is with us. We grudge no man a fortune in civil life if it is honorably obtained and well used. It is not even enough that it should have been gained without doing damage to the community. We should permit it to be gained only so long as the gaining represents benefit to the community. This, I know, implies a policy of a far more active governmental interference with social and economic conditions in this country than we have yet had, but I think we have got to face the fact that such an increase in governmental control is now necessary.

No man should receive a dollar unless that dollar has been fairly earned. Every dollar received should represent a dollar's worth of service rendered—not gambling in stocks, but service rendered. The really big fortune, the swollen fortune, by the mere fact of its size acquires qualities which differentiate it in kind as well as in degree from what is possessed by men of relatively small means. Therefore, I believe in a graduated income tax on big fortunes, and in another tax which is far more easily collected and far more effective—a graduated inheritance tax on big fortunes, properly safeguarded against evasion and increasing rapidly in amount with the size of the estate.

The people of the United States suffer from periodical

financial panics to a degree substantially unknown among
the other nations which approach us in financial strength.
There is no reason why we should suffer what they escape.
It is of profound importance that our financial system
should be promptly investigated, and so thoroughly and
effectively revised as to make it certain that hereafter our
currency will no longer fail at critical times to meet our
needs. . . .

Of conservation I shall speak more at length elsewhere.
Conservation means development as much as it does protection. I recognize the right and duty of this generation to
develop and use the natural resources of our land; but I
do not recognize the right to waste them, or to rob, by
wasteful use, the generations that come after us. I ask
nothing of the nation except that it so behave as each
farmer here behaves with reference to his own children.
That farmer is a poor creature who skins the land and
leaves it worthless to his children. The farmer is a good
farmer who, having enabled the land to support himself
and to provide for the education of his children, leaves
it to them a little better than he found it himself. I believe
the same thing of a nation.

Moreover, I believe that the natural resources must be
used for the benefit of all our people, and not monopolized
for the benefit of the few, and here again is another case
in which I am accused of taking a revolutionary attitude.
People forget now that one hundred years ago there were
public men of good character who advocated the nation
selling its public lands in great quantities, so that the nation
could get the most money out of it, and giving it to the
men who could cultivate it for their own uses. We took the
proper democratic ground that the land should be granted
in small sections to the men who were actually to till it

and live on it. Now, with the water-power, with the forests, with the mines, we are brought face to face with the fact that there are many people who will go with us in conserving the resources only if they are to be allowed to exploit them for their benefit. That is one of the fundamental reasons why the special interests should be driven out of politics. Of all the questions which can come before this nation, short of the actual preservation of its existence in a great war, there is none which compares in importance with the great central task of leaving this land even a better land for our descendants than it is for us, and training them into a better race to inhabit the land and pass it on. Conservation is a great moral issue, for it involves the patriotic duty of insuring the safety and continuance of the nation. Let me add that the health and vitality of our people are at least as well worth conserving as their forests, waters, lands, and minerals, and in this great work the national government must bear a most important part. . . .

Nothing is more true than that excess of every kind is followed by reaction; a fact which should be pondered by reformer and reactionary alike. We are face to face with new conceptions of the relations of property to human welfare, chiefly because certain advocates of the rights of property as against the rights of men have been pushing their claims too far. The man who wrongly holds that every human right is secondary to his profit must now give way to the advocate of human welfare, who rightly maintains that every man holds his property subject to the general right of the community to regulate its use to whatever degree the public welfare may require it.

But I think we may go still further. The right to regulate the use of wealth in the public interest is universally admitted. Let us admit also the right to regulate the terms and conditions of labor, which is the chief element of wealth, directly in the interest of the common good. The fundamental thing to do for every man is to give him a chance to reach a place in which he will make the greatest possible contribution to the public welfare. Understand what I say there. Give him a chance, not push him up if he will not be pushed. Help any man who stumbles; if he lies down, it is a poor job to try to carry him; but if he is a worthy man, try your best to see that he gets a chance to show the worth that is in him. No man can be a good citizen unless he has a wage more than sufficient to cover the bare cost of living, and hours of labor short enough so that after his day's work is done he will have time and energy to bear his share in the management of the community, to help in carrying the general load. We keep countless men from being good citizens by the conditions of life with which we surround them. We need comprehensive workmen's compensation acts, both State and national laws to regulate child labor and work for women, and, especially, we need in our common schools not merely education in book-learning, but also practical training for daily life and work. We need to enforce better sanitary conditions for our workers and to extend the use of safety appliances for our workers in industry and commerce, both within and between the States. Also, friends, in the interest of the working man himself we need to set our faces like flint against mob-violence just as against corporate greed; against violence and injustice and lawlessness by wage-workers just as much as against lawless cunning and greed and selfish arrogance of employers. If I could ask but one thing of my fellow countrymen, my request would be that, whenever they go in for reform, they remember the two sides, and that they always exact justice from one side as much as from the other. I have small use for the public servant who can always see and denounce the corruption of the capitalist, but who cannot persuade himself, especially before election, to say a word about lawless mob-violence. And I have equally small use for the man, be he a judge on the bench, or editor of a great paper, or wealthy and influential private citizen, who can see clearly enough and denounce the lawlessness of mob-violence, but whose eyes are closed so that he is blind when the question is one of corruption in business on a gigantic scale. . . .

In 1911, when discontented Republicans gathered to form the National Progressive Republican League, there were those who thought that Robert M. LaFollete, the Republican but Progressive Senator from Wisconsin, might walk off with the Republican nomination in 1912. But the LaFollette boom collapsed. When the Progressives found their delegates were disqualified at the Chicago Convention, they seceded to form the Progressive party and made Roosevelt their candidate.

TR had no intention of playing safe in the three-cornered race for the Presidency. As early as December 13, 1910, in a speech before the New Haven Chamber of Commerce, he admitted that:

The criticism has been made of me that I am a radical. So I am. I couldn't be anything else, feeling as I do. But I am a radical who most earnestly desires to see the radical programme carried out by conservatives. I wish to see industrial and social reforms of a far-reaching nature accomplished in this country, and I wish to see them accomplished, not under the leadership of those who will

materially profit by them, but under the leadership of
those who will lose rather than profit by them. I want to
see just such men as you here, whom I am now addressing,
taking the lead in solving those problems. I wish to see that
for two reasons. In the first place for your sakes, and in
the next place for the sake of the nation. I believe most
emphatically in the progress which shall be gradual and not
by leaps and starts. I believe most emphatically in the progress which shall be sane, and therefore I wish to see our
people as a whole combine the firm resolution to go forward with the firm resolution to test each step and see
that that step really does represent movement forward
and not to one side.

And at Carnegie Hall on March 20, 1912 he warned that re-
actionaries who failed to give an inch might have to yield a mile:

I prefer to work with moderate, with rational, conservatives, provided only that they do in good faith strive
forward toward the light. But when they halt and turn
their backs to the light, and sit with the scorners on the
seats of reaction, then I must part company with them. We
the people cannot turn back. Our aim must be steady, wise
progress. It would be well if our people would study the
history of a sister republic. All the woes of France for a
century and a quarter have been due to the folly of her
people in splitting into the two camps of unreasonable con-
servatism and unreasonable radicalism. Had pre-Revolu-
tionary France listened to men like Turgot, and backed
them up, all would have gone well. But the beneficiaries

of privilege, the Bourbon reactionaries, the short-sighted ultra-conservatives, turned down Turgot; and then found that instead of him they had obtained Robespierre. They gained twenty years' freedom from all restraint and reform, at the cost of the whirlwind of the red terror; and in their turn the unbridled extremists of the terror induced a blind reaction; and so, with convulsion and oscillation from one extreme to another, with alternations of violent radicalism and violent Bourbonism, the French people went through misery toward a shattered goal. May we profit by the experiences of our brother republicans across the water, and go forward steadily, avoiding all wild extremes; and may our ultra-conservatives remember that the rule of the Bourbons brought on the Revolution, and may our would-be revolutionaries remember that no Bourbon was ever such a dangerous enemy of the people and of freedom as the professed friend of both, Robespierre. There is no danger of a revolution in this county; but there is grave discontent and unrest, and in order to remove them there is need of all the wisdom and probity and deep-seated faith in and purpose to uplift humanity we have at our command.

Friends, our task as Americans is to strive for social and industrial justice, achieved through the genuine rule of the people. This is our end, our purpose, The methods for achieving the end are merely expedients, to be finally accepted or rejected according as actual experience shows that they work well or ill. But in our hearts we must have this lofty purpose, and we must strive for it in all earnestness and sincerity, or our work will come to nothing. In order to succeed we need leaders of inspired idealism, leaders to whom are granted great visions, who dream greatly and strive to make their dreams come true;

who can kindle the people with the fire from their own burning souls. The leader for the time being, whoever he may be, is but an instrument to be used until broken and then to be cast aside; and if he is worth his salt he will care no more when he is broken than a soldier cares when he is sent where his life is forfeit in order that the victory may be won. In the long fight for righteousness the watchword for all of us is spend and be spent. It is of little matter whether any one man fails or succeeds; but the cause shall not fail, for it is the cause of mankind.

We, here in America, hold in our hands the hope of the world, the fate of the coming years; and shame and disgrace will be ours if in our eyes the light of high resolve is dimmed, if we trail in the dust the golden hopes of men. If on this new continent we merely build another country of great but unjustly divided material prosperity, we shall have done nothing; and we shall do as little if we merely set the greed of envy against the greed of arrogance, and thereby destroy the material well-being of all of us. To turn this government either into government by a plutocracy or government by a mob would be to repeat on a larger scale the lamentable failures of the world that is dead. We stand against all tyranny, by the few or by the many. We stand for the rule of the many in the interest of all of us, for the rule of the many in a spirit of courage, of common sense, of high purpose, above all in a spirit of kindly justice toward every man and every woman. We not merely admit, but insist, that there must be self-control on the part of the people, that they must keenly perceive their own duties as well as the rights of others; but we also insist that the people can do nothing unless they not merely have, but exercise to the full, their own rights. The worth of our great experiment depends upon its being in good faith an experiment—the first that has ever been tried—in true democracy on the scale of a continent, on a scale as vast as that of the mightiest empires of the Old World. Surely this is a noble ideal, an ideal for which it is worth while to strive, an ideal for which at need it is worth while to sacrifice much; for our ideal is the rule of all the people in a spirit of friendliest brotherhood toward each and every one of the people.

Nor was he restrained when he spoke at Orchestra Hall, Chicago, in June:

When I undertook this contest I was well aware of the intense bitterness which my re-entry into politics would cause, I knew that the powers that prey would oppose me, with tenfold the bitterness they would show in opposing any other Progressive candidate, simply because they do not fear any other Progressive candidate, whereas they very greatly fear me. I knew also that they would directly or indirectly influence very many men who pride themselves upon belonging to and indeed typifying what they regard as the educated and respectable classes. But it has been to me a matter of melancholy concern to see the effect that these influences have produced upon so many men in the Northeast, and in cities like New York, Boston, and Philadelphia, who lead lives that are on the whole rather pleasant, rather soft, and who are free from all possibility of the pressure of actual want. It has been a matter of concern to me to see how bitter and irrational has been the opposition to us among a very large proportion of these men, the men who are to be found in the most noted clubs, in the centres of big business, and in the places especially resorted to by those whose chief desires are for ease and pleasure. We have with us a small percentage of the heads of great corporations and of great corporation lawyers, including I believe almost every man of either class sufficiently high-minded and far-sighted to see that in the long run privilege spells destruction, not only to the class harmed by it but the class possessing it. We welcome the presence of these men. Every honest man whatever his fortune, should be our ally. The great majority of capitalists, however, and of the big corporation lawyers so intimately connected with them, are naturally hostile to us. Their hostility did not surprise me. The men who are most benefited by privilege unless they are exceptionally disinterested and far-sighted, cannot be expected to feel friendly toward those who assail privilege. But associated with them are many men whose selfish interest in privilege is far less obvious. I genuinely regret that we have had with us so small a percentage of the men for whom life has been easy, who belong to or are intimately associated with the leisured and monied classes; so small a proportion of the class which furnishes the bulk of the membership in the larger social business and professional clubs, and which supplies the majority of the heads of our great educational institutions and of the men generally, who take the lead in upholding the cause of virtue when only the minor moralities and the elegancies of life are at issue. My concern and regret are primarily for these men themselves. They could do us good by joining with us, for it is earnestly to be wished that this movement for social justice shall number among its leaders at least a goodly proportion of men whose leadership is obviously disinterested, who will themselves receive no material benefit from the changes which as a matter of justice they advocate. Yet the good to the people would be small compared to the good which these men would do to their own class by casting in their lot with us as we battle for the rights of humanity, as we battle for social and industrial justice, as we champion the cause of those who most need champions and for whom champions have been too few. I have been puzzled at the attitude of the men in question. They are often the men who in the past have been very severe in their condemnation of corruption, in their condemnation of bossism, and in railing at injustice and demanding higher ideals of public service and private life. Yet when the supreme test comes they prove false to all their professions of the past. They fear the people so intensely that they pardon and uphold every species of political and business crookedness in the panic-struck hope of strengthening the boss and special privilege and thereby raising a powerful shield to protect their own soft personalities from the public. They are foolish creatures; the people would never harm them; yet they still dread the people. They stand with servile acquiescence behind the worst representatives of crooked business and crooked politics in the country, and by speech or by silence they now encourage or condone the efforts of our opponents to steal from the people the victory they have won and to substitute boss rule for popular rule. Some of these men have in the past assumed to be teachers of their fellow men in political matters. Never again can they speak in favor of a high ideal of honesty and decency in political life, or of the duty to oppose political corruption and business wrong-doing; for to do so would expose them to the derision of all who abhor hypocrisy and who condemn fine words that are not translated into honorable deeds.

Apparently these men are influenced by a class consciousness which I had not supposed existed in any such strength. They live softly. Circumstances for which they are not responsible have removed their lives from the fears and anxieties of the ordinary men who toil. When a movement is undertaken to make life a little easier, a little better, for the ordinary man, to give him a better chance, these men of soft life seem cast into panic lest something that is not rightly theirs may be taken from them. In unmanly fear they stand against all change, no matter how urgent such change may be. . . .

Opposed undyingly to these men are the men of faith and vision, the men in whom love of righteousness burns like a flaming fire, who spurn lives of soft and selfish ease, of slothful self-indulgence, who scorn to think only of pleasure for themselves, who feel for and believe in their fellows, whose high fealty is reserved for all that is good, that is just, that is honorable. By their very nature these men are bound to battle for the truth and the right. They do not address themselves only to the cultured and exclusive few. They prize character even more than intellect. They know well that conscience is not the privilege merely of the men of wealth and cultivation, and they make their appeal to all men alike in the name of the great fundamental qualities, and qualities that every man should have, the qualities of generosity and unselfishness, of fearless honesty and high courage. . . .

Friends, here in Chicago at this time you have a great task before you. I wish you to realize deep in your hearts that you are not merely facing a crisis in the history of a party. You are facing a crisis in the history of a nation and what you do will have an appreciable effect throughout the world at large. Here in America we the people have a continent on which to work out our destiny, and our faith is great that our men and women are fit to face the mighty days. Nowhere else in all the world is there such a chance for the triumph on a gigantic scale of the great cause of Democratic and popular government. If we fail, the failure will be lamentable, and our heads will be bowed with shame; for not only shall we fail for ourselves, but our failure will wreck the fond desires of all throughout the world who look torward us with the fond hope that here in this great Republic it shall be proved from ocean to ocean that the people can rule themselves, and thus ruling can gain liberty for and do justice both to themselves and to others. We who stand for the cause of the uplift of humanity and the betterment of mankind are pledged to eternal war against wrong whether by the few or by the many, by a plutocracy or by a mob. We believe that this country will not be a permanently good place for any of us to live in unless we make it a reasonably good place for all of us to live in. The sons of all of us will pay in the future if we of the present do not do justice to all in the present. Our cause is the cause of justice for all in the interest of all. The present contest is but a phase of the larger struggle. Assuredly the fight will go on whether we win or lose; but it will be a sore disaster to lose. What happens to me is not of the slightest consequence; I am to be used, as in a doubtful battle any man in used, to his hurt or not, so long as he is useful, and is then cast aside or left to die. I wish you to feel this. I mean it; and I shall need no sympathy when you are through with me, for this fight is far too great to permit us to concern ourselves about any one man's welfare. If we are true to ourselves by putting far above our own interests the triumph of the high cause for which we battle, we shall not lose. It would be far better to fail honorably for the cause we champion than it would be to win by foul methods the foul victory for which our opponents hope. But the victory shall be ours, and it shall be won as we have already won so many victories, by clean and honest fighting for the loftiest of causes. We fight in honorable fashion for the good of mankind; fearless of the future; unheeding of our individual fates; with unflinching hearts and undimmed eyes; we stand at Armageddon, and we battle for the Lord.

Disappointed with Taft, TR feared the worst from Woodrow Wilson. In a speech at San Francisco on September 14 he made plain his misgivings:

In one of his campaign speeches Mr. Wilson made a sweeping assault on the Progressive platform and programme and defined his own position as to social and industrial justice. According to the stenographic report of his speech, Mr. Wilson stated that there is no hope for social reform through the platform of the Progressive party, saying: "In the very platform itself is supplied the demonstration that it is not a serviceable instrument. They do propose to serve civilization and humanity but they cannot serve civilization and humanity with that kind of government. . . . The history of liberty is a history of the limitation of governmental power, not the increase of it."

And he then continues to uphold what he calls "representative" government and "representative" assemblies as against the platform that we propose, and also to uphold the Democratic proposals for dealing with labor and the trusts as against the Progressive proposals.

Mr. Wilson is fond of asserting his platonic devotion to the purposes of the Progressive party. But such platonic devotion is utterly worthless from a practical standpoint, because he antagonizes the only means by which those purposes can be made effective. It is idle to profess devotion to Progressive principles and at the same time to antagonize the only methods by which they can be realized in actual fact.

The key to Mr. Wilson's position is found in the statement I have just quoted, when he says that "The history of liberty is a history of the limitation of governmental power, not the increase of it."

This is a bit of outworn academic doctrine which was kept in the schoolroom and the professorial study for a generation after it had been abandoned by all who had experience of actual life. It is simply the *laissez-faire* doctrine of the English political economists three-quarters of a century ago. It can be applied with profit, if anywhere at all, only in a primitive community under primitive conditions, in a community such as the United States at the end of the eighteenth century, a community before the days of Fulton, Morse, and Edison. To apply it now in the United States at the beginning of the twentieth century, with its highly organized industries, with its railways, telegraphs, and telephones, means literally and absolutely to refuse to make a single effort to better any one of our social or industrial conditions.

Moreover, Mr. Wilson is absolutely in error in his statement, from the historical standpoint.

So long as governmental power existed exclusively for the king and not at all for the people, then the history of liberty was a history of the limitation of governmental power. But now the governmental power rests in the people, and the kings who enjoy privilege are the kings of the financial and industrial world; and what they clamor for is the limitation of governmental power, and what the people sorely need is the extension of governmental power.

If Mr. Wilson's statement means nothing, then he ought not to have made it.

If it means anything, it means that every law for the promotion of social and industrial justice which has been put upon the statute-books ought to be repealed, and every law proposed should be abandoned, for without exception every such law represents an increase of governmental power. Does Mr. Wilson mean to repeal the interstate commerce commission law? If not, does he deny that it represents a great increase of governmental power over the railroads? Let him take whichever horn of the dilemma he chooses. Either his statement is not in accordance with the facts or else he is bound, if it is in accordance with the facts as he sees them, to include in his programme the repeal of the Interstate Commerce Commission Act.

Again, every Progressive State in the Union has passed laws for factory inspection; every such law means an increase of governmental power. Is Mr. Wilson in favor of repealing those laws? If he is not, then what does he mean by saying that the history of liberty is the history of the limitation of governmental power?

The fact is that his statement is a mere bit of professorial rhetoric, which has not one particle of foundation in the facts of the present day.

Again, we propose to limit the hours of working girls

to eight hours a day; we propose to limit the hours of working men in continuous industries to eight hours a day, and to give them one day's rest a week. Both of these proposals represent an increase in the exercise of governmental power, an extension of governmental power. Does Mr. Wilson mean that he is against this extension? If not, then his sentence which I have just quoted and which represents the key-note of his speech, means nothing whatever.

In other words, Mr. Wilson's promise is either a promise that is not to be kept or else it means the undoing of every particle of social and industrial advance we have made and the refusal to go forward along the lines of industrial and social progress.

TR fought a gallant fight, and when a fanatic shot him in the right breast at Milwaukee on October 14, insisted on giving his speech as scheduled. "It takes more than that to kill a bull moose," he bragged.

In November Wilson, who polled only forty-two per cent of the vote, was the overwhelming victor in the Electoral College. Roosevelt, who carried six states, got twenty-seven per cent of the votes. Taft trailed; with only Utah and Vermont in his pocket, he scored no more than twenty-three per cent.

TR, who thought Wilson "a perfect trump" at the time of his election as President of Princeton, was positive that he would be an undependable man in the White House. To his Irish friend Horace Plunkett TR wrote that:

Wilson is a good man who has in no way shown that he possesses any special fitness for the Presidency. Until he was fifty years old, as college professor and college president he advocated with skill, intelligence and good breeding the outworn doctrines which were responsible for four fifths of the political troubles of the United States. He posed as, and believed himself to be, a strong conservative, and was being groomed by a section of Wall Street as the special conservative champion against me and my ideas. Then he ran as Governor of New Jersey, and during the last eighteen months discovered that he could get nowhere advocating the doctrines he had advocated, and instantly turned an absolute somersault so far as at least half of these doctrines was concerned. He still clings to the other half, and he has shown not the slightest understanding of the really great problems of our present industrial situation. . . .

In 1913 TR made a brave effort to forget politics by exploring the River of Doubt in the jungles of Brazil. But he never could forget his defeat at the polls, and what rankled most of all was the rejection by the Republican Convention of delegates loyal to him. He found it hard to forgive Taft, or for that matter Elihu Root. Root, who had served Roosevelt as Secretary of War and later as Secretary of State, stuck by Taft in 1912.

To the New York newspaperman Henry Luther Stoddard TR wrote in the fall of 1916:

Over a year ago Taft and I were both pallbearers at the funeral of Professor Lounsbury of Yale. He came up, spoke to me, and shook hands with me. In my judgment it would have been simply silly for me to refuse to be a pallbearer for Professor Lounsbury on the ground that Taft was also to be one; and it would have been merely bad manners on my part for me to refuse to recognize him when he came up to speak to me. The newspapers made a great hullabaloo about it at the time. They themselves have utterly forgotten the incident, and are now making another hullabaloo over the Union League Club meeting; and in a short time they will forget that exactly as they have forgotten the other incident.

The Union League Club is to give a reception to Mr. Hughes. Among the members of that Club who will be at that reception are a number of men, including Elihu Root, who shared Taft's guilt four years ago. Indeed, if there must be a choice between them, I think that Root's offense was as rank as Taft's and more wanton. It would, in my judgment, have been absurd for me to say that I would refuse to meet Taft, when I have already met Root and many others. My belief is that for me to refuse to come to the Union League Club for the Hughes reception because Taft was to be there, would be a very, very unwise thing.

But what was the guilt of Taft and Root compared with that of Woodrow Wilson?

TR, who could not comprehend Wilson's initial reluctance to bring America into the First World War on the side of the Allies, could not help taking the stump for the cause of Preparedness. On November 3, 1916, at Cooper Union, the Ex-President made a bitter reference to "Shadow Lawn," the summer White House:

There is no more evil lesson that can be taught this people than to cover up failure in the performance of duty in the present by the utterance of glittering generalities as to the performance of duty in the nebulous future. With all my heart I believe in seeing this country prepare its own soul and body so that it can stand up for the weak when they are oppressed by the strong. But before it can do so it must fit itself to defend its own rights, and it must stand for the rights of its citizens. During the last three years and a half, hundreds of American men, women, and children have been murdered on the high seas, and in Mexico. Mr. Wilson has not dared to stand up for them. He has left them suffer without relief, and without inflicting punishment upon the wrong-doers. When he announces that in some dim future he intends to stand up for the rights of others, let him make good in the present by now standing up for the rights of our own people. He wrote Germany that he would hold her to "strict accountability" if an American lost his life on an American or neutral ship by her submarine warfare. Forthwith the *Arabic* and the *Gulflight* were sunk. But Mr. Wilson dared not take any action to make his threat effective. He held Germany to no accountability, loose or strict. Germany despised him; and the *Lusitania* was sunk in consequence. Thirteen hundred and ninety-four people were drowned, one hundred and three of them babies under two years of age. Two days later, while the dead mothers with their dead babies in their arms lay by scores in the Queenstown morgue, Mr. Wilson selected the moment as opportune to utter his famous sentence about being "Too proud to fight." Mr. Wilson now dwells at Shadow Lawn. There should be shadows enough at Shadow Lawn; the shadows of men, women, and children who have risen from the ooze of the ocean bottom and from graves in foreign lands; the shadows of the helpless whom Mr. Wilson did not dare protect lest he might have to face danger; the shadows of babies gasping pitifully as they sank under the waves; the shadows of women outraged and slain by bandits; the shadows of Boyd and Adair and their troopers who lay in the Mexican desert, the black blood crusted round their mouths, and their dim eyes looking upward, because President Wilson had sent them to do a task, and had then shamefully abandoned them to the mercy of foes who knew no mercy. Those are the shadows proper for Shadow Lawn; the shadows of deeds that were never done; the shadows of lofty words that were followed by no action; the shadows of the tortured dead. . . .

A little while, and TR was beseeching Wilson for permission to recruit a division of infantry for battle in France. His request denied, TR wrote Secretary of War Newton D. Baker:

You decline my application on the ground of lack of military training and experience; and yet you are summoning, and have summoned, to the field numbers of militia officers, as division and brigade commanders, who have not had one tenth my experience. My dear sir, you forget that I have commanded troops in action in the most important battle fought by the United States army during the last half century, and that I have commanded a brigade in the campaign of which this battle was an incident.

This, like his other letters, was to no avail. Nor did a call at the White House change Wilson's mind. So the leader of the charge at San Juan Hill stayed home, while his four sons did their part at the front.

On July 17, 1918 TR received word that Quentin, the youngest, was killed in flight over the German lines. In October the Ex-President wrote this tribute to "The Great Adventure" for the Metropolitan Magazine:

Only those are fit to live who do not fear to die; and none are fit to die who have shrunk from the joy of life and the duty of life. Both life and death are parts of the same Great Adventure. Never yet was worthy adventure worthily carried through by the man who put his personal safety first. Never yet was a country worth living in unless its sons and daughters were of that stern stuff which bade them die for it at need; and never yet was a country worth dying for unless its sons and daughters thought of life not as something concerned only with the selfish evanescence of the individual, but as a link in the great chain of creation and causation, so that each person is seen in his true relations as an essential part of the whole, whose life must be made to serve the larger and continuing life of the whole. Therefore it is that the man who is not willing to die, and the woman who is not willing to send her man to die, in a war for a great cause, are not worthy to live. Therefore it is that the man and woman who in peace-time fear or ignore the primary and vital duties and the high happiness of family life, who dare not beget and bear and rear the life that is to last when they are in their graves, have broken the chain of creation, and have shown that they are unfit for companionship with the souls ready for the **Great Adventure**. . . .

Woe to those who invite a sterile death; a death not for them only, but for the race; the death which is insured by a life of sterile selfishness.

But honor, highest honor, to those who fearlessly face death for a good cause; no life is so honorable or so fruitful as such a death. Unless men are willing to fight and die for great ideals, including love of country, ideals will vanish, and the world will become one huge sty of materialism. And unless the women of ideals bring forth the men who are ready thus to live and die, the world of the future will be filled by the spawn of the unfit. Alone of human beings the good and wise mother stands on a plane of equal honor with the bravest soldier; for she has gladly gone down to the brink of the chasm of darkness to bring back the children in whose hands rests the future of the years. But the mother, and far more the father, who flinch from the vital task earn the scorn visited on the soldier who flinches in battle. And the nation should by action mark its attitude alike toward the fighter in war and toward the child-bearer in peace and war. The vital need of the nation is that its men and women of the future shall be the sons and daughters of the soldiers of the present. Excuse no man from going to war because he is married; but put all unmarried men above a fixed age at the hardest and most dangerous tasks; and provide amply for the children of soldiers, so as to give their wives the assurance of material safety.

. . . At this moment there are hundreds of thousands of gallant men eating out their hearts because the privilege of facing death in battle is denied them. So there are innumerable women and men whose undeserved misfortune it is that they have no children or but one child. These soldiers denied the perilous honor they seek, these men and women heart-hungry for the children of their longing dreams, are as worthy of honor as the men who are warriors in fact, as the women whose children are of flesh and blood. If the only son who is killed at the front has no brother because his parents coldly dreaded to play their part in the Great Adventure of Life, then our sorrow is not for them, but solely for the son who himself dared the Great Adventure of Death. If, however, he is the only son because the Unseen Powers denied others to the love of his father and mother, then we mourn doubly with them because their darling went up to the sword of Azrael, because he drank the dark drink proffered by the Death Angel.

In America to-day all our people are summoned to service and sacrifice. Pride is the portion only of those who know bitter sorrow or the foreboding of bitter sorrow. But all of us who give service, and stand ready for sacrifice, are the torch-bearers. We run with the torches until we fall, content if we can then pass them to the hands of other runners. The torches whose flame is brightest are borne by the gallant men at the front, and by the gallant women whose husbands and lovers, whose sons and brothers are at the front. These men are high of soul, as they face their fate on the shell-shattered earth, or in the skies above or in the waters beneath; and no less high of soul are the women with torn hearts and shining eyes; the girls whose boy-lovers have been struck down in their golden morning, and the mothers and wives to whom word has been brought that henceforth they must walk in the shadow.

These are the torch-bearers; these are they who have dared the Great Adventure.

TR was a sick man in February, 1918. Sent to Roosevelt Hospital, he was home again in a month. But on Armistice Day he was back at the hospital. Released on Christmas Eve, he went home to Sagamore Hill. At four in the morning of January 6, 1919 he died.

Sources and Index

CHAPTER 1 Boyhood and Youth

Works XXII (*An Autobiography*), Pages 3-4, 6-7, 8-10, 10-11, 11-13, 14-16, 17-19, 22-23, 23-25, 26-28, 29-31, 32-33; *Letters* I, 1, 23; *Memorial,* Theodore Roosevelt Association.

CHAPTER 2 The Vigor of Life

Works, XXII, Pages 34-36, 38-39, 49-51, 54-58.

CHAPTER 3 Practical Politics

Works, XXII, Pages 66, 67-68, 68-69, 70-72, 72, 73-74, 77-78, 78-79, 79, 80-82, 83, 84, 86, 87-88, 88-89, 91-93, 93-94, 95-98, 103-104, 104, 104-106; *Letters* I, 118.

CHAPTER 4 In Cowboy Land

Works XXII, Pages 112-114, 114, 115-129, 138, 138-9, 141, 143-144, 144-146, 146-147, 148-149, 153-154; *Letters,* I, 148, 150, 153.

CHAPTER 5 Applied Idealism

Works XXII, Pages 155, 156-157, 158-159, 159, 160-161, 161-162, 163, 164-165, 165-166, 176-177, 178, 179-180, 180-181, 182-183, 183, 184-185, 185-186, 186-187, 187-189; *Letters* I, 224, 354 A, 475.

CHAPTER 6   The New York Police

Works XXII, Pages 202, 203-204, 204-205, 207, 224-225, 227, 230-231, 239-242; *Letters*, I, 637; Henry James, *Charles W. Eliot*, II, Page 159; *Works*, XVI, Pages 394-395; *Works*, XIV, Pages 129-130, 134-135, 141-142, 142-143.

CHAPTER 7   The War of America the Unready

Works XXII, Pages 246, 246-247, 248-249, 250, 251, 252, 253-254, 254-255, 255-256, 256-257, 257, 258, 260, 261-263, 263-264, 272-273, 274, 278-280, 281-282, 283-285, 285-287, 288-291, 291-297, 304, 305; *Letters* I, 718, 732.

CHAPTER 8   The New York Governorship

Works XXII, Pages 307, 307-308, 308-311, 311-312, 312, 313, 318, 318-319, 320, 321-322, 324-326, 328, 329-331, 332-334, 335-336, 340-341, 342-343, 346, 353-355; *Works* XV, Pages 267-268, 281; *Letters* II, 1404.

CHAPTER 9   Outdoors and Indoors

Works XXII, Pages 359, 371-373, 373-375, 375-378, 379-381, 382-392, 392, 393-394.

CHAPTER 10   The Presidency: Making An Old Party
             Progressive

Works XXII, Pages 395-398, 399, 402-403, 404-405, 411, 412-413, 443-444; *Works* XXI, Pages 489-490; *Letters* III, 2567; *Works* XXI, Insert between Pages 516 and 517, pages 553-554, 567-568.

CHAPTER 11   The Natural Resources of the Nation

Works XXII, Pages 446, 447-448, 448, 448-449, 449, 449-450, 450-451, 451-452, 453-457, 457-458, 458-459, 460, 460-461, 463, 464-465, 469, 477-479.

CHAPTER 12   The Big Stick and the Square Deal

Works XXII, Pages 481, 481-482, 482-484, 485-488, 489, 490-491, 491-493, 493-494, 495, 497-499, 499, 502-503, 503-504, 504-505, 505,

506, 507-508, 509-509, 513; *Letters* III, 2386; VI, 4678; V, 3922; *Works* XVIII, Pages 571-573; *Letters* V, 3696.

CHAPTER 13 Social and Industrial Justice

Works XXII, Pages 526-527, 527-528, 529-530, 530-531, 531-532, 532-533, 533-536, 539-540, 546-547, 551-554, 561-562; *Letters* IV, 3363, V, 4171; *Works* VI, Pages 435, 436, 438, 441.

CHAPTER 14 The Monroe Doctrine and the Panama Canal

Works XXII, Pages 571-572, 572-573, 574-575, 575-576, 576, 578-579, 579-580, 582-584, 585, 591-592, 592-593, 593-594, 594-596, 596-597, 600-602; *Letters* VI, 5143.

CHAPTER 15 The Peace of Righteousness

Works XXII, Pages 604, 606-607, 611-617, 622-623, 633; *Letters* V, 3668, 3898.

CHAPTER 16 Hunter and Historian

Works V, Pages 70-75; XIV, Pages 463-470; *Letters* VII, 5521; *Works* XV, Pages 353-355; XIV, Pages 5-6, 8-10, 15-16, 18-19, 25-26, 27-28; *Letters* III, 2941.

CHAPTER 17 Armageddon and Afterward

Letters VI, 4834, 4958; VII, 5282, 5328; *Works* XIX, Pages 16-21, 22-23, 24-25; XVIII, 104-105; XIX, Pages 221-224, 307-310, 313-314, 316-317, 419-422; *Letters* III, 2364, VII 5751, VIII, 6143; *Works* XX, Pages 525-526; *Letters* VIII, 6203; *Works* XXI, Pages 263, 265-266, 266-267.

Works refers to the Memorial Edition of the Works of Theodore Roosevelt, published by Charles Scribner's Sons in twenty-four volumes in 1924. *Letters* refers to *The Letters of Theodore Roosevelt*, edited by Elting E. Morison, in eight volumes, Harvard University Press, 1951-1954. The numbers following the volumes cited of the letters refer to the numbers of the letters cited, not to page numbers. James's biography of Eliot was published in two volumes by Houghton Mifflin in 1930.

Henry F. Pringle's *Theodore Roosevelt: A Biography*, Harcourt, Brace, 1931, is a delightful book that has proved to be invaluable to the compiler of this volume. For a more comprehensive account of Roosevelt in his early years, see Carleton Putnam, *Theodore Roosevelt: The Formative Years 1858-1886*. Scribner's, 1958.

Adams, Brooks, 112-116
Adams, Charles Francis, 264
Adams, Henry, 115, 283
Adams, John, 242
African Game Trails, 298
Ahlwardt, Rector, 103-104
Algeciras Conference, 196, 288, 294
Alger, Russell A., 123-124
Altgeld, John Peter, ix, 111-112
American Historical Association, 318, 324
American Museum of Natural History, 16
American Tobacco Company, 228, 231, 239-240
Armageddon, 345
Astor, Mrs. William, 84
Austen, Jane, 177

Bacon, Robert, 255
Baer, George F., 263-264
Baker, Newton D., 352
Ballinger, R. A., 199-200, 327
Bismarck, Otto von, 115, 313
Black Horse Cavalry, 49-50
Blaine, James G., 56-57

Bonaparte, Charles, 228, 234-235
Brace, Charles Loring, 9
"Bronco Buster," 171
Bryan, William Jennings, ix, 111-112, 146, 150
Bryce, James, 77, 197
Buchanan, James, 198-200
"Bull Moose," 10, 348
Bulloch, Anna, 11, 23
Bulloch, Archibald, 5
Bulloch, Irvine, 11
Bulloch, James Dunwoodie, 11
Bulloch, Martha Stewart Elliott, 10
Bullock, Seth, 33, 190
Bunau-Varilla, Philippe, 280
Bunyan, John, 246, 304
Bureau of Forestry (United States Forest Service), 213-215
Bureau of Mines, 250
Burroughs, John, 266
Bury, John B., 243

Cannon, Joseph G., 202
Carlyle, Thomas, 304, 309, 318, 321
Carnegie, Andrew, 243, 314
Chaffee, Gen. A. R., 132, 140
Chaucer, Geoffrey, 98-99
Cigarmaker's Union, 52-54
Civil War, 10-11, 39, 94, 115, 117-118, 123, 201, 321, 328
Cleveland, Grover, 48-49, 54, 57, 86, 225, 254
Conservation and Reclamation, 209-221
Costello, Michael, 44, 47-48
Croker, Richard, 149
Curtis, George William, 5
Cutler, Arthur, 18

Dante, Alighieri, 173, 304
Darwin, Charles, 305, 319
Davis, Richard Harding, 129-130
DeConstant, d'Estournelles, 287
DeLesseps, Ferdinand, 280

Democratic Party, 39-40, 42, 44, 46, 57, 100, 146-147, 150, 158, 161-162, 346
Dewey, Admiral George, 120-121
Dickens, Charles, 206, 305
Dow, William, 28, 63

Edmunds, George F., 56
Edward VII, 310
Elevated Railway, 47-49
Eliot, Charles W., 18, 109-111, 115
Elkhorn, 58, 60, 62-63
Evans, Admiral R. D., 171, 243
Evening Post, New York, 110, 264
Everybody's Magazine, 265

Farragut, Admiral David, 181
Ferris, Joseph 60, 201
Ferris, Sylvane, 60, 72-74
First United States Volunteer Cavalry, *see* Rough Riders
First World War, 350
Franchise-Tax Bill, 161-164, 264
Frankfurter, Felix, 238-239
Frederick the Great, 313, 321
French Panama Company, 274, 277, 279-280
Frick, H. C., 234-236

Garfield, James A., 219-220
Gary, E. H., 234-236
George, Henry, 44, 86
Goethals, Col. G. W., 282
Gorgas, Dr. William, 282
Gorman, Arthur, 110
Gould, Jay, 49 f.
Grant, Ulysses S., 166
"Great Adventure," 353-355

Hague Tribunal, 274, 287, 297, 314
Half-Breed, 46, 55
Hamilton, Alexander, 43, 222

Hamilton Club, 166-167
Hannah, Mark, 93-94, 164-165
Harriman, E. H., 229 f.
Harris, Joel Chandler, 173, 188
Harrison, Benjamin, 86, 225, 327
Harvard College, 18-24, 28, 36-37, 109, 110, 115, 125, 241, 264, 324
Havemeyer, Henry O., 239
Hawthorne, Nathaniel, 309
Hay, John, 276-277, 282-285, 287
Hay-Herran Treaty, 275-277, 281
Hay-Pauncefote Treaty, 274, 276
Haymarket Riot, 84, 111
Henry, Prince, 314
Hepburn, Peter, 183
Hepburn Rate Bill, 232, 237, 331
Hess, Jake, 38, 41-42
Hewitt, Abram S., 86
Hill, David B., 46, 146
Hill, James J., 229 f, 243, 264
History of Naval War of 1812, 19
Hitchcock, E. A., 214
Holmes, Oliver Wendell, Sr., 240, 304
Holmes, Oliver Wendell, Jr., 240-243
How the Other Half Lives, 101
Hughes, Charles Evans, 350
Huxley, Julian, 305, 319

Inland Waterways Commission, 218
Interstate Commerce Commission, 232, 330-331

Jackson, Andrew, ix, 198-200, 252
James, Henry, 99, 283
Jefferson, Thomas, 222, 274
Jusserand, Jean-Jules, 33, 294-295

Keats, John, 304, 310
Kelly, Peter, 44-45
Kipling, Rudyard, 99, 309

Knight, E. C., 226-229, 240
Knox, P. C., 217, 227-228, 285

LaFollette, Robert M., 336
Lambert, Alexander, 189
Law of Civilization and Decay, 112-116
Lawton, Gen. Henry, 132-134
Lee, Arthur Hamilton, 327
Lincoln, Abraham, ix, 43, 56, 150-151, 166, 173, 194-195, 198-200,
    222, 252, 263, 313, 323, 326
Lodge, George Cabot, 305
Lodge, Henry Cabot, 109, 117, 121, 168, 196, 240, 282, 288, 326
Loeb, William, Jr., 193, 238-239
Long, John, 27
Long, John Davis, 143
Long, William J., 265-267
Longfellow, Henry Wadsworth, 177, 304, 309-310
Longworth, Alice Roosevelt, 24
Louis-Philippe, 116
Louis XV, 116
Louisiana, 171-172
Lounsbury, Thomas R., 306, 349-350
Low, Seth, 293
Lusitania, 351-352

MacMonnies, Frederick, 172
Madison, James, 115
Mahan, Capt. Alfred T., 118, 142, 304
Maine, 120
Maroquin, J. M., 277
Marshall, John, 241-242
Matthews, James Brander, 99, 265
Maximilian, Emperor, 175
Mayflower, 171, 290
McClure, S. S., 247
McIlhenny, John, 202
McKinley, William, ix, 93-94, 120, 141, 150, 165, 192-194, 242,
    270, 327
Merriam, Hunt, 19, 21

Merrifield, William, 60, 72-73
Meyer, George, 73-74
Meyer, George von L., 293
Miles, Gen. Nelson, 127
Millet, Frank, 221
Mitchell, John, 253-255, 293
Moltke, Helmuth von, 115
Monocacy, 121
Monroe Doctrine, 268, 270-271
Moody, William H., 228
Morgan, J. P., 229 f, 234, 243
Muckraker, 246-248
Mugwumps, 109
Murray, Joseph, 39-42

Napoleon I Bonaparte, 85, 296
Nashville, 278
Nat'l Association of Manufacturers, 262
Nat'l Child-Labor Committee, 250
Nat'l Conservation Commission, 219
Nat'l Progressive Republican League, 336
"New Nationalism," 328, 331-334
Newell, F. H., 209, 211
Newlands, Francis G., 209, 212
Nibelungenlied, 172, 177, 304
Nicholas II of Russia, 293, 314
Nobel Peace Prize, 293, 296
Northern Securities Company, 227-229, 239-240, 264

Odell, B. B., 147
Olympia, 122
O'Neill, William, 43-44
Oyster Bay, 18, 171 f

Panama Canal, 213, 268, 272-282, 284-285, 288, 294, 296
Panic of 1907, 212, 233-236
Parker, Alton B., 146-147, 263
Parkman, Francis, 306, 324
Parr, Richard, 238-239

Payne-Aldrich Tariff, 327
Peary, Admiral Robert, 173, 243
Pennsylvania coal strike, 252-259
Perkins, George W., 255
"Pigskin Library," 303-305
Pinchot, Gifford, 209-211, 213, 216, 327
Platt, Thomas, 146-164, 169
Plunkett, Horace, 348
Poe, Edgar Allan, 174, 304, 310
Portsmouth, treaty, 172-173, 196, 290, 293
Powell, John Wesley, 209
Pure Food and Drug Act, 237

Quay, Matthew, 94-97
Quigg, L. E., 147-149

Reclamation Act, 209, 213
Remington, Frederic, 58
Republican National Convention 1900, 164-166
Republican National Convention 1912, 336
Republican Party, 37-42, 55-57, 111, 146-148, 150-153, 157-158,
    161-162, 164, 169, 194-196, 242, 327, 336
Revolutionary War, 95
Rhodes, James F., 243
Riis, Jacob, 101, 105-106
Robinson, Douglas, 147
Roosevelt, Alice Lee, 24-25
Roosevelt, Anna, 8, 12, 57, 83-84
Roosevelt, Archibald, 202
Roosevelt, Corinne, 22-23
Roosevelt, Cornelius Van Schaack, 3, 6, 18
Roosevelt, Edith Carow, 23, 29, 171, 179-181, 184-185, 188-189,
    202
Roosevelt, Elliott, 12, 23
Roosevelt, Ethel, 203-204, 207-208
Roosevelt, Kermit, 201-202, 206, 298-299, 301-302
Roosevelt, Margaret Barnhill, 3-4
Roosevelt, Martha Bulloch, 4, 8-13, 22-23
Roosevelt, Robert, 11

Roosevelt, Theodore, the Elder, 3, 7-14, 18-20, 23-24, 26-27

Roosevelt, Theodore
  Nominated to New York Assembly, 41; Elected, 42;
      As New York Assemblyman, 31, 42-55
  In the Badlands, 58-80, 83
  As Civil Service Commissioner, 86-91, 97, 103
  As New York Police Commissioner, 100-109, 207
  As Assistant Secretary of the Navy, 117, 119-128, 142,
      182
  As Rough Rider, 123-141
  Nominated Governor of New York, 146-149; As
      Governor, 30, 153-166, 169
  Nominated Vice President, United States, 166; Suc-
      ceeds McKinley, 193
  As President, 5, 9, 29-35, 60, 76-77, 81, 93-97, 110,
      171-172, 183, 192-199, 201-208, 210-222, 225-259,
      263-297
  As Progressive candidate, 336-348

Roosevelt, Theodore, Jr., 208
Roosevelt, Quentin, 202, 353
Root, Elihu, 234, 283, 285, 287, 349-350
Roswell, 5
Rough Riders, 123-141, 146, 171, 352
Russo-Japanese War, 289-293
Ryan, Thomas F., 264

Sagamore Hill, 29, 170-171, 171 f, 172, 178-179, 183, 190, 356
Saint-Gaudens, Augustus, 172, 220
Santo Domingo, 272
San Juan Hill, 134-136, 353
Sargent, John Singer, 173
Schurz, Carl, 110, 264-265, 296
Scott, Sir Walter, 177, 304
Selous, Frederick, 189, 243
Sewell, William, 28, 63
"Shadow Lawn," 350-351
Shafter, Gen. William, 127, 139-141
Shakespeare, William, 176-177, 304
Shelley, Percy Bysshe, 304, 310

Sherman, John, 143
Sherman Anti-Trust Law, 223, 225-226, 327
Smith, Hopkinson, 173
Spalding, Bishop John L., 256
Spanish-American War, 77, 80-82, 94, 117-142, 145, 147, 195, 269, 297, 352
Sprague, Henry L., 246
Spring-Rice, Cecil, x, 29, 97, 143, 243
Square Deal, 328-331, 333-334
Stalwarts, 46, 55
Standard Oil Company, 228, 230-231, 239-240
Sternberg, Baron Speck von, 29
Stimson, H. L., 238-239
Stoddard, Henry Luther, 349
Straus, Oscar, 293
Strong, William L., 100-101
Sugar Trust, 225-227, 237-240
Sumner, Brig. Gen. Samuel, 132-134, 136, 140
Swift, Louis, 245
Symonds, Marcus, 173

Taft, William Howard, 198-200, 210, 215, 298, 326-327, 345, 348-350
Tammany Hall, 39, 44, 46, 52, 100, 110, 149
Taney, Roger, 242
Tennessee Coal & Iron Company, 235
Tennis Cabinet, 32-33, 172, 196
Tennyson, Alfred, Lord, 304, 309-310
Thomas Hart Benton, 98
Tolstoi, Count Lev, 84-85
Trevelyan, Sir George Otto, 310, 312-313, 324

Wadsworth, James Walcott, 244
War and Peace, 84-85
War of 1812, 318
Washington, George, 242, 313, 323, 326
Westbrook, T. R., 49 f, 49-50
Wharton, Edith, x
Wheeler, Gen. Joseph, 132, 137

White, Henry, 293
White, Stewart Edward, 29
Whitman, Walt, 309
Wilcox, Ansley, 193
Wilderness Hunter, The, 267
Wilhelm II, 292, 310, 312-315
Wilson, Woodrow, 345-353
Winning of the West, The, 267
Winsor, Justin, 324
Wister, Owen, 58, 263
Wood, Leonard, 30, 34, 123-125, 127-128, 131-132, 138, 140-141, 182, 269
Woodruff, Timothy, 154, 165
Wright, Carroll, 257

Young, Gen. S. B., 132